The
Next
Hurrah

The Next Hurrah

The Communications Revolution in American Politics

Richard Armstrong

BB
BEECH TREE BOOKS
WILLIAM MORROW
New York

Grateful acknowledgment is made for permission to reprint the following:

Table 1: Summary of Donor Acquisition Mailings and Table 2: Summary of Resolicitation Program from "The Direct Mailbox: Launching an Effective Fundraising Effort" by Roger Craver, *Campaigns and Elections*, Spring 1985. Copyright © 1985 *Campaigns and Elections*. Reprinted with permission. All rights reserved.

Table 3: "Please, please, Mister Postman," reprinted with permission from *The Washington Monthly*. Copyright by THE WASHINGTON MONTHLY CO., 1711 Connecticut Avenue, N.W., Washington, D.C. 20009; (202) 462-0128.

Table 4: Sample Assembly District—Voter Database Fields from "New Techniques in Voter Contact" by Frank Tobe, *Campaigns and Elections*, Summer 1984. Copyright © 1984 *Campaigns and Elections*. Reprinted with permission. All rights reserved.

Library of Congress Cataloging-in-Publication Data

Armstrong, Richard, 1952–   The next hurrah: The communications revolution in American politics/Richard Armstrong.
    p. cm.
    Bibliography: p.
    Includes index.
    ISBN 0-688-06783-2
    1. Electioneering—United States—Technological innovations.
2. Mass media—Political aspects—United States.   3. United States—Politics and government—1981–   I. Title
JK2281.A76   1988   87-33283
324.7'3'0973—dc19   CIP

Printed in the United States of America

First Edition

1 2 3 4 5 6 7 8 9 10

BOOK DESIGN BY JAYE ZIMET

The word "book" is said to derive from *boka*, or beech.
The beech tree has been the patron tree of writers since ancient times and represents the flowering of literature and knowledge.

To Sharon

Preface

I'm a junk-mail writer.

There, I said it.

Most people in my business don't like to use that term. Our trade publications, when forced to mention it at all, usually spell it "j**k m**l." But I've never minded the phrase too much. You see, I'm not just a run-of-the-mill junk mail writer. I'm a specialist. I specialize in political fundraising and advocacy. Ever since I got my first job as a summer intern in the mailroom of the Republican National Committee, I've been involved with political direct mail. I've written for congressmen, senators, governors, and presidents. I've written over the signatures of Barry Goldwater, Jerry Ford, and Bob Hope. I've written for organizations ranging from Defenders of Wildlife to Mothers Against Drunk Driving, from the Sea Turtle Rescue Fund to the National Republican Senatorial Committee. I've probably written many of the political fundraising letters you've received in your own mailbox . . . letters that, I'm sure, you promptly threw away.

One day it occurred to me that for all the paper we ourselves have expended in this business, very little has been expended on us. With the exception of a few how-to books and some articles in our own trade publications, hardly anything has been written about political direct mail. This remains true despite the fact that direct mail has had an enormous effect on

American politics, an effect that still hasn't been fully understood by its practitioners, much less the press.

The press *has* taken note of Richard Viguerie, the "wizard" of political direct mail, but he is the exception that proves the rule. I'm sure Mr. Viguerie would be the first to agree that his story, as important as it is, is not the whole story of political direct mail. To regard direct mail as strictly a conservative phenomenon, or as a tool of the "New Right," is a big mistake.

Telemarketing, the direct mail of the telephone, is another important political tool that has been utterly ignored by the press. When I became involved in a professional way with the cable television industry, I noticed cable TV was also being used by political candidates without receiving much notice from the media. And as I looked more deeply into the subject of new political technologies, I saw that computers, satellites, and computer-based telecommunications were all having a substantial impact on American politics. But again, with a few exceptions, they had hardly received any notice in the news media or the publishing world.

So I decided to write this book.

I'm not a scholar, a journalist, a political scientist, or a historian. I'm not even what you would call a "top political consultant," although it's been my privilege to work with some of them. I'm just a junk-mail writer who has tread this peculiar ground and from time to time wondered what it was all about. In the process I've come up with some ideas, some opinions, some theories, and some observations . . . and, like anyone who works in an obscure but (I think) important industry, I want to share them. My book is based on a combination of personal experience, interviews, research, and sheer speculation. It's opinionated, subjective, biased, and, I'm afraid, a little fatuous from time to time. If it has one saving grace, it is that it's the first book that deals extensively with most of these subjects and is intended for a general readership.

So if I've stumbled now and then, wandered around dazed and confused, made mountains out of molehills and molehills out of mountains, and generally done a poor job of mapping the territory, I hope you'll forgive me as you would forgive a laboratory mouse working his way through an unfamiliar maze. I fully expect others will follow me and do a better job than I did. In fact, I sincerely hope they do. We need many more books on the political use of direct mail, telemarketing, cable TV, satellites, and computers. We could probably get by very nicely with fewer books about the political use of television.

I owe a tremendous debt of gratitude to the people who agreed to let me interview them for this book. They are, without exception, very busy people whose talent and intelligence is matched only by their generosity: Ray Strother, James Aldige, Bob Odell, Larry Sabato, Roger Ailes, Joanne Emerson, Tim Roper, Bruce Eberle, Stephen Winchell, Frank Tobe, Charlie Judd, Roger Craver, Bob Harty, Rod Smith, Richard Wirthlin, Mark Hinkle, Sherry Taffer, Charlie Welsh, Bob Alter, John Florescu, Richard Parker, Richard Viguerie, Charlie Cadigan, Bruce McBrearty, Robert Vastine, Jonathan Robbin, John Falcone, Matthew Reese, Tom Wheeler, Victor Kamber, Tom Collins, Dean Phillips, Tom Palma, Frank Greer, Brian Lamb, Eddie Mahe, Peter Hart, Tom Belford, Jim Eury, Ed Dooley, Kay Lautman, John Phillips, David Andelman, and Kim Spencer.

Unless otherwise noted, all the quotes in this book come from those interviews.

From this group, I would like to single out two people: Ed Dooley, who is the kind of interviewee every writer prays for; and Larry Sabato, who was not just a great interview but also an inspiration.

Ed was not content with merely sitting for a two-hour interview about the use of cable television and satellites in politics, but he took it upon himself to send me copies of memos, speeches, articles, and press releases . . . and to make himself enormously helpful in a dozen different ways.

Larry Sabato puts me in mind of that wonderful quote of Isaac Newton's: "If I have been able to see farther than others, it was because I stood on the shoulders of giants." Professor Sabato's *The Rise of Political Consultants* is the definitive book on political campaign technology. It is, I'm proud to say, the only book other than this one to deal substantially with political direct mail. And it is a book without which mine would not have been possible. When it comes to campaign technology, Professor Sabato is the giant on whose shoulders everyone else must stand.

I also owe a great debt to the trade press since, as I've said, many of the subjects covered here have not yet percolated their way up to the consumer media. In particular I would like to thank the publishers of *Campaigns & Elections, Direct Marketing, Fund Raising Management, Who's Mailing What!*, and *DM News* for providing much of the raw material on which this book is based. I would also like to thank the editors of *The National Review* for publishing my article on the political use of cable television. It was the seed from which this book ultimately grew.

To my agent Richard Pine, my dear friend and editor Jane Meara, and the mysterious Jim Landis, who buys my books without ever meeting me in person—sort of like the guy on that old TV show *The Millionaire*—I say, "Hey look, we did it again!"

And finally, much thanks to my research assistant, Matthew Frey—today a humble graduate student at Columbia University, tomorrow one of the great political scientists of the post-television age!

RAA
New York City

Contents

The medium is the message.

—Marshall McLuhan,
Understanding Media

The new electronic interdependence is re-creating the world in the image of a global village.

—Marshall McLuhan,
Understanding Media

FIRST WOMAN: What do you think of that war in the Middle East?
SECOND WOMAN: Honey, when I got home last night I was so tired I didn't even bother to turn it on.

—Overheard on a bus
by the author in 1967

1

Introduction:
Punch/
Counterpunch

When political reporters get hold of something, they
like to tear it apart and chew on it like a pack of wild dogs.

During the 1986 election cycle, the raw meat that was driving reporters into a feeding frenzy of righteous indignation was
something they called "negative advertising." Political TV ads
that directly attacked the opponent were leading the country
into a new era of dirty politics, or so it was repeatedly charged.
Headlines like these adorned publications ranging from the (smart
enough to know better) *New York Times* to (look who's talking)
Advertising Age:

"MUD: THERE SEEMS TO BE MORE OF IT THIS YEAR"
"POLS ACCENTUATED THE NEGATIVE"
"IT'S HIGH NOON NOW FOR POLITICAL MUDSLINGERS"

New York Times political columnist Tom Wicker said the
1986 campaigns were "the nastiest, least relevant, most fraudulent campaigns"[1] in history. A group calling itself The Committee for the Study of the American Electorate chimed in with the

theory that "demagogic and distorted political advertising"[2] was the main reason behind the drop in voter turnout. Charles Guggenheim, himself a political media consultant, published a widely quoted *mea culpa* on the *New York Times* op-ed page. And even George Will, a man who usually doesn't allow himself to be carried away by the latest media hype, succumbed to making this incredibly insupportable statement:

"What is new [about the 1986 campaigns] is not just the amount of negativism, it is the niggling tendentiousness of it."[3]

Niggling tendentiousness?

What about John Quincy Adams's charge that Andrew Jackson had murdered six innocent men? Was that not niggling enough for Mr. Will, or not tendentious enough?

Or how about the charges of bigamy and adultery in the same 1828 campaign, a campaign in which Adams called Jackson "a barbarian and savage who could scarcely spell his own name" and in which the Jackson partisans responded by labeling Adams a pimp?

Some reporters who knew better than to say negative campaigning was new in 1986 implied instead that it was the advent of television that made the difference. The negative charges themselves weren't new, so this particular argument went, it was the power of *television* to promulgate attacks farther and wider than ever before that was unprecedented in American politics.

"Don't confuse all this with traditional mudslinging," wrote Tom Wicker, as if traditional mudslinging were as wholesome as apple pie. "The stuff flying through the political air this year not only is smellier than that; today's guttersniping is doubly repellent—perhaps doubly lethal—because it's carried farther along the low road, with greater force and to more voters, by the candidates' use of television, primarily the thirty-second spot."[4]

Indeed, the poor thirty-second spot became so widely vilified during the 1984–86 election cycle that it was the subject of several pieces of reform legislation, a congressional investigation, a specially impaneled "jury" of advertising professionals, and, of course, the impassioned rhetoric of the politicians themselves. Barry Goldwater called negative advertising "the most disgusting development in politics in my lifetime."[5] Howard Baker said, "it's the sleaziest new element in politics."[6] And John Danforth, who led the congressional movement for regulating political ads, said, "They demean the candidates. They disgust the public. They destroy our sense of fairness. They transform the democratic process into guerrilla warfare . . . it's a sickening . . . revolting mess."[7]

Sickening and revolting it may be, but "new" it definitely was not. In 1986, political spot advertising on television was approximately thirty-four years old, having made its major debut in the presidential campaign of 1952. Even back then, some of Eisenhower's pioneering sixty-second spots were decidedly negative. He charged, for example, that the Truman administration had left America woefully unprepared for war in Korea. Not to be outdone, Stevenson's partisans produced an ad that linked the moderate Eisenhower to his archconservative GOP rival Robert Taft. The ad featured the voices of Taft and Eisenhower cooing at each other in such a way as to suggest they were in bed together, or at least very much in love. These were among the first political ads ever produced for television, and they were negative.

By 1960, John F. Kennedy felt comfortable enough with negative advertising to run a spot that featured a clip from one of Eisenhower's press conferences. In it, a reporter asked the president if he could name an occasion when Vice President Nixon had made an impact on administration policy. Ike replied, "If you give me a week, I might think of one." JFK's media advisers made sure every American who owned a TV set had heard that unfortunate remark by election day.

Negative advertising on television reached its peak in 1964, some twenty-two years before it became a *cause célèbre* in the press. Lyndon Johnson's advertising campaign was created by Doyle Dane Bernbach during that agency's golden years and featured an ad (aired only once) that strongly implied Goldwater would start a nuclear war; another ad (never aired) that tied Goldwater to the Ku Klux Klan; a third that featured the Eastern Seaboard being sawed off and cast out to sea (inspired by one of Goldwater's many facetious remarks); and a fourth that showed a little girl eating an ice cream cone laced with strontium 90 and cesium 137, the presumed result of Goldwater's commitment to nuclear testing.

Since nothing produced in 1986 even came close to that level of venality, why did the national press suddenly decide negative political spots were new and unprecedented? What made them "discover" a story that had been sitting under their noses for more than three decades?

Actually, the press was not entirely off-base in making a fuss about negativity in 1986 because where there's smoke there's fire. But the press was clearly guilty of mistaking cause and effect. What was really reaching an advanced stage in that year was not negativity but something that for lack of a better word I will call "reactivity." And this, in turn, was being fueled *not* by the advent of television advertising but by *new technologies* in television that were subtly changing the way political campaigns used the medium.

What was really "new" about political television in the 1980s— and especially in 1986—was that it was cheaper, more plentiful, and much more immediate than it had ever been before. These effects were the direct result of new video production technologies, new distribution technologies, new technologies in the generation of "free media," new technologies in media buying, and new technologies in polling—all of which combined to make campaigns seem more "negative" but that actually made them more "reactive."

New video production technologies. Nothing has changed the business of political advertising on television more than the advent of videotape. Although many media consultants still prefer to work with film because it has a softer and more dramatic look, shot-on-video commercials have become increasingly common—especially in situations where the campaign needs to save money or time. Video "tap" systems are commonly used on the set to show the director what he has just shot, enabling him to reduce the number of takes needed to get the shot he wants. In postproduction, film is now transferred to videotape immediately after being developed so color adjustments, editing, and special effects can be done on the more flexible video medium.

"Nowadays we can do in four easy hours what used to take us about four hard days," says media consultant Raymond Strother.

Strother was among the first political consultants to make use of another key production technology, something known generically as "digitalized video effects" and also known by such colorful brand names as "Mirage," "Paint Box," and "Abacus." Although each of these machines has its own set of capabilities, all of them use a computer to break video images into their component dots and reorganize those dots at the command of the user. A "Mirage," for example, can take a shot of the candidate and send it spiraling down a whirlpool, split it down the center, smash it into a thousand pieces, roll it into a ball, or transform it into a human stick figure. With "Paint Box," the user "dips" an electronic stylus into a palette of colors and literally paints an image on the video screen.

Strother used "Mirage" in a spot he produced for Gary Hart's presidential campaign only one day after the British-made machine first arrived in the United States.

"We let the medium and the message merge," said Strother, "because we used this new hardware and software to prove that Hart was a man of change, a new generation of leadership."

The press dutifully picked up on this, making lots of noise about Hart's "high-tech" commercials and even suggesting they were instrumental in his surprise victory in the New Hampshire primary. But the press, as usual, was missing the forest for the trees.

It's very unlikely the voters paid any attention to Hart's special effects since video animation had been seen on American television for years. The opening of basketball games on CBS Sports and the introduction of ABC's *Thursday Night at the Movies* are two of the most vivid examples. The difference is that such animated effects used to take months of work by highly trained (and highly paid) video artists. Now they can be done in two minutes, for less than five hundred dollars, by a semiskilled production assistant sitting at the controls of a "Mirage." What was new and exciting about Gary Hart's ads were not the ho-hum electronic "page turns" but the fact that such page turns could be done so quickly and at such low cost. Using digitalized video equipment, it's now possible for media consultants to go into a postproduction studio for an hour and create a visually interesting ad out of thin air. The low cost means *more* ads can be produced, and the quick turnaround time means they get on the air faster.

New distribution technologies. Also contributing to that quick turnaround are new technologies in video distribution and delivery. Whether it's something as simple as overnight letters or as complex as satellite uplinks, the pace of communication between media consultants and their clients has picked up consid-

erably in recent years. Media guru Tony Schwartz is probably
the ultimate example. Schwartz and his associate Bob Landers
lease four hours of satellite time every day to produce radio ads
written by Tony in New York and performed by Bob in Carls-
bad, California. Schwartz sends the ad copy to Landers by facsimile machine or computer modem. Landers rehearses alone
for a few minutes and then walks into his recording studio, located just off the kitchen of his house in California. After the
satellite connection is made, Landers reads the ad while Schwartz
records it in high-fidelity. After two or three takes, the ad is
ready for broadcast. The whole process often takes less than
thirty minutes.

Of course, Schwartz's frequent use of satellites is based on
two factors not shared by other media consultants: (1) he hates
to travel; and (2) he insists on using Landers for virtually all of
his voice-over work. Nevertheless, most media consultants these
days use satellites occasionally to deliver a commercial from
their production studios in Washington or New York to their
clients around the country. And with Federal Express, facsimile
machines, and computer-based telecommunications, the lag time
between what T. S. Eliot called "the idea and the reality" is now
scarcely more than a day.

New technologies in "free media." Satellites have also played
a role in the growth of something media consultants call "free
media," or more recently, "earned media." The subject of free
media received much attention from the press in 1984 primarily
because the Reagan White House, under the guidance of Michael Deaver, was widely acknowledged to be highly skilled at
it. Free media, quite simply, is the business of urging, encouraging, and *helping* the media—especially the electronic media—
to cover the campaign. Activities designed to generate free media
range from staging rallies against patriotic backdrops (as Reagan so often did) . . . to carrying around a physician's skeleton
to dramatize the fact that one's opponent "has no backbone"
(as one Texas gubernatorial candidate did) . . . to having the
candidate spend each day of the campaign "working" on a different job, like driving a truck or teaching kindergarten (as several successful candidates have done). Thanks to Reagan's skillful
but blatant use of free media, the press finally caught up with
the story in 1984 and began complaining about how it was being

"manipulated." But in truth, the press had been manipulated since Estes Kefauver pioneered the use of free media in his presidential campaign of 1952. What was new and different in the 1980s was that the press was not just being manipulated, it was actually being *supplanted.*

Radio and television "actualities"—many of them delivered by satellite—are to the electronic media what press releases are to the print media. Nowadays, candidates in effect "cover" their own campaign. Staffers are hired to follow the candidate around with cassette recorders and minicams, taping anything that resembles news. These tapes are then delivered to radio stations, television stations, and cable systems by telephone, by satellite, or by hand, where they will find their way on to the air—often without much editorial comment. In the print media it's very rare for a press release to be published intact. But with radio and television actualities, it happens all the time. And, for the most part, the press regards it as a service!

Again, speed and low cost make radio and television actualities so useful in a political campaign. Using actualities, a campaign can respond to events very quickly and at virtually no expense. When Candidate A makes a gaffe by saying, for example, he doesn't think Poland is under Soviet domination, Candidate B can record an indignant rebuttal to that point of view, complete with many pious references to the brave Polish people. Candidate B's assistant then calls up every radio station in the state and says, "I have twenty seconds of Candidate B responding to the Polish gaffe. Would you like to take it?" The radio station, especially if it's a small one without any political reporters on staff, usually says yes. Within the hour, Candidate B's response will be on the air.

As charges and countercharges fly back and forth over the airwaves, the press may notice an apparent rise in the negativity of the campaign. But what has really risen is the campaign's "reactivity," its sheer technological ability to respond.

New technologies in media buying. Computerized media buying is another factor driving the cost of political television downward and sending the quantity of commercials produced in a typical campaign higher. Television commercials nowadays are targeted to specific interest groups, and computers are used to analyze the ratings of TV shows not just by the number of people who are watching but also by the *kind* of people who are watching. In the past, a political campaign might buy time on a highly rated (and therefore expensive) program just to make sure it was hitting every voter in the district. But today's political media buyer decides exactly what kind of voter he wants to reach and uses a computer to match his target voter to the audience profiles of various programs. This usually winds up saving money on the purchase of airtime, and the money saved is often invested in more commercials.

New technologies in polling. Finally, new technologies in polling have contributed to significant changes in political spot advertising. In the past, most campaigns could afford to do only three major opinion polls during a campaign. But with the advent of computer software for polling (see Chapter Nine), it has become common for even small campaigns to run "tracking polls" nightly as the campaign nears its end. Since tracking polls concern themselves only with the direction, or the flow, of public opinion late in the campaign, they require neither the large number of interviews nor the highly skilled analysis of the early polls that are used to set the campaign's overall theme.

In most cases, tracking polls are used to measure the effect of the campaign's television commercials and the opponent's. New commercials will be written and aired almost daily to reflect the movement in each evening's tracking polls. If Candidate A, for example, appears to be rising in the polls by charging that his opponent wants to cut Social Security benefits, Candidate B may deem it advisable to go on the air with an ad saying "My momma gets Social Security, and I'd never cut my momma's benefits."

"It used to be you'd take a poll, set up a media plan, and six months later find out how it worked," says media consultant Robert Squier. "Nowadays you can send out your media, check out how it worked by the very next day, and fine-tune the message accordingly."[8]

When you put all these factors together—new production technologies, new delivery systems, computerized media buying, radio and television actualities, and the marriage of tracking polls to last-minute commercials—what you get are political television messages (both free and paid) that are faster, cheaper, easier to produce, and therefore much more plentiful than ever before. The result is no longer an "advertising campaign," at least not in the way we generally understand that term, but a kind of nonstop political debate, or argument, that takes place *on television.*

"We used to have one election on Election Day," says Robert Squier. "With the tracking polls and the instant production of new spots, you now have one 'petite election' after another and have what amounts to an ongoing dialogue carried out by way of thirty-second TV."[9]

But "dialogue" is perhaps too nice a word to describe something that usually looks more like a prizefight.

In the 1986 South Dakota U.S. Senate campaign, for example, Democrat challenger Tom Daschle and Republican incumbent James Abdnor waged a battle where flailing punches and counterpunches were landed so often that the entire campaign became a kind of video blur. After one or two rounds of feeling each other out with positive ads, Daschle landed first with a spot that quoted Abdnor saying farmers might have to settle for lower prices. Abdnor retaliated with a stiff counterpunch accusing Daschle of "mixing apples and oranges." Then he followed up with a shot to the chin accusing Daschle of putting up a "smoke screen." Daschle fell back on the ropes and appealed to the referee, running an ad that quoted Abdnor's previous two ads and demanding an apology. Sensing blood, Abdnor moved in with a hard uppercut that tied Daschle to Jane Fonda. This rocked Daschle badly, and again Abdnor followed with a combination—a stiff jab just below the belt that accused Daschle of missing an important House Agriculture Committee vote because he was too busy raising money in Florida. Reeling and almost out on his feet, Daschle let go with a wild punch that was as risky as it was creative—an ad showing Abdnor's high-priced media advisers sitting around a conference table trying to dream up ways to smear Tom Daschle. It was a knockout. Abdnor never recovered. He weakly tried to hit Daschle for a bad vote on a highway bill, but the tracking polls showed the punch never landed. As Election Day approached, Daschle hammered away at the old Democratic standby, Social Security. But by that time, Abdnor was too weak to respond.

Tony Schwartz says the modern media campaign is like guerrilla warfare. "Someone takes a shot at you, you move aside and take a shot back.[10]

"If you plan your fight six months in advance," Schwartz says, "it's really no fight. It's a dance."[11]

The 1984 U.S. Senate race in North Carolina between incumbent Jesse Helms and former Governor James Hunt was no dance, either. It was another classic example of the punch/counterpunch television campaign. Widely noticed for its high level of negativity, what was really interesting about the Hunt-Helms race was its incredibly high level of technological *reactivity*. Charges and countercharges were flying back and forth over the airwaves, in the mail, and on the telephone almost daily. "The ads took on a life of their own," wrote *Washington Post* political reporter Bill Peterson. "Hunt would air a commercial attacking Helms for opposing a bipartisan plan to rescue Social Security. Helms replied with an ad of his own. Hunt answered it with another ad; Helms countered with a new ad."[12]

There's no question that such a technological capacity to respond quickly has a tendency to drive the tone of a campaign into the gutter. But to say that the ultimate effect of such technology is to create more negativity is missing the whole point. Theoretically, reactive advertising could be positive. Indeed, during the 1986 Pennsylvania gubernatorial race, Richard Scranton thought he could take advantage of the rising furor about negative advertising by announcing he was removing all of his attack ads from the air. His next series of commercials featured prominent Pennsylvanians talking about what a nice man Scranton was because he had put an end to the negative campaigning. But his opponent, Robert Casey, responded in a matter of days with his *own* set of upbeat ads featuring, among other things, pictures of happy children picking flowers.

In fact, just two years after the Hunt-Helms race had turned North Carolina into a bloody political battlefield, Terry Sanford and James Broyhill waged a U.S. senatorial campaign in the same state that was just as reactive as the Hunt-Helms campaign but that was generally acknowledged to be far more positive in tone. Each man criticized the other's positions on the issues, but both did it accurately, fairly, and decently.

The truth is it doesn't really make any difference if reactive ads are negative *or* positive. The content of these ads is entirely meaningless. A reactive political advertising campaign is like an argument that takes place in the backseat of a car between two small children:

"Billy hit me."
"I did not."
"You did, too."
"Did not."
"Did."
"Didn't."
"Did."

After eight hours of listening to this in a hot car, Mommy and Daddy scarcely pay any attention to the *content* of the argument. The content is meaningless. But the *effect* is very meaningful—especially if Daddy's nerves are frayed to the point where he drives the car into a telephone pole.

Marshall McLuhan would, I think, be the first to agree that the content of a message is irrelevant; it's the medium carrying the message that's important. Negativity is neither a new development in American politics nor a particularly significant one. What *is* new and significant is that political campaigns nowadays, for all intents and purposes, actually *take place on television.* And since the form of communication will help shape the content ("the medium is the message"), ultimately the punch/counterpunch TV campaign is bound to have an effect on American politics. Good or bad, we don't yet know.

Clearly, television already *has* changed American politics quite a bit. But I disagree with those who believe its effect on politics has been to demean it. On the contrary: When it comes to the questions of tone, dignity, accuracy, honesty, attention to the issues, substance over image, and so on, TV has had a highly salutary effect on American politics. It's inconceivable in today's television age that a candidate would attack his opponent for having fathered an illegitimate child or accuse his opponent of being a pimp. Despite television's reputation for being an "image" medium, I think it's very unlikely that a modern candidate could create a blatantly false and misleading image like William Henry Harrison's "Log Cabin and Hard Cider" campaign of 1840. Even Abraham Lincoln's image as a rail-splitting frontiersman probably wasn't close enough to reality to stand up to the unblinking eye of television. Today's image campaigns must be fundamentally grounded in truth. And today's attack ads must be scrupulously researched and fairly presented. A scurrilous attack on television runs the risk of sparking backlash from the opponent, the press, and the public itself that is potentially devastating to the candidate who airs it. So television actually has a kind of built-in self-correction mechanism that prevents politics from getting too dirty or too dishonest.

The real effect of television on American politics has sprung from the nature of the technology itself. Indeed, TV's impact on American politics has only been a continuation of the effect of radio, since technologically the two media are essentially the same. Although each has its own unique set of strengths and weaknesses, it makes no sense to draw a distinction between radio and TV. Both are forms of broadcasting.

In simple terms, broadcasting is a medium that reaches many people at once with a brief message transmitted in a pattern radiating outward from a central point, like ripples in a pond. Broadcasting is, therefore, highly centralized rather than regional. It reaches a mass audience rather than a targeted one. Its message is delivered instantaneously rather than over a period of time.

Before the advent of broadcasting, political communication was limited by both distance and speed. In William Henry Harrison's campaign of 1840, for example, giant leather balls were painted with slogans and rolled from town to town by Harrison's volunteers. The candidate's voice could be heard only as far as he himself was willing and able to travel. Political communication, therefore, could move only as fast as a horse, or later, a locomotive. Although the candidate was able to talk with groups of voters in rallies and through the print media, these were groups defined not by a common interest or common demographics but only by a common home. As a result, American politics was largely determined by *regional* interests. National policy was a matter of negotiating and resolving those competing interests. Our regionalism was, in fact, so pervasive that in 1860 we went to war over it.

A revealing contrast between the political impact of communication technology in the nineteenth century and in the twentieth can be made by comparing the War of 1812 with the Vietnam War. In 1815, hundreds of soldiers died in a battle that took place *after* the war ended. While news of the peace treaty was slowly wending its way across the Atlantic, Andrew Jackson led his men into the bloody Battle of New Orleans.

One hundred fifty years later, American troops won an important victory during the Tet Offensive of 1968. But the battle was widely perceived as an American defeat. Early television reports of greater-than-expected enemy strength led many to believe that the Americans had been routed. Somehow the story that the Americans eventually won the battle never quite caught up with earlier reports that they were outmatched. And the perception of a huge American loss at Tet began a chain of events that eventually turned the American people against the war in Vietnam, ultimately causing the United States to withdraw.

In 1815, hundreds of lives were lost because communications technology was too slow. By 1968, a war was lost in part because communications technology had become too fast.

With the advent of national radio networks in the early 1930s, American politics became more centralized, more nationalistic, and more populist than ever before. The ship of state was no longer steered along the carefully negotiated lines of regional interests but on what was perceived to be the most popular course among the people at large. The federal government assumed greater and greater power as it centralized authority in Washington and placated the mass radio audience with populist programs like Social Security and the "New Deal." Strictly regional policies, like segregation in the South, became harder and harder to maintain under the national scrutiny of broadcasting. Meanwhile, radio led to stronger feelings of national unity and pride. People became Americans first and citizens of their state second. In many ways, World War II was a war of rampant nationalism waged on the airwaves by skillful radio personalities. What Roosevelt, Hitler, Churchill, and Mussolini all had in common was a hypnotic talent with the microphone.

But more than enough has been written about the effect of broadcasting on politics. It is not my intention to duplicate that material in this book. What interests me is that the newer technologies of political communication will *also* have an effect on American politics. Yet these technologies, for the most part, have not been written about at all.

The impact of direct mail, cable television, satellites, computers, telemarketing, and the "new electronic media" on American politics—like the impact of television itself—will be felt regardless of what messages these technologies are used to convey. When it comes to content, we might as well assume the new technologies will carry pretty much the same junk as the

leather balls in William Henry Harrison's campaign or the hand-
bills of Andrew Jackson's. The content of political communication hardly ever changes. But the overall effect of each new
communication technology is significantly different from what
has gone before.

Direct mail, for example, has utterly revolutionized American politics in the past thirty-five years, although the press has
scarcely noticed it. Direct mail has drastically changed the role
of the national political parties . . . created an enormous shadow
government of special-interest groups in Washington . . . completely revolutionized the nature of campaign finance . . . abet-
ted the rise of political action committees . . . created a new
form of political advertising . . . changed the way incumbents
communicate with their constituents . . . and dramatically al-
tered the nature of lobbying. In short, it has had a myriad of
misunderstood and dimly understood effects on politics in the
United States. Yet as of this writing, only one book has been
published in this country that contains as much as a single chapter
on political direct mail.

Meanwhile, there is *no* book dealing with the political use of
cable television, even though cable TV has made its presence
felt in national politics since 1982 and is now an important part
of the media mix in many local campaigns.

There is *no* book on satellites in politics, even though satellites have revolutionized the business of generating free media,
created politically oriented television networks, and subtly affected international politics.

There is *no* book on political telemarketing, even though the
telephone has been used in American politics for more than a
century and is being used today in a manner and on a scale that
is unprecedented in history.

There is *no* book on the computer in politics, even though
most political campaigns nowadays are fully computerized, and
America is, in fact, entering a new era of "machine politics" in
America . . . where the machine is a personal computer.

Nor is there any book that deals substantively with the use
of computer-based telecommunications, videocassettes, videodiscs, teletext, and videotext in politics. Alone among these "new
electronic media," bidirectional cable television has been the
subject of many books and magazine articles. But that's because
bidirectional cable television looks and sounds a lot like "Big

Brother," and there's never any shortage of writers who want to scare you about the future. Ironically, bidirectional cable TV probably is the *least* worthy item of discussion, since it now seems unlikely that a sufficient number of such systems will be built to have any political impact whatsoever.

If these new technologies are mentioned in the press at all, they are usually discussed in terms of "who is ahead?" But the question of who's ahead is as meaningless as the question of content! One side is ahead for a little while; then the other side catches up. What difference does it make? The important question is the one that never gets asked:

"What's it doing to us?"

I'm not even sure the question has been properly answered for television yet. And it probably *won't* be answered if the press continues to focus on content. What was new and interesting about the political use of television in 1986 was not negativity but the fact that an evolutionary process that began in 1952 seemed to be nearing its apex.

Ever since 1952, people have gotten most of their information about political campaigns from television. Almost from the very beginning, newspapers and campaign events began to play a secondary role. But by 1986, with the growing use of free media and the advent of punch/counterpunch political spots, it was no longer a question of using television to convey information about the campaign. Nowadays, for all intents and purposes, political campaigns *happen* on television.

Debates, rallies, meetings, whistlestop tours, stump speeches, and the rest still exist. But they are like flying buttresses on a contemporary church. Flying buttresses used to be important because they held up the church's walls. Nowadays the walls are held up by reinforced concrete, but the flying buttresses remain as a kind of decoration. So it is with most of the events and activities we associate with a political campaign. Those that remain are used primarily to dress the set for television commercials and free media.

In 1986, for example, Arizona congressman John McCain decided to launch his U.S. Senate campaign by going on an old-fashioned whistlestop tour. But unlike the whistlestop tours that earned a place in history for William Jennings Bryan and won a famous upset victory for Harry Truman, McCain's train made only two stops—one at the point of departure and one at the destination. The train didn't make any stops along the way because it would have been too hard to manufacture crowds of McCain supporters at each little station and too difficult for the film crews to set up. The real objectives of the exercise, as outlined later by a McCain staffer in a magazine article, were threefold: "(1) [to] create interest and excitement in the campaign; (2) [to] generate positive electronic media coverage in the state's two largest media markets; and (3) [to] permit our own film crews to record the excitement and interesting visuals for later use in McCain television commercials."[13] No one had any illusions about using the tour to persuade voters, since virtually everyone who was invited to attend the event was a McCain supporter or a GOP loyalist anyway.

But the ultimate example of my point that modern campaigns *happen* on television was an incident that occurred ten years before McCain's whistlestop tour, in the 1976 presidential race.

During a debate ostensibly held at the invitation of the League of Women Voters, ostensibly for the benefit of several thousand people at the Walnut Street Theater in Philadelphia, the TV sound cables suddenly failed. Not the public-address system, mind you, but the TV audio system. And so for nearly twenty minutes, Jerry Ford and Jimmy Carter stood at attention like a pair of wooden soldiers while TV technicians furiously tried to restore the sound. If the debate wasn't happening on television, then it wasn't happening. Period.

There is no such thing as a political campaign anymore, at least not in the flag-waving, button-wearing, baby-kissing sense of that word. Nowadays, many candidates make no public appearances at all during the final weeks of a campaign—the period that used to offer the most intense activity—because they are too busy talking on the telephone to raise money for more commercials. Such traditional activities as shaking hands at the factory gate, visiting the local diner, touring nearby farmland, and marching in Labor Day parades are done entirely for the benefit of the TV cameras—the cameras the candidate bought and paid for, plus the ones he is simply trying to manipulate.

"In California," said one Alan Cranston aide after the 1986 election, "a political rally is two or three people gathering around a television set."[14]

That remark really says it all—except, ironically, for the fact that California probably is the one place in the nation where this is *least* true. California has too many different densely populated media markets to have total political saturation on TV. Many congressional candidates in the Los Angeles area, for example, can't afford to use television at all. The states where political campaigns *really* take place entirely on television are states like South Dakota, Idaho, and Wyoming, where broadcast time is cheap and plentiful.

Campaigns no longer take place in public houses, as they did in Patrick Henry's day. They don't take place on the stump of a fallen tree, as they did in the day of William Jennings Bryan. Gone are the days when Lyndon Johnson could announce his candidacy from the back of a flatbed truck or Harry Truman could pull off an upset victory from the back of a train. Campaigns no longer happen in Mayor Daley's smoke-filled rooms or on Franklin Roosevelt's flag-draped podiums. Even the thoroughly modern shopping mall may be a thing of the past, politically speaking. In 1972, a congressional candidate in Maryland was arrested for campaigning in a shopping mall. Mall owners around the country are cracking down on politicians because they're afraid that if they let candidates pass out campaign literature in their malls, they're going to have to let the Ku Klux Klan do the same. And so far, the U.S. Supreme Court agrees.

When shopping malls go, the technique of campaigning in public as a way of winning votes (as opposed to a way of attracting television coverage) will be completely obsolete. And American politics will have completed a long march from the streets to our living rooms. Not that this is necessarily a bad thing, or even particularly unusual. After all, one way of looking at this progression is simply to say that politicians always go wherever the people are. When the people were in the pubs, the politicians delivered speeches in the pubs. When people spent a lot of time in train stations, politicians talked from the back of trains. When people started sitting at home watching TV, politicians went on TV.

The difference is that while political campaigns still take place "publicly" (more publicly, in fact, than ever before), they no longer take place *in public*. Almost by definition, politics used to be the most intensely social of all human activities. Now it is among the most private. Sex used to be the one topic that was most carefully avoided in polite conversation. Now it's politics. And no wonder! Politics isn't the kind of thing you want to share with strangers, or even friends. Politics is something you do in the privacy of your own home, with your T-shirt on, with a beer in your hands, with your shoes off. It's like belching.

That's where television has left us.

And that's where the new technologies begin.

One

Direct
Mail

2

The Lazy Man's Way to Riches

Young Dick Sears stared at the unopened package sitting on his desk and wondered what he should do with it. After all, he had been the railroad station agent at North Redwood, Minnesota, for less than a year, and nothing like this had ever happened before. A package arrives, obviously filled with valuable items, and nobody claims it! Should he send it back? Should he keep it a little longer? Should he open it himself and find out what's inside?

Letting his curiosity get the better of him, Dick opened the box and found six gold-filled watches. Priced at twelve dollars each and shipped COD to anyone who wanted them, the watchmaker presumably wanted to do business with the jeweler in North Redwood, Minnesota. But North Redwood was a town of just three houses, and it had no jeweler. What it did have, however, was a very clever railroad station agent.

"Maybe I could buy these watches myself," Dick said to no one in particular, "and sell them to the other agents down the line. After all, I have a list of their names in my stationmaster's book. I know they are all responsible men, making a good income. And in the railroad business," he mused, "you can always use a good watch."

So Dick began to write letters. And in doing so, he discovered a talent he never knew he had. He was a good salesman—especially on paper. His writing was personal and persuasive. Offering the watches to his fellow station agents at fourteen dollars each, Dick quickly got enough orders to pay the watchmaker's COD while pocketing twelve dollars for himself.

"How long has this being going on?" he may have asked himself when he realized he'd stumbled onto such an apparently easy way to make money. And the answer would have surprised him: not very long at all. Although this kind of marketing had its roots in ancient times, and despite the fact that one of Dick's contemporaries, a man named Aaron Montgomery Ward, was already enjoying success with a similar business in Chicago, history credits Dick with being one of the pioneers of this new form of advertising. Years later, it would come to be known as "direct marketing" or "direct response." In Dick's day it was known by the humbler and more descriptive term of "mail order."

Direct marketing encompasses a variety of advertising media, the most common of which is the one Dick used: direct mail. But whether buyer and seller communicate by letter, telephone, radio, television, or print, the essence of direct marketing—and the characteristic that distinguishes it from the kind of advertising most of us are familiar with—is that the customer's name and address are "captured" by the seller. The information thus gleaned from the response to a direct-mail campaign can be measured, analyzed, statistically projected, and, most important, used again.

Which is exactly what Dick did.

He wrote *back* to the agents who bought from him before. No longer perfect strangers, as they were before they bought his watch, now they were loyal customers, customers about whom Dick knew a great deal. He knew, for example, that they had some disposable income. He knew they were experienced with ordering things by mail. He knew they liked getting letters. And he knew that they owned a brand-new watch, a watch that might, perhaps, look nice with a shiny new chain.

So Dick ordered chains.

And the R. W. Sears Watch Company began to grow. So much

so, in fact, that Dick Sears placed a want ad for someone to fix
the watches that were occasionally returned to him in response
to his ironclad guarantee. The man who responded to the ad
was named A. C. Roebuck.

The success of Sears, Roebuck & Company was based on a
single key ingredient vital to any direct-mail campaign, an ingredient that Sears himself managed to use better than any marketer before or since: *trust.*

A sales transaction that takes place by direct mail is an act
of faith, both from the point of view of the buyer and, in many
cases, the seller. In the early days, Sears sold most of his merchandise COD, and the mail-order ads he ran in pulp magazines
to generate orders invariably began with the famous headline
"SEND NO MONEY." By shipping the merchandise cash-on-de-
livery, Sears was placing a certain trust in his customer's good
intentions. But more often, it was the mail-order *buyer* who took
the bigger leap of faith. Without seeing or touching the merchandise, the buyer sent money to a distant address on the
strength of the promises made to him by a stranger. The ability
to create that confidence, that bond of trust between buyer and
seller, may have been Richard Sears's greatest legacy to the world
of mail order. He did it with ironclad guarantees, with depend-
able products, and with an enormous degree of personalization.
As a result, Sears, Roebuck & Company quickly became one of
the most hallowed institutions in America. "There are three people in this world you can trust completely," said rural politicians
of the day: "Jesus Christ; Sears, Roebuck; and me!"

But even Jesus Christ faced temptation. And so did Richard
Sears. Wherever a bond of trust exists, there exists alongside it
the potential for betrayal. The deliberate creation of a sense of
confidence and the ultimate betrayal of that confidence is, after
all, the definition of a "con" game. And at one point in his career, even the scrupulously honest Richard Sears did not resist
the tempting power of the confidence he had so carefully wrought
in his rural audience. Historian Daniel Boorstin writes:

> "An Astonishing Offer" which [Sears] announced in rural week-
> lies in 1889 was illustrated by a drawing of a sofa and two
> chairs, all of "fine lustrous metal frames beautifully finished
> and decorated, and upholstered in the finest manner and with
> beautiful plush" which "as an advertisement only" and only for

the next sixty days would be sent to anyone who remitted ninety-five cents "to pay expenses, boxing, packing, advertising, etc." Customers who sent in their money received a set of doll's furniture as specified; they had not noticed in the first line of the advertisement, in fine print, the word "miniature."[1]

To borrow from George Lucas, Sears had glimpsed "the dark side of the Force."

Nobody tells Joe Karbo's story better than Joe Karbo himself. It's a story he has told in hundreds of magazines to millions of eager readers over the years.

"I didn't have a job and I was worse than broke. I owed more than fifty thousand dollars, and my only assets were my wife and eight children. We were renting an old house in a decaying neighborhood, driving a five-year-old car that was falling apart, and had maybe a couple of hundred dollars in the bank. Within one month, after using the principles of *The Lazy Man's Way to Riches*, things started to change—to put it mildly. I live in a home that's worth over $250,000. I own my 'office.' I own a lakefront 'cabin' in Washington. I own two oceanfront condominiums. I have two boats and a Cadillac. I have a net worth of over a million dollars. But I still don't have a job!"[2]

How did he do it? Well, that's what Joe was hoping you would ask. Because the answer is contained in his ten-dollar book, which, he candidly explains, costs him only fifty cents to print. "Why should you care if I make a $9.50 profit," he asks, "if I can show you how to make a lot more?"[3] In fact, Joe is so certain you'll get rich by reading his book, he's willing to make this rather unusual guarantee: "I won't even cash your check or money order for thirty-one days after I've sent you my material. If you don't agree that it's worth at least *a hundred times* what you invested, send it back. Your *uncashed* check or money order will be put in return mail."[4] It's not quite as firm a guarantee as Dick Sears's "SEND NO MONEY," but almost.

What eventually arrives in the mail is an ordinary looking paperback book, slightly more than 150 pages long, priced, in the upper right-hand corner, at $1,000.00—"not the selling price," Joe explains, "but guaranteed to be what it's worth to you at the very least!"[5] It is somehow characteristic of Joe Karbo not to stop selling even after the book is sold, and, in fact, the book keeps on selling right up to its last page.

What's inside *The Lazy Man's Way to Riches* could be charitably described as a lengthy pep talk. The book is divided into two sections. In the first section, Joe outlines a program of relaxation techniques, concentration drills, and goal-setting exercises of the sort that could be found in any good in-flight magazine. He calls this program "Dyna-Psyc" and confides that these principles were first revealed at top-secret enclaves of high-ranking executives from "really big corporations"[6] at "mountain or desert retreats"[7] during the 1950s. After about sixty pages of this, though, Joe realizes that he has his reader all dyna-psyched up with nowhere to go, so he prepares to unveil his real money-making ideas in Book Two.

Book Two begins by disclosing two vital secrets (Chapter One: "Eliminate the Negative" and Chapter Two: "Accentuate the Positive"), but the author doesn't really get hot until Chapter Three, when he is ready, at last, to talk about what he calls "The World's Most Exciting Business."

"It's called the Direct Response Business. And probably no other business has so many people who started from scratch and became millionaires. You know some of the giants: Sears, Roebuck; Montgomery Ward; Spiegel's; and I'm sure you could list a dozen more household names."[8]

From this point on, Karbo's book becomes a short course on mail order, offering advice which, in the opinion of some, could be described as ranging from the absurdly oversimplified to the unnecessarily detailed. Lost in this soup of friendly advice, cheerful bromides, and occasional facts, perhaps only the most alert reader realizes the underlying principle behind the lazy man's way to riches. The reader has responded to a direct-response ad promising to make him rich, and in return for his ten-dollar check, he has been taught how to run direct-response ads. About one of every ten readers asks for his money back—a fact that bothers Joe Karbo not one bit.

An ex-actor and former advertising man who lost his family's entire bankroll trying to produce his own television show, Joe Karbo woke up one morning to find himself utterly broke and in debt. Sitting with his wife and eight kids around the kitchen table, Karbo worked out a budget plan and decided to learn everything he could about debt reduction. The result was a booklet titled *The Power of Money Management,* which he wrote, published, and sold through direct-response ads headlined "Get Out of Debt in Ninety Minutes—Without Borrowing!"

He sold a hundred thousand copies.

Thus every word in Karbo's *The Lazy Man's Way to Riches* ad is scrupulously true. He really was broke. He really did make millions. He really will show you how to do the same. Yet one out of every ten readers is dissatisfied, and the only startling thing about that statistic is that it isn't higher.

Interestingly, Karbo's book arrives in the mail with three other advertisements enclosed. The first is headlined "WINNING AT THE RACES MAY NOT BE YOUR IDEA OF FUN, BUT . . ." The second says "AFTER YOU'VE READ JOE'S BOOK . . . READ THIS!" (it offers to tell you how to find merchandise for your new mail-order business). The third shouts, "GET OUT OF DEBT IN NINETY MINUTES—WITHOUT BORROWING!"

In the mail-order business, advertisements like these are referred to as "bouncebacks," and they illustrate a fundamental direct-marketing principle: The person most likely to buy from you is the person who just did. The more recently the customer bought, the more likely he can be persuaded to buy again. Once the seller has made the investment necessary to acquire a new customer—often at a loss—he now is in a position to make a profit either by selling more products to the same customer or by *selling the customer* to someone else. In direct marketing, this never-ending process of reselling past customers and selling their names to other direct marketers is known as "milking the list." And Joe Karbo's mailing list is one of the milkiest around.

But the *most* responsive mailing list in America is not Joe Karbo's list of money-seekers; it's a political list. It was compiled by a man a lot like Richard Sears: hardworking, entrepreneurial, honest, kind, and God-fearing. Like Sears, his generosity to his employees is legendary. Like Sears, he's a country boy who made his fortune among the city slickers.

Indeed, he is a man who was made very much in the image of a Richard Sears . . . with just enough Joe Karbo thrown in to make him interesting.

Richard Viguerie's hands were numb.

He had been sitting in the same chair in the same musty government office for hours, for days, for weeks on end, transcribing names and addresses, one by one, from the official records of the clerk of the U.S. House of Representatives to his own wrinkled yellow pads. Occasionally his eyes looked up furtively and caught the stares of file clerks who had at first ignored him but who now, after the days had turned into weeks and the weeks into months, looked at him with vague suspicion.

Their worries increased when Viguerie, his hands finally paralyzed with writer's cramp, hired housewives to come in and continue the transcribing under his supervision. "Those clerks didn't know what I was doing," Viguerie remembers, "but it just didn't *seem* right to them. It was sort of like the Russian who took a wheelbarrow full of dirt out of the factory every night. The bosses would say, 'Comrade, we know you're stealing something,' and they would search through the dirt. But they never found anything. They couldn't figure it out until one day they realized he was stealing wheelbarrows!

"So after I did it for about three or four months," Viguerie says with a chuckle, "they changed the rules and said we couldn't do it anymore. But by that time we had about 12,500 names."

And by that time the "New Right" had been born.

Richard Viguerie himself was born in 1933 in Golden Acres, Texas, near Houston, the son of a middle-management executive at Shell Oil Company and a practical nurse. Although his parents were religious and conservative by nature, neither was very political, so it was something of a surprise when young Richard showed an interest in politics. "In college, my big political heroes were 'the two Macs'—Douglas MacArthur and Joseph McCarthy."[9]

A life in politics was Richard's goal from a very early age, but he had several false starts in finding the proper route. At first he thought he'd make money in engineering, then retire early and run for Congress. But he couldn't hack the algebra necessary to become an engineer, so he switched to law. But after a semester and a half of C's and D's in law school, he gave up on that, too, and went into the Army. "As you can see," Viguerie later wrote, "I was not exactly burning up the track and setting records. I was what you would call a late bloomer. But I always knew I was going to do important things that would make a big difference in people's lives."[10]

Viguerie started to make a difference when he stopped studying politics and started practicing it. He got involved with

John Tower's first campaign for the U.S. Senate in Texas. A young conservative Republican in a Democratic state, Tower was running against Lyndon Johnson in 1960. Johnson (typically) had cross-filed and was running for reelection to the Senate at the same time he was running for vice president with JFK. "Double your pleasure, double your fun," went the slogan Viguerie coined in his first known piece of political copywriting. "Vote against LBJ twice!"

It was during this campaign that Viguerie wrote his first direct-mail fundraising letter. It worked pretty well, he remembers. "I was kind of intrigued by it."[11]

But it was a different kind of direct-response advertisement that gave Richard Viguerie his biggest break—a small classified ad in William F. Buckley's conservative journal *The National Review*. The ad said that a national conservative organization was looking for field men in its New York office. So Richard Viguerie took the red-eye to New York.

The "conservative organization" turned out to be Young Americans for Freedom (YAF), an organization of young conservatives that was less than a year old but already twenty thousand dollars in debt. Viguerie was hired, and not surprisingly his first assignment was fundraising. At first he went about the task in the conventional manner, visiting wealthy old conservatives and begging them for money. But while he enjoyed some success with this approach, the painfully shy Texan found asking people for money face-to-face very difficult.

Perhaps remembering the letter he had written for John Tower a few years earlier, Viguerie began to contact YAF donors by mail. It "seemed to work," he recalls, "so I wrote more and more letters and before many months, direct mail was my whole focus."[12]

Viguerie had become so fascinated with direct mail that he made a very unusual career move. By this time he was executive director of YAF. But to spend more time working on direct mail, he urged the board of directors to find a new executive director so he could become a full-time direct-mail coordinator. Like Sears, Karbo, and many others before him, Viguerie was "hooked" on direct marketing. After only a few months in the new position, he decided what he really wanted to do was start his own direct-mail agency.

With a loving wife and a growing family, Viguerie found himself in a position not unlike the one Joe Karbo faced when he discovered the lazy man's way to riches. Viguerie had a grand total of four thousand dollars in the bank. He took about one tenth of that and decided to start his own company. The Richard A. Viguerie Company was founded on four hundred dollars and an idea.

The idea was to go to the office of the clerk of the U.S. House of Representatives and copy down the names and addresses of everyone who had given fifty dollars or more to the Goldwater for president campaign.

In January 1965, as Viguerie began the laborious process of transcribing those names, being a conservative in America was about as far underground as one could get, politically, without completely leaving the mainstream of American life. Barry Goldwater had been crushed at the polls, repudiated by the intellectual establishment, and ridiculed in the media. John F. Kennedy was approaching a state of apotheosis in the public mind, while Lyndon Johnson had begun to promote the panoply of liberal programs known as the "Great Society." On college campuses, the most significant political movement of the decade was taking shape—opposition to the Vietnam War. And growing anger about the war brought with it a wide range of other anti-establishment activities and attitudes that today we can recall just by invoking the phrase "the sixties." It was a time when conservatives spent a lot of time indoors . . . licking their wounds, worrying that Barry Goldwater might have been their last chance, wondering if they would ever again get the opportunity to voice their ideas about how the country should be run. In the late sixties the typical conservative was not the kind of person who would be inclined to parade his political views down Main Street, nor even confide them to a stranger at a cocktail party. But he was exactly the kind of person who would respond to a direct-mail letter from a like-minded individual. Indeed, the mere arrival of such a letter, the mere affirmation that there were other people out there just like him would be a welcome event in any conservative's household at the time.

As forlorn as the conservative movement appeared to be in 1965, Richard Viguerie believed there were thousands, perhaps millions of conservatives who could be rallied to support political candidates and causes. The problem was: How do you reach them?

"Imagine this thing is a microphone," Richard Viguerie said to me as he picked up a paperweight in his office and held it near his mouth. "We conservatives didn't have access to this microphone," he said, holding his hand between the paperweight and his lips. "Our message was blocked. But one day we discovered a pass through that microphone—direct mail.

"If the media wasn't talking about the Panama Canal, if the media wasn't talking about common situs picketing, or abortion, or high taxes, then we could do it through the mail. We discovered that we could go out there and mail these millions and millions of letters. We could get our people to write their congressmen, call their senator. We could change the national agenda. So liberals would be talking about *our* issues, politicians would be dealing with *our* issues. We could do all this and have it pay for itself."

Surveying the political scene in 1965, Viguerie saw that there were already a number of prominent conservative writers, columnists, and spokesmen in the public eye. And he decided that if he chose to follow their path he would probably "not amount to a hill of beans." [13]

"But I realized that what we [conservatives] didn't have was someone who could take the ideas, the writings and the books and market them to the people. . . . So I set out to become the best marketer I could be. I determined to learn how to successfully market ideas to millions." [14]

In doing so, Viguerie customarily awoke at 5:30 A.M. and spent as many as four hours a day studying the history and principles of commercial direct mail before turning to the daily business of running his agency. But the hard work paid off. Although Richard Viguerie did not invent political direct mail—by the time his company was founded in 1965, the Republican National Committee had been active in direct mail for nearly thirteen years—he brought to his chosen field the techniques, strategies, and gimmicks that had been evolving in commercial direct marketing since Richard Sears sold his first watch. Fellow political consultants snickered at Viguerie and regarded him with a mixture of ridicule, jealousy, and downright disdain. In particular, his emotional, hard-sell, gimmicky letters were objects of scorn. But Viguerie, being an avid student of direct-marketing history, probably remembered the classic mail-order ad for music les-

sons headlined "They Laughed When I Sat Down at the Piano—
But When I Started to Play . . ."

They laughed when Richard Viguerie sat down at the typewriter, but when he started to write . . . the money rolled in.

Yet far more important than the copywriting gimmicks Viguerie borrowed from commercial direct mail was the way he
borrowed the commercial mailer's fondness for "milking the list."
Starting with just 12,500 names, Viguerie realized that the key to
his agency's future—and in fact the future of the "New Right"—
was to find more names.

"That was the hardest part of the business at the time," Viguerie recalls. "There were no names out there. I mean, I knew
something about direct mail and copywriting and so forth, but
there were no conservative contributors. That's why those 12,500
Goldwater names became the most important asset of The Viguerie Company. With this list I was able to go to clients and
say, 'Hey, I can raise you some money.'"

But he also said, in effect, let's take some of that money and
use it to find *new* contributors, and since we're doing all this at
my risk, why don't we *share* the names? In fact, that is roughly
how Viguerie's early contracts with his clients were written: Viguerie accepted most of the risk in launching a direct-mail campaign, but in return for that risk, he assumed an unusual level
of control over the question of how much would be reinvested
in finding new donors. And he also assumed joint ownership of
the names. So the list of 12,500 conservative names Viguerie and
his team of housewives painstakingly copied from the clerk of
the House grew . . . and grew . . . and grew. Viguerie's "master
file" came to include some twenty million names, about four
million of which were active donors to conservative causes. Diversifying and milking in a way that would make Joe Karbo proud,
The Viguerie Company eventually reached a high watermark of
three hundred employees, with a mailing list subsidiary, a lettershop subsidiary, a computer company, a publishing company,
and most recently a pizza parlor. Richard Viguerie is anything
but lazy. But he had found the lazy man's way to riches.

These three stories—Richard Sears's rise to preemin-
ence in merchandising, Joe Karbo's path to personal wealth, and
Richard Viguerie's road to power—illustrate three themes that

recur frequently in the history of both political and commercial direct mail. They are: the "flimflam," the "entrepreneurial," and the "underground."

Direct mail is a highly entrepreneurial business, one with the potential of growing to fabulous heights from very humble beginnings. It is a business with a greater-than-average potential for deception. And it is a business that operates silently and beneath the surface. As such it appeals to a certain type of seller and a certain type of buyer, or, in the case of political direct mail, a certain kind of candidate and a certain kind of voter.

These three strains are all closely related and intertwined. The entrepreneur, for example, is attracted to direct mail because it requires so little overhead and capital investment. It allows him to move quickly and take advantage of opportunities as they occur. Yet this also provides him with at least the opportunity to behave fraudulently. Post office boxes can be opened and closed in a day. New companies can be started for the price of a box of stationery. Thus the mail-order entrepreneur is always tempted to sell snake oil, to take advantage of his customers (or his voters) in a way that simply wouldn't be possible in an aboveground medium like television. He can feed on the darkest, most hidden motivations of his customers, because they, too, approach direct mail as a silent and anonymous way of doing business. It is a shy person's medium, a medium for people who feel somewhat "out of it."

Modern direct mail was born, in fact, out of a sense of political and geographical disenfranchisement. When Aaron Montgomery Ward first set up shop in a loft above a livery stable, America's population was roughly 60 percent rural and 40 percent urban. Thus the number of people living far away from plentiful retail outlets was greater than the number of people living close to them. Farmers at the time—almost as they do now—saw themselves squeezed between the high prices of local general stores on the one hand, and the low payments they received for produce on the other. "Eliminate the middleman!" became the political battle cry of a generation of American farmers. And in 1867, thousands of farmers across the country came together to form an organization designed to lower the cost of merchandise. They called it the "Patrons of Husbandry," but it soon came to be known simply as the "Grange."

Montgomery Ward's masterstroke was to have himself declared the official supply house to the Grange. By mailing his catalog to the Grange's nationwide list of members, he plugged his young mail-order business into a power line of political frustration, geographical disenfranchisement, and sheer consumer demand. These people were not only frustrated, angry, and ready to buy, but they were innocent, lonely, and shy to boot! It was not uncommon for Ward to receive dozens of letters in every day's batch of incoming mail proposing marriage to "the girl wearing hat No. 1524 on page 153 of your catalog." It boggles the mind to imagine what Richard Viguerie could have done with this list.

Today, with rural electrification, rural free delivery, super-highways, radio, and television, rural Americans are as tuned into the mainstream of American life as their friends in the city. But there is a new kind of disenfranchisement, not geographically based but psychologically and perhaps sociologically rooted. Millions of Americans are afraid, angry, lonely. They feel persecuted, frustrated, left behind. Wrapped in what Viguerie himself describes as their "cocoons," they are left alone in the privacy of their own homes with only their inner thoughts and their checkbooks to keep them company.

The typical political direct-mail donor has a remarkably homogeneous demographic and psychographic profile, apparently without regard to whether he or she is politically on the right, on the left, or in the middle. Both liberal and conservative direct-mail consultants agree that their typical donor is older than the average American (forty-five or more), slightly more educated than average, with considerably more disposable income. He tends to be from the professional or business classes; tends to be a registered voter; an active citizen; and more often than not, something of an extremist.

Even the political moderates who respond to direct mail (and there *are* some) tend to be extreme—extreme in their passion, extreme in their level of commitment to a cause. "What I call the left is almost nonexistent in direct mail," says leading liberal consultant Roger Craver. This is because there are no lists around to reach the the truly radical. "So I call the people who respond to our appeals 'the extreme middle.'"

But no matter where the direct-mail donor sits on the political fence, he shares with fellow contributors—both left and right—an amazingly consistent pattern of emotions, attitudes, and feelings. It is a psychographic profile that makes him particularly susceptible to the skillful manipulations of a talented direct-mail fundraiser.

Webster defines "alienation" as a feeling of being isolated, and in this sense, alienation is a key element of both commercial and political direct mail. Montgomery Ward and Richard Sears depended on the sheer physical isolation of a rural audience to build their mail-order catalogs into multimillion-dollar enterprises. Today's political direct mailer depends on a different kind of isolation—not geographical, but emotional.

Look, for example, at the elderly couple who sit at home every evening, not because they live far away from restaurants and shows but simply because they are afraid to go out at night. They turn on the TV, but all they can find are half-hour sex comedies and dramas about abortion, child molestation, and incest. The eleven-o'clock news comes on: A bunch of foreigners are spitting on the American flag. They go to bed, but they don't sleep well because the teenagers in the neighborhood are awake all night playing stereos and drag-racing through the streets. In the morning they read the newspaper and learn that their congressman has sent a friendly letter to the Communist dictator of Nicaragua. At 10:30 A.M. the morning mail arrives. Inside is their Social Security check. But with inflation, they know the check buys less today than it did just a few years ago. Also in their mail is a letter from Richard Viguerie. They are ready to hear what he has to say.

The direct-mail donor is an angry person. And Viguerie, for one, sees nothing wrong with that. "There is a value in being angry about things. There's a lot of things in this world to be angry about. Some of the leaders we love and respect the most were the ones who made us angry about things. Martin Luther King made us angry about segregation, for example. There is value in having people call to our attention the fact that there are injustices in the world."

Yet much of this anger arises not so much from a sense of injustice as it does from a deep feeling of political frustration. Direct-mail donors "are frustrated with the status quo," says former Viguerie employee James Aldige. "They want a change and/or a new direction in politics. . . . In a lot of cases, they lack confidence in the present political leaders. . . ."[15]

Many direct-mail donors have the feeling that life is passing them by, that they have somehow missed the boat. There is a vague yearning in their hearts, especially among conservative donors, for an America that once was, or perhaps that never was but should have been.

In many cases the direct-mail donor also is afraid. Herschell Gordon Lewis, one of the top free-lance direct-mail copywriters on the commercial side, has identified "fear" as one of only four main reasons why people respond to direct mail. (The others, he says, are "exclusivity," "greed," and "guilt.") This comes as no news to political direct marketers, who have been preying on the fears of their donors for years: fear of higher taxes, fear of growing interest rates, fear of crime, fear of losing Social Security benefits, fear of communism.

Perhaps because of these fears, the direct-mail donor feels a strong need to be involved, to be part of something bigger and more powerful than himself.

"People are surprised but pleased to see themselves reflected back in material that comes from far away and from someone they don't personally know," says direct-mail consultant Richard Parker. "It gives them a chance to associate their personal beliefs with candidates or organizations who espouse those beliefs."

In light of this, it isn't surprising that political direct-mail experts have discovered that the single most effective enclosure in any direct-mail letter is a membership card. Ironically, the personalized membership card retains its power even though the reality of membership in most direct-mail–funded organizations is somewhat hollow. "Mass membership without mass action"[16] is how political scientist Larry J. Sabato describes it. At most, membership in a political organization entitles the donor to receive a newsletter and, occasionally, some free gifts. The biggest "benefit" of membership is, in fact, the privilege of receiving more direct mail.

Yet donors respond rabidly to the plastic membership cards because the typical direct-mail donor wants to be involved . . . but not *too* involved. "They are not broadly engaged in politics," says Sabato. "The most active political people tend to give directly to candidates or parties rather than through the mail. But [the direct-mail donor] can be 'turned on' by a controversy or threat." In other words, the direct-mail donor is interested in political issues and wants to get involved, but he doesn't want to get his hands dirty making phone calls, stuffing envelopes, or canvassing the neighborhood. He is, after all, shy.

Richard Parker, former publisher of *Mother Jones* magazine, author of *The Myth of the Middle Class,* and now a leading liberal direct-mail consultant, sees the direct-mail donor's motivation in terms of what he regards as an ongoing class struggle.

"What you have in the New Right," says Parker, "is a push for the enfranchisement of the small-business and small-town professional classes." According to Parker, these people felt cut out of the negotiation that took place between big business, big labor, and big government on the major issues of the last twenty years—civil rights, Vietnam, the war on poverty, and so on. "As a result, there was a rise of resentment on their part. When you've been cut out of the decision-making process entirely, you have a lot of anger and vindictiveness."

Parker's class theory would serve to explain one of the most perplexing anomalies in the world of political direct mail: namely, that Richard Viguerie himself, archconservative ideologue and multimillionaire businessman, is, temperamentally and philosophically, anti-establishment. "He's a very strange combination of anti-establishment populist and right-wing conservative," says Larry Sabato. And so Viguerie remains perennially on the outside, endlessly criticizing the institutions and individuals one would expect him to support. "Ronald Reagan probably spits when he hears the name Richard Viguerie," says Sabato with a grin.

So, in many cases, a political direct-mail campaign is a form of communication from one political outsider to another. Men like Viguerie on the right and Roger Craver, his counterpart on the left, have formed vast computer files of direct-mail donors who can be rallied to support *any* candidate or *any* cause that fits their ideological biases. But the frustrating thing about trying to wield genuine political power with a group of direct-mail donors is that they don't really *like* to win. They *like* being on the outside. They like being persecuted, alienated, angry, frustrated, and lonely.

"Direct-mail [contributors] are the opposite of the rest of the world, of the political fat cats who give money to the politicians who look like winners," Roger Craver told *DM News,* "or even sports fans who get more involved as their team gets closer to victory."[17] Liberal causes do well in direct-mail fundraising when they seem to be losing in society and in electoral office.

As an example, Craver told me about his experiences managing the direct-mail program for Morris Udall's quixotic campaign for president in 1976. According to Craver, Mo Udall consistently raised more money in direct mail *after* he dropped out of the race than he did when things were going well. Direct-mail donors are "almost theological" in their commitment to principles, says Craver. "They are not as interested in winning and losing as they are in supporting a candidate who upholds the values and principles for which they stand."

And if there's nothing direct-mail donors like better than a candidate who will go down in flames while fighting for a good cause, they certainly found the right boy in 1972.

It all began in 1967 with a telephone call to, of all people, Richard Viguerie.

"I explained to the senator that we were poles apart ideologically and he'd want someone more akin to his philosophy," Viguerie recalls. "We had a good long chat. It was clear that he had an appreciation of the power of direct mail."[18]

The 1972 George McGovern campaign for president of the United States has been enshrined in the mythology of political campaign technology as the first, the best, and by far the most creative use of direct mail in politics. Although it was certainly not the first, probably not the best, and at least not any longer the most creative, it was indeed a significant moment in the history of political direct mail—if for no other reason than it represented the first complete synthesis of the "entrepreneurial," the "underground," and the "flimflam" themes of direct marketing in a political campaign.

McGovern himself was the first person in his campaign to show an entrepreneurial flair. The senator from South Dakota has always drawn a lyrical connection between his own massive direct-mail program and the historical fact that Thomas Jefferson was the first U.S. president to announce his candidacy by mail. But unless McGovern spent that long telephone conversation with Richard Viguerie chatting about early American history, he was far more sophisticated about the use of direct marketing in politics—even at that early stage—than he ever let on. Most likely it was Viguerie himself who advised the senator that the smartest thing he could do in preparing for a large-scale direct-mail effort would be to start collecting names. And that's exactly what McGovern did.

Viguerie explains:

> In 1969, after his reelection [to the Senate], McGovern told liberal organizations and candidates he wanted to help them raise money. He was generous. He signed a lot of fundraising letters. He wanted only one thing—the names and addresses of people who responded to those mailings.
>
> So in January of 1971, when George McGovern announced for president, he had a tremendous head start—a mailing list of thousands of people who had responded to an appeal for contributions for liberal causes—primarily to end the Vietnam War.[19]

Although McGovern may have been the first to come up with this idea, it is a very common practice among politicians today. When asked to sign a fundraising letter for some worthy organization, political or otherwise, senators and congressmen often will ask for the names and addresses as a quid pro quo for their signature. By doing so, George McGovern compiled— at no expense to himself—a valuable "in-house" list of approximately sixty thousand direct-mail donors who were sympathetic to his stand on a wide range of issues.

Who were these people? Well, interestingly enough, if what we know about the typical direct-mail donor holds true, they were probably *not* the long-haired campus activists with whom we associate the core of George McGovern's support. It's almost impossible to raise money through the mail from young people, much less the kind of footloose young people who dominated the protest movement of the late sixties. McGovern's original list probably was composed mostly of older, more established, relatively high-income Americans. The were probably married, with good jobs, enjoying a high standing in the community, and with lots of children and grandchildren—specifically, children and grandchildren nearing draft age.

By 1971, when George McGovern was preparing to announce his candidacy for president, the war in Vietnam was no longer a matter for polite debate or dignified editorials. It was reaching into American homes, creating fear, anger, and division around suburban kitchen tables where, a few years earlier, the biggest problem had been deciding what kind of cookies go best with milk. Mothers were worried about their draft-age sons. It seemed as if every mother knew someone's boy who was "over there," or someone's son who had been killed. At an underground level, it appears likely that George McGovern's message had much more effect than his showing at the polls twenty-one months later would indicate. These affluent, middle-class, pro-establishment Americans would probably no more dream of revealing at a neighborhood cocktail party that they intended to vote for George McGovern than they would announce they had just purchased a copy of Joe Karbo's *The Lazy Man's Way to Riches.* But privately sending off a check in the mail was another matter, especially if it meant that little Billy wouldn't have to go to Vietnam.

Armed with his precious in-house list and outfitted with a political philosophy suited to the interests of the growing underground antiwar movement, George McGovern was poised on the verge of a direct-mail success. But one element was missing. It would be, in fact, the one element that would truly distinguish the McGovern campaign and make it a part of political direct-mail history: namely, the infusion of commercial direct mailers. It was these people who—for the first time—brought all the techniques, the science, the gimmicks, and the sheer huckster-ism of the mail-order marketplace into a political campaign.

"I was a little embarrassed to be working where I was," said the soft-spoken Tom Collins as he and I sat out on the porch behind his Manhattan apartment one spring afternoon and I listened to him reminisce about his early years in the direct-mail business.

"I came to New York when I was twenty-one years old, looking for a job in advertising or publishing. I just couldn't get anywhere. Finally I sent a letter to a small agency called Schwab & Beatty, because I'd heard they did a lot of book advertising, and I *loved* books. So they hired me. And that agency turned out to be the granddaddy of all direct-marketing agencies.

"But for the first few years, we had accounts like the Charles Atlas body-building program and the Sherwin Cody School of English . . . real corny stuff. And my idea of advertising was, you know, 'Lucky Strike!' But as time went on I decided if I'm going to do this, I'm going to do it well."

And that's exactly what Tom Collins did. But as he began his rise to becoming one of the industry's most celebrated copywriters, and a partner of one of its largest firms (Rapp & Collins), Collins also was nurturing a private interest in politics. Among other activities, he ran as a Stevenson delegate in Great Neck, New York.

Given his interest in politics, it was not surprising when one day in 1970 Tom Collins received a call from one of his own clients asking him if he would like to get involved in the McGovern campaign. The man's name was Morris Dees, and like Richard Sears, he was a bright young small-town boy who had made his fortune in mail order.

A clever and entrepreneurial Southerner, Dees had shown a knack for direct marketing as early as his college days, when he organized what was probably the first "Send a birthday cake to your kid" service to appear on campus. From there his business diversified into publishing cookbooks designed as mail-order fundraising tools. That, in turn, led to a variety of publishing and direct-marketing activities that eventually made Fuller & Dees one of the largest mail-order companies outside of New York and Chicago.

Active in Democratic politics, Morris Dees was friendly with McGovern. And when McGovern's staff informed the senator that his silly notion of announcing his candidacy by mail, just like Thomas Jefferson had done, was technically impossible, McGovern called the only direct-mail expert he knew (other than Richard Viguerie)—Morris Dees.

Tom Collins re-creates what happened next:

" 'Can you help us get this mailing out?' said McGovern."

"Morris said, 'Fine, where's the letter?' "

" 'There is no letter,' said McGovern. 'But one of our people will put something together.' "

" 'Wait a second, Senator. This is direct mail. You can't have just anybody sit down and write a letter. You've got to get a professional.' "

And so it was that Tom Collins went from writing about kicking sand in the face of ninety-seven-pound weaklings to writing about kicking sand in the face of Richard Nixon.

Whether it was ultimately inspired by Thomas Jefferson or by that other great revolutionary populist, Richard Viguerie, McGovern's idea to announce his candidacy by mail proved to be a stroke of genius. In addition to his house list of sixty thousand names, McGovern had another sixty thousand names generated by an antiwar TV program he had produced with Senator Mark Hatfield. These 120,000 names, merged with a series of lists rented and borrowed from outside sources, brought the size of McGovern's first mailing to 250,000. It cost thirty thousand dollars to mail a seven-page letter to each of these people.

Three hundred thousand dollars came back.

Rarely does a first mailing—a "prospect mailing," as it's called in the business—yield such an enormous profit. But whether it does or does not, the key to making real money lies, as you will recall, in "milking the list." So Dees, like Joe Karbo, bounced back to his new customers quickly. He sent all fifteen thousand donors to the first mailing a letter inviting them to join something he called "The Presidential Club."

"This was an idea of Morris Dees," Tom Collins told a reporter for *Direct Marketing* magazine shortly after the fact, "and Morris has a most wonderful promotional sense. That's why he was able to retire twenty years earlier than I've been able to. The idea was to write these contributors . . . and say we are looking for a dedicated group of people who would be willing to give ten dollars a month from now until convention time. We did a mailing to our donor file of fifteen thousand and got about a 12 percent response. We got about two thousand people who agreed to send us ten dollars a month and gave them a coupon book just like an installment loan, a different month on each coupon, so that every month they would send us a coupon and ten dollars."[20]

By the time of the Democratic National Convention in July 1972, George McGovern had raised approximately four million dollars by direct mail. But the best was yet to come. For the general election campaign in the fall, the McGovern for President Committee set out to raise at least eight million dollars in less than seventy days.

"We had a meeting of all the fundraising people during the convention," Collins recalls, "and they were going around the room one by one and asking us how much money we thought we could raise by election day. When they got to me, they said, 'Tom, how much can we expect from direct mail?' And I gulped and said, 'Eight million dollars!' Afterward I thought, 'Oh, my God, what have I done?'"

But as it turned out, Collins's estimate was low.

Raising large sums of money by direct mail has more in common with designing a sophisticated investment program than it does with conducting an advertising campaign. And in this respect, the McGovern committee was fortunate to have the skills of Collins's business partner Stan Rapp.

"Stan constructed this sixty-day cash flow," Collins recalls, "that predicted 'on such-and-such a date we will mail five hundred thousand letters and it will pull a 1.2 percent response and that will give us X amount in cash, and then we will use that money to mail so many letters' . . . and so on. It was incredibly intricate. He put this thing together almost overnight, and his predictions proved to be uncannily accurate—that is, until late in the campaign, when we started running *ahead* of the plan."

True to form, McGovern's direct-mail donors responded better as it became clear the senator was a sure loser.

More than fifteen million letters were mailed on behalf of the McGovern for President Committee in the fall of 1972, and a wide variety of different formats and creative approaches were tried. But the finest of these, and perhaps the most ingenious mailing of the entire campaign, was the one Collins and Dees created as a bounceback to the hundred thousand people who had given to McGovern prior to the convention. They called it the F.M.B.M. letter—"For McGovern Before Miami." Joe Karbo would have loved it.

"In appreciation of your past help," it said, "we would like to send you a souvenir of those unforgettable days when the odds against us seemed hopeless and only your steadfast support kept the campaign going. It is a sterling silver lapel pin that says "F.M.B.M."—standing for For McGovern Before Miami. Since production will be limited to one pin for each before-Miami supporter, we want to be certain yours does not go astray. So please check your name and address on the enclosed shipping label, correct it if necessary, and return it to us for your pin."[21]

Collins explains the psychology behind this approach: "Obviously, we couldn't afford to send everyone a piece of sterling silver without a contribution. And I felt if we said something like, 'Send us your donation and we'll send you a pin,' it would've seemed ungrateful. So we said, 'We're *going* to send you this pin, but we didn't want to just send it to you without your knowledge because it's a very valuable pin. We wanted you to check your name and address first to make sure we have it correctly here.' And the theory was that they would want the pin, but what kind of a crumb would say 'Send me the pin' and not send any more money? So that was the psychology behind it, and it was extremely successful."

Presumably, if the donor was reading the letter, then his address was essentially correct. Yet it was the manner in which the donor was asked to send in his contribution that Collins and Dees reached their peak of ingenuity.

"Here's an idea," the letter said, "for maximizing your effectiveness. Here are four blank checks, each dated one month apart. By filling out all four (or you can use your own checks, of course), you can send us four monthly contributions all at once, and we won't cash the last three until they come due."[22] Printed on a computer form included with the mailing were four checks, each personalized with the donor's name and address, and *postdated* August 1, September 1, October 1, and November 1, 1972.

This was what Joe Karbo would have called "a very unusual guarantee." And it worked. Twenty-five percent of the hundred thousand donors who received this mailing responded, with an average gift of forty dollars. The mailing grossed one million dollars. And it helped to bring the total amount of money raised by George McGovern after the convention to a grand total of twelve million dollars, or four million dollars higher than Tom Collins's off-the-cuff estimate.

In the words of Joe Karbo, it's "the most exciting business in the world!"[23]

Direct mail has two roles in politics: advertising and fundraising. The distinction between these roles is often blurred—deliberately—because many direct-mail experts like it that way. Specifically, they like to use direct mail's value as an advertising medium to help mask its deficiencies as a medium of fundraising.

To understand why, one first must understand why direct mail can be a difficult, expensive, time-consuming, and frustrating way to raise money.

Imagine for a moment that we are not interested in finding political direct-mail donors but rather in finding fish. Not just any kind of fish, mind you. We're looking for the fan-tailed Liberalfish, a very rare breed.

How do we find it?

Well, there's only one way, and it's not easy. You have to rent a boat, hire a crew, get a map, go into the ocean, find a spot where you know the Liberalfish tends to congregate, and drop your net.

Later, when you pull up the net, you're apt to find all sorts of creatures trapped inside it. Maybe there will be a swordfish, some tuna, about twenty flounder, and perhaps, if you're lucky, one Liberalfish.

All that work for one fish? Is this any way to raise money? No. In fact, you probably *lost* money finding that one fish. But wait: You're not finished yet. Let's take that one Liberalfish, keep it alive, and put it in your aquarium back home.

Now, you go back into the ocean and drop the net again. This time you get two Liberalfish, and you put them in the aquarium. The next day you get none. (As the Haitians say, "Every day is a fishing day, but not every day is a catching day.") The following day you hit it big. Three Liberalfish. In the aquarium they go.

After several months of this you are broke, tired, angry, and ready to tell me that my method of finding Liberalfish just doesn't work. So when I wake you up one morning and say, "Let's go fishing," you look at me with murder in your eyes. But today is different—because today we're going to go fishing *in the aquarium.* And in the aquarium, the Liberalfish are biting like crazy!

This little story is a fair description of the difficult two-step process that political direct mailers must go through to find and cultivate donors. In the first phase—the "prospecting" phase—the direct mailer rents lists on which he suspects he will find people who are interested in his cause. He sends out letters urging them to contribute, but not surprisingly, he gets only 1 or, at most, 2 percent of the recipients to respond. In most cases he *loses* money on these prospecting mailings. In fact, he considers himself very lucky to break even.

However in the second phase—the "renewal" phase—the direct mailer writes back to the people who have given to him before. Now he gets results that are comparable to fishing in an aquarium. After all, everybody on this list, his "house" list, is familiar with the organization and supportive of its goals. Compared with prospecting for new donors, renewing past donors is inexpensive, profitable, and downright easy.

Direct-mail consultant Tim Roper explains in more detail how the prospect/renewal concept works in practice:

"Let's say you manage to find a thousand new donors with your prospecting mailing. Maybe you only broke even in the process, but it's a success. Because now you have a thousand new contributors you didn't have before, and it didn't cost you a thing.

"Now, let's suppose you mail to these thousand new contributors, and you spend a fair amount on the letter—oh, about fifty cents apiece, or five hundred dollars for the whole mailing. On the average, 20 percent of these people will respond, and they will give an average of twenty-five dollars each. So now you've raised five thousand dollars at a cost of five hundred dollars, or a net profit of forty-five hundred dollars. There's your money!"

Voilà!

Only it doesn't always work out that way.

In fact, to make a direct-mail campaign work out as neatly as Roper describes takes not only skill, talent, creativity, experience, and a fair amount of luck, it also takes *time*. Lots of it. For a political candidate to use direct mail effectively, he needs to begin prospecting for new donors eighteen to twenty-four months before election day. Not many candidates have that kind of foresight. Many of them come straggling through the consultant's door a few months before the election, begging for help. That's why most political direct-mail consultants prefer to work with advocacy groups and political-action committees (PACs) instead of candidates. And that's why those who *do* work for candidates spend a lot of time talking about how wonderful direct mail is as an *advertising* medium.

"Of course, it's an advertising medium," says Larry Sabato. "But so are billboards. And billboards are one of the most useless expenditures you can make. The question in my mind is, how cost-effective is it compared to the other means of advertising?"

After twenty years of selling the sizzle instead of the steak, the question of how effective direct mail is as an advertising medium rarely comes up in Richard Viguerie's mind. By calling his company an advertising agency and regarding direct mail solely as a self-liquidating form of advertising, Viguerie has locked his firm into a no-lose proposition with its clients:

You lost money? Don't worry. Think of all the free advertising you're getting.

You made money? Don't look so surprised. We knew all along you'd make money.

Heads, I win; tails, you lose.

When viewed in the most charitable light, direct mail offers a variety of added benefits to the political candidate besides raising funds. It can be an organizational tool, a polling device, a means of recruiting volunteers, and a way to get out the vote. But the consultant who emphasizes these ancillary benefits to the detriment or to the exclusion of fundraising is a consultant with one hand firmly planted in the client's pocket.

Nevertheless, when direct mail is used *only* as an advertising medium—without any attempt to raise funds—the evidence shows it can be quite persuasive. This kind of direct mail is called, appropriately, "persuasion mail."

But Roger Craver has an even better name for it.

He calls it "the water moccasin of politics."

Like a water moccasin, persuasion mail is silent, it is poisonous, and it has a forked tongue.

One of the greatest attractions of persuasion mail from the politician's point of view is that it is by far the most insidious advertising medium in the world. Attack your opponent's record on television, and he will respond in kind. Attack your opponent in the mail, and he will never even know what hit him. At the local level, a candidate who is skilled in the use of persuasion mail can lock up the election before his opponents realize he is in the race. Indeed, one of the great advantages of direct mail as a political tool—and here I include fundraising mail as well— is its ability to give the savvy candidate a silent head start on his opponents.

"If you put an ad on TV," says Larry Sabato, "everyone knows what you're up to, including the opposition. But with direct mail, you've got a silent killer. No one knows how extensive the effort is."

This cloak of silence can be used to mask the real intent of an organization from the public, if that is what's needed to build credibility and acceptance before seeking to raise money. And the silence of persuasion mail permits a wider range of expression than any other advertising medium, making it a potentially poisonous weapon in the hands of the unscrupulous candidate.

Democratic Congressman George E. Brown, Jr., of California, for example, wondered why his opponent was being so quiet. With twelve days left before the election, there hadn't been as much as a peep of campaign activity from the opposition camp. Then, slightly less than two weeks before election day, at the rate of one a day, they began to arrive: direct-mail "hit pieces."

The first said that Brown didn't really live in the district, that he kept a small hotel room there for appearance sake, and that his "real home is in Virginia—three thousand miles away!"[24]

Next came a rather jaundiced look at Brown's voting record. It seems Brown had "refused to vote against the mailing of pornography to children . . . voted to allow scientific experiments on live fetuses . . . and advocated a national program to fund sterilization."[25]

In the days that followed, voters in San Bernardino County were treated to a wide variety of revelations about Brown, including the charge that he advocated sex between students and teachers and that he had voted in favor of legalizing sodomy.

Ironically, these letters came not from Brown's opponent but from the National Republican Congressional Committee—one of the three main arms of the national Republican Party in Washington. As such, they were mailed at the nonprofit postage rate to which political parties are entitled but political candidates are not. Brown can be forgiven for being particularly angry that the taxpayer was helping to subsidize this smear campaign against him.

Brown alerted the local newspapers, but with only a few days left until the election, the damage had been done. "Even when the newspapers jump on a direct-mail piece and reprint it in its entirety," says Tim Roper, "it doesn't have the same impact as it did when the recipient first reads it. Sometimes a piece of direct mail is the only source of information that people have about your candidate. They don't read newspapers. They may not be very educated. So they read your letter, and they believe it."

Finally, like the water moccasin, persuasion mail has a forked tongue. It's capable of speaking to one set of voters from one side of its mouth and to another set from the other side. We've already seen how direct mail's capacity for "targeting" is used in fundraising mail to rifle the appeal to those deemed most likely to respond. In persuasion mail, the same capacity is used to tell different groups of people exactly what each group wants to hear. "In the old days," says Tim Roper, "candidates used to give one speech in one town and give a different speech in the next town. Nowadays, when they try that, they get caught by the news media. But it's very hard to get caught doing that in direct mail."

The simplest and most obvious way to target persuasion mail is geographically. In large metropolitan areas like New York City or Los Angeles, where the broadcast media cover dozens of congressional districts, local candidates find direct mail a cost-effective way to reach only the people who are capable of voting for them. For a congressional candidate on Long Island to buy a spot on New York City television, for example, he would have to pay to reach nineteen people who could *not* vote for him for every one person who could.

Persuasion mail also can be targeted *demographically* to reach voters of a certain age, income, sex, or religion. In his bid for the governorship of New York, for example, Republican Lew Lehrman sent one letter to Jewish voters in which a third party endorsed Lehrman by saying "he speaks our language." But at the same time, a second letter went out to Catholic voters that spoke heavily in the language of tuition tax credits and anti-abortion. In fact, during the last week of the campaign, Lehrman mailed no less than three million letters, segmented to a variety of different audiences and carrying a variety of different messages. Twelve percentage points down in the polls before the letters were mailed, Lehrman closed to lose the election by only three.

Finally, persuasion mail can be targeted *psychographically*, by the voter's own personal interests and concerns. A candidate can mail to farmers, bakers, bankers, and candlestickmakers, telling each of them whatever they want to hear. "This kind of persuasion mail has an enormous potential to be destructive when it's used unethically," says Roger Craver.

"Let's say you're running for town council right here in Falls Church," Craver hypothesizes, "and you've got a list of mobile-home owners in the Falls Church area. So you create an organization. Get yourself some stationery and call yourself, oh, let's say, 'The Falls Church Mobile-Home Association.' Now, you write a letter and say, 'Dear Dick: Do you know that Roger Craver, who is running for town council, has pledged to pass legislation banning mobile homes in Falls Church? Well, I don't want to leave my home. And I know you don't . . .' and so on. All of this might be a total fabrication, but there's no damn way the opposition is going to see this as easily as they would if you put it on television."

Rod Smith of the National Republican Senatorial Committee sums up psychographically targeted persuasion mail rather neatly when he says, "You take a poll, you find out what people are thinking, and you just vomit back what they're thinking."

But in fairness, direct mail's capacity for precision targeting has its positive side as well. While consulting on the late Harold Washington's race for mayor of Chicago, Roger Craver realized his candidate was being hurt badly in middle-class white neighborhoods by a trumped-up charge of tax evasion. In truth, the matter involved only a few hundred dollars, and there was considerable evidence it was politically motivated. So Craver sent a letter targeted to middle-class and upper-middle-class whites in which he carefully laid out all the facts in the case over four long pages.

"This was the kind of thing you just couldn't do on television," says Craver. "In order to tell a factual story on TV, you need lots of time. To treat it superficially would only reinforce the prevailing perception."

Of course, if I had been working for Washington's opponent, I would have advised him to send a letter to middle-class blacks saying, "*You* have to pay taxes . . . why doesn't Harold Washington?"

You see, in the old days, the only way to sling mud at your opponent in a political campaign was to pick up a bucket of the stuff and throw it at him. But with today's direct-mail technology, you can nail the bastard right between the eyes.

3

High-Tech
Origami:
How Direct
Mail Works

Tom Bradley never knew what hit him.

A popular black mayor of Los Angeles, Bradley was the favorite in his race for governor of California against a rather bland attorney general by the name of George Deukmejian. But for Tom Bradley, election day 1982 was one of those days when you do everything right and everything still goes wrong.

The day began well enough. Exit polls conducted by the television networks and local pollsters showed him ahead by a clear margin. On the strength of those polls, TV reporters projected him the winner. As it turned out, the exit polls were exactly right. More than seven million Californians went to their polling places in 1982, and they gave Tom Bradley a distinct majority of 19,886 votes.

But something funny happened to Tom Bradley on the way to Sacramento.

He won at the polls.

But he lost in the mail.

* * *

It all started three months earlier when John Myers, the executive director of the California Republican Party, and his brilliant direct-mail consultant, Tim Roper, decided to put a new twist on an old idea. The old idea was a "slate mailing." Perhaps the most common form of political persuasion mail, a slate mailing is a list of officially endorsed candidates mailed by political parties to registered voters shortly before the election. Many voters are confused by the array of choices presented to them inside the voting booth, and a slate mailing helps alleviate the confusion while reminding party loyalists which candidates have earned their party's endorsement.

The new twist Roper and Myers added to their traditional slate mailing was based on a law recently passed by the California state legislature. Ironically, it was a law the Democrats had initiated and the Republicans had bitterly opposed. To vote by absentee ballot in California prior to 1978, it always had been necessary for a voter to write a letter to his County Board of Elections explaining why he would be unable to vote at the polling place. But the new law said this was no longer necessary. It said, in effect: "If you want to vote absentee, fine. Just write in and ask for an absentee ballot, and we'll send it to you—no questions asked." Even more significant, a key provision of the law said it was now permissible for a *third party* to make the application on behalf of the voter. If Grandma is sick, for example, Grandpa can apply for the absentee ballot on her behalf. Having passed this law in 1978, California Democrats promptly forgot about it.

"But we Republicans are elephants," said John Myers, "and we never forget."[1]

Myers and Roper decided to include an official application for an absentee ballot in their slate mailing to registered Republicans in the fall of 1982. There was only one problem. There was no such thing as an "official absentee ballot application." The new law, after all, had said the voter need only write a note requesting the ballot. But Roper was a direct-mail expert, and if there's one thing direct-mail experts are good at, it's taking a worthless piece of paper and making it look as valuable and official as the Magna Carta.

"URGENT! IMPORTANT VOTER INFORMATION EN-CLOSED" said the headline on the outer envelope. And underneath it there was a short line browbeating the beleaguered postman: "ATTENTION POSTMASTER—TIME DATED LEGAL DOCUMENTS ENCLOSED, EXPEDITE FOR IMMEDIATE DELIVERY." Above, in the area usually reserved for the return address, was Deukmejian's name and title, plus the address of the California Republican Party, all arranged in such a way as to suggest the letter was official business from the office of the attorney general. The words "California Republican Party," for example, were set in fine type in upper and lower case. Just underneath it, the words "STATE ADMINISTRATIVE OFFICE" were set in bold type with solid caps. While the mail would be processed at the party's headquarters in Burbank, a Sacramento return address was given. And underneath it were the words, "OFFICIAL DOCUMENTS, GEORGE DEUKMEJIAN, ATTORNEY GENERAL, CALIFORNIA." All of this was set in a typestyle widely used by state and federal agencies.

Inside the envelope was a rather long letter from George Deukmejian, a short letter from President Reagan, a postage-paid return envelope, a "candidate guide" (the slate), and Roper's *pièce de résistance*—the "OFFICIAL ABSENTEE BALLOT APPLICATION." As designed and written by Roper, the application looked like something from the Internal Revenue Service. Printed in black, blue, and red, it provided three spaces for registered voters to sign their names and receive absentee ballots.

"Here's your personal Absentee Ballot Application," said the copy. "The person named below can simply sign in the blue shaded area and mail this form to apply for an Absentee Ballot.

"If there are other Republicans in your household, simply ask them to print their names and addresses in the other two boxes provided, and then sign in the additional blue-shaded areas.

"Once you've received your Absentee Ballot, you can vote in the privacy of your own home and avoid long lines, parking problems and yet help our Republican candidates win on November 2!"

Using state-of-the-art technology in computer printing, each application was preprinted with the voter's name and address in large capital letters. All the voter had to do was sign his name and mail it back in the postage-paid envelope.

But letting it go at that would have been too easy! In the terms of direct-mail fundraising, the mailing couldn't be considered a real success unless it also raised money. So Roper enclosed a reply card asking the recipient for an "emergency contribution to the California Republican Party to help wage this special election drive." And to show the donor exactly what was at stake, Roper used his computer to create a personalized slate. Taking its cue from the Zip code of each recipient, the computer was able to print exactly which GOP candidates would appear on the voter's own ballot—from the Republican candidate for United States senator (Pete Wilson) all the way down to the Republican candidate for the local tax-assessment board.

"The chairman took a lot of criticism for sending out a slate mailing so early in the campaign," said Roper. "But we had to mail it early to give the absentee-ballot idea time to work. So we told people to stick the slate on their refrigerator."

The bulk of Deukmejian's letter concentrated on urging the recipient to send back his ballot application. "Simply drop your ABSENTEE BALLOT APPLICATION in the postage-paid envelope I've enclosed for you," it said. The postage-paid envelope was addressed to something called "THE VOTE-BY-MAIL CENTER," which happened to be located at the address of the California Republican Party.

"We weren't ready for the deluge of returns," a party official told *The California Journal*. "Within a few days after the mailer hit, we had nearly a hundred thousand applications at the party's Burbank headquarters."[2]

Working at a frenzied pace, Roper and other party staffers sorted the applications into fifty-eight different batches, one for each county in California. "We'd open the envelopes, drop the applications in boxes marked by county, and the next day we'd send the boxes to the Board of Elections in each county." A few days later, county officials sent each voter his or her absentee ballot.

The California Republican Party sent this mailing to 2.5 million registered Republicans in the state, and it cost approximately $350,000 to do so. But since it raised $288,000 in contributions, the *net* cost was only $62,000. And by adding thousands of new Republican donors to the mailing list, the California Republican Party eventually will realize a profit from it. By any measure, the mailing was a huge success. But its real impact was not felt until the evening of November 2.

Tom Bradley must have choked on his champagne that night. With the TV anchormen projecting him as the winner and his own exit polls saying he had a clear lead, Bradley probably felt his heart sink as the absentee ballots were counted. Nearly a half million absentee ballots had been filed, a whopping 6.5 percent of the total vote. Tom Bradley received 189,112 absentee votes. George Deukmejian got 302,343. Tom Bradley won at the polls by a margin of 20,000 votes. George Deukmejian won in the mail by a margin of 113,000. When it was all added up, Deukmejian had won the governorship by ninety-three thousand votes.

For Mayor Tom Bradley, it was one of those days.

But for Tim Roper, "It was one of those days when I really kick my heels in the air."

To pull off a direct-mail miracle like the one Tim Roper engineered in California, it's almost imperative that you get to know a man like Bob Harty.

A short, energetic, good-looking man, it's almost impossible not to like Bob Harty on sight and sound. And that personal charm undoubtedly serves him well in his job, which is to act as the chief salesman and troubleshooter for a full-service direct-mail production company called the Communications Corporation of America.

Nestled in the foothills of the Blue Ridge Mountains in a town called Culpeper, Virginia, CCA is a for-profit direct-mail firm that grew out of a not-for-profit political organization—The American Security Council. About thirty years ago, a small group of major corporate defense contractors decided it would be in their best interest—and presumably in the best interest of the country as well—if there were a voice in the public sector to keep the American people advised of the nation's weakening defense posture and the growing need for more arms. They called the organization "The American Security Council." And to run it, they hired a bright young man who had already risen high in the ranks of Dick Sears's watch company, or, as it was known by that time, Sears, Roebuck. Like Richard Sears, John Fisher realized very early that the success of his new venture would depend greatly on direct marketing.

In a tiny office on Capitol Hill, he began writing direct-mail letters to conservative Americans who were deeply concerned about what they saw as a growing weakness in America's will to maintain the upper hand in the arms race. Fisher was a talented copywriter and a skillful direct-mail manager, but from the point of view of his suppliers, he also was a demanding client. He insisted on tight deadlines and errorless printing, and he was often disappointed.

Eventually Fisher decided the only way to maintain complete control over his direct mail was to bring more and more production facilities in-house. And from that point it was only a matter of time before he started selling his production services to others. Fisher called his young production company "The Communication Corporation of America," and he hired his son, Steve, to run it. Under the younger Fisher's management, CCA grew impressively. Although it is by no means the only facility of its kind in the country, or even the largest, it is in some ways the best. CCA is on the cutting edge of direct-mail technology. And that's why I was so pleased when Bob Harty agreed to give me a tour of it.

In truth, most direct-mail campaigns are won or lost long before a man like Bob Harty even sees them. That's because success in direct mail has less to do with computers, laser printers, and state-of-the-art technology than it does with good, old-fashioned arithmetic—the kind you do with a sharp pencil, a good eraser, and lots of patience.

Financial Strategy

"Direct-mail fundraising is first and foremost a process of financial management," wrote Roger Craver in the political trade journal *Campaigns & Elections*. "While the creative and technical functions are important, they must take place in the context of an overall financial strategy."[3]

Craver's statement probably is the most overlooked principle in political direct mail and the most common reason why the majority of direct-mail campaigns fail. Assembling such a strategic plan, however, requires both a fundamental understanding of the mathematics of direct marketing and enough

Table 1

Summary of Donor Acquisition Mailings

Time Period	Quantity	Resp. Rate	Avg. Gift	Gross Income	Gross Cost	Net Income
April 1985	100,000	1.0%	$22	$22,000	$25,000	$(3,000)
June 1985	500,000	0.9	22	99,000	125,000	(26,000)
September 1985	500,000	0.9	22	99,000	125,000	(26,000)
January 1986	500,000	1.2	22	132,000	125,000	7,000
February 1986	500,000	1.2	22	132,000	125,000	7,000
TOTAL	2,100,000	1.05	22	484,000	525,000	(41,000)
New Donors Acquired	22,000					

practical experience to realize that even the most careful estimates seldom match real-life results. Given the complex, almost scientific nature of the task, it's amazing how many candidates are willing to entrust their direct-mail campaigns to volunteers and relatives. Almost every professional direct-mail consultant has a story about candidates who insist direct mail doesn't work. When pressed on the matter, the disillusioned politicians often confess that while they hired top-flight talent to do their TV commercials, they left the direct mail to anyone who walked through the door.

One of the reasons why the candidate's brother-in-law is apt to be mystified by direct-mail fundraising is that a professionally designed direct-mail campaign invariably begins by losing money. In the prospecting, or donor acquisition phase, mailings are conducted at a net loss, or—with luck—on a break-even basis. It is not until the renewal, or resolicitation, phase when direct mail begins to show a profit. In the accompanying tables, Roger Craver has designed a hypothetical direct-mail fundraising campaign for a candidate who has wisely decided to begin prospecting twenty-one months before the election. Table 1 shows the results of the prospecting mailings. Table 2 shows how the original donors responded when they were asked to give again.

The program begins in April, a year and a half before the election, when the first prospecting mailing of a hundred thousand pieces is tested on a variety of liberal lists. This initial "test phase" is designed to determine which lists are the most effective for the candidate and which of several different versions of copy work best. One of every hundred people who received this mailing responds and they make an average contribution of twenty-two dollars. Thus the mailing grosses twenty-two thousand dollars at a cost of twenty-five thousand dollars, or a net loss of three thousand dollars. At this point the candidate's brother-in-law is likely to give up and tell his friends, "Direct mail doesn't work." But Roger Craver is just getting warmed up. To him, three thousand dollars is an acceptable loss.

Like the mad salesman who loses money on every sale but makes it up on volume, Craver now takes his money losing proposition and "rolls it out" to five hundred thousand names. In doing so he drops any lists that were unproductive the first time, and he uses only the copy that worked best before. Because of the statistical projectability of direct mail, he is reasonably certain the results he gets on this larger "rollout" mailing will be similar to what he got on his earlier test mailing. Indeed, they are. Roughly one of every hundred people respond, and the average gift is the same as before, twenty-two dollars. Now Craver has made $99,000 at a cost of $125,000—or a net loss of $26,000. This is when the candidate's wife suggests to her husband that there is a woman in her garden club who might be able to do a better job with the direct-mail program than Mr. Craver.

But by August, slightly more than one year before the election, Craver is ready to stop fishing from the ocean and start fishing from the aquarium. In Table 2 we see the results of his first renewal mailing. His first two prospecting mailings have yielded a "house list" of fifty-five hundred loyal donors. When he mails to these proven supporters in August, nearly one of every *ten* respond, and they kick in with an average gift of twenty-five dollars, three dollars more than before. This mailing grosses $13,750 at a cost of $2,750—for a net *profit* of $11,000. Things are looking up.

In September, Craver wades into the ocean again for more prospecting. Another half-million-piece mailing yields the same results as before, at a loss of twenty-six thousand dollars. But forty-five hundred more precious names are added to the house list, which is resolicited profitably again in October. In January

Table 2

Summary of Resolicitation Program

Time Period	Quantity	Resp. Rate	Avg. Gift	Gross Income	Gross Cost	Net Income
August 1985	5,500	10.0%	$25	$13,750	$2,750	$11,000
October 1985	7,500	10.0	25	18,750	3,750	15,000
December 1985	10,500	10.0	25	26,250	5,250	21,000
January 1986	10,500	10.0	25	26,250	5,250	21,000
February 1986	10,500	10.0	25	26,250	5,250	21,000
March 1986	16,500	10.0	25	41,250	8,250	33,000
April 1986	22,000	10.0	25	55,000	11,000	44,000
May 1986	22,000	10.0	25	55,000	11,000	44,000
June 1986	22,000	8.0	24	42,240	11,000	31,240
July 1986	22,000	8.0	24	42,240	11,000	31,240
August 1986	22,000	8.0	23	40,480	11,000	29,480
September 1986	22,000	9.0	25	49,500	11,000	38,500
Late Sept. 1986	22,000	9.0	25	49,500	11,000	38,500
October 1986	22,000	10.0	25	55,000	11,000	44,000
TOTAL	241,000	9.1	25	541,460	118,500	422,960
Total Program	2,341,000	—	—	1,025,460	643,500	381,960

and February, the first two months of the election year, Craver "drops" his final two prospecting mailings. Notice that the results are slightly better this time. There are two likely reasons for this: (1) in the course of three earlier prospecting mailings, Craver has refined his list strategy and copy approach to the point where he is now enjoying a slight increase in response; and (2) more people want to make political contributions in an election year than in the year before.

With nine months left to go before election day, Craver begins an intensive renewal effort. And here is another occasion when the candidate (or his amateur advisers) and the professional direct-mail consultant are likely to disagree. "You can't keep mailing letters to these poor people," says the candidate. "They'll get mad at me. They won't give anymore." But experience shows that a loyal contributor, if handled properly, will give . . . and give . . . and give . . . until he drops dead or suffers bankruptcy, whichever comes first. When it comes to resoliciting previous donors, professional direct mailers follow a simple rule: Don't stop doing it until you stop making money.

That is especially true when the resolicitation can be tied to actual events, as is most dramatically the case in the heat of a presidential primary campaign. Craver's chart shows him renewing previous donors once a month, but a presidential candidate in the spring primaries may mail to his house file as often as once a week.

"We won by a slim margin in New Hampshire," the candidate writes with a gathering sense of urgency, "but the polls show us down by five points in Florida. If I don't get your special contribution of fifteen dollars by next Tuesday, I'm afraid life on this planet, as we know it, will cease to exist." Collins and Dees used this technique very effectively for McGovern in the spring of 1972.

This kind of schedule calls for pinpoint timing and extremely tight deadlines, but in most political campaigns the problem is not keeping up with events but manufacturing them. Mailing once a month during the election year becomes a creative challenge for the direct-mail copywriter who, by the end of August, will be making suggestions like, "Why don't we try a letter from the candidate's dog?"

No matter what creative gimmicks are employed, however, the essence of the financial strategy at this stage of the campaign will be to "upgrade" the donors—in other words, to urge them to give bigger checks than before. For the sake of simplicity, Craver's chart does not show the effect of donor upgrading, but success in this vital effort is what distinguishes a modestly profitable direct-mail campaign from a real winner.

To carry our "fishing" analogy one step farther, upgrading donors is like dropping large amounts of food into the aquarium every day in the hope of fattening the fish for an eventual kill. In direct-mailing fundraising this is done by feeding the loyal contributor large doses of flattery, computer personalization, and constant requests for increasingly larger sums of money. One direct-mail consultant appropriately calls this process "the care and feeding of a donor." And nobody feeds their donors like the

National Republican Senatorial Committee.

From the donor's point of view, sending fifteen dollars to the Senatorial Committee in response to a prospect mailing about rising inflation or high taxes must feel like accidentally stumbling into a secret society. The donor begins in the outer circle, where he will be treated with respect but without much affection. From time to time he will receive a prospect letter inviting him to carry his membership forward another degree and come one step closer to the inner circles of power in Washington. If he goes along with the idea, he soon will receive letters addressed "Dear Friend," in which the word "Friend" has been crossed out by a laser printer and his first name printed above it in imitation handwriting. In time he will be given a secret "800" telephone number he can call to get the latest information on what's happening in Washington. By the time he is giving ten thousand dollars to the RNC's Eagles Club, the contributor will be made to feel like he is one of Ronald Reagan's closest personal friends and that scarcely anyone in Washington dares to make a move without consulting him.

The Republican Senatorial Committee's "Presidential Task Force" went as far as to fly to Europe so they could send a renewal letter back to their donors in the United States, postmarked in Normandy and timed to coincide with the anniversary of D-Day. Signed by Strom Thurmond, the letter began, "The beaches here in Normandy are quiet, but you and I know this scene looked drastically different forty years ago. I was there on that day. . . ."

Somehow the letter managed to get from that lyrical opening back to urging the donor to renew his membership in the Task Force.

But no matter how much creative energy is expended in the effort to upgrade previous donors, the key to getting bigger contributions is simply to ask for them. Direct mailers have found that loyal donors are amazingly inclined to give exactly the amount you ask them for—which is why it's so important to keep big donors separated from the smaller ones. "Don't ask a person who has given you a hundred dollars for twenty-five," warns Roger Craver. "You're likely to get it!"[4]

Offer Strategy

Having laid the groundwork of a financial plan, the direct mailer next turns his attention to his "offer strategy," or in the case of political mail, his candidate's position. "Positioning" is a marketing theory that states that the best way to establish a place for your product in the consumer's mind is to *relate* it to the other products already there. Given that Hertz is the obvious leader in the car rental business, for example, Avis found a profitable position for itself by saying, "We're number two."

In general advertising, once the positioning strategy for a particular product has been determined, the advertiser must remain committed to it for a substantial time. But in the silent and underground world of direct mail, positioning is a much more dynamic process.

"In direct marketing," says direct-mail expert Ed Nash, "we have the ability to refine our positioning very precisely, to measure the results, and to make dramatic changes from one advertisement to another. We can, in effect, be all things to all people. . . ."[5]

After demonstrating how one product can have several different positions, Nash concludes by saying, "None of these positions are necessarily right or wrong, but all of them are different, and all of them give you something to say about your product that differentiates it from the competition. The position that is almost always wrong is 'right in the middle. . . .'"[6]

So it goes in political direct mail, where the only wrong way to position the candidate is as a moderate. Although it is always easier to raise money with a candidate on either end of the political spectrum, the clever direct-mail strategist has many ways of using the techniques of positioning to make his candidate seem more extreme than he really is. If the candidate is a moderate Republican, for example, the direct mailer may choose to portray the Democratic opponent as a radical left-winger in order to gather support from the right. Sometimes a candidate can take advantage of the silence of direct mail and simply portray himself as more extreme than his opponent, even if he really isn't. In George Bush's campaign for the Republican presidential nomination of 1980, for example, Bush frequently sent direct-mail letters that out-Reaganed Reagan. Many candidates will establish a strong position by identifying themselves with a single issue, as in "I am the anti-abortion candidate!" This is the political equivalent of saying, "Nyquil is the nighttime cold medicine." Finally, the candidate may simply latch on to any issue, personality trait, or characteristic that helps distinguish himself from the rest of the field and play it to the hilt.

John Anderson probably was the ultimate "positioned" candidate. Finding himself pitted against a half-dozen other contenders for the 1980 Republican presidential nomination, all of whom held roughly the same conservative views, Anderson decided to position himself as the one liberal candidate in the field. For a while it became more important for Anderson to distinguish himself from the competition than it was to articulate his real thoughts on the issues. If all the Republican candidates got together and decided the sky was blue, Anderson would issue a press release saying it was green. He went as far as to come out against school prayer, even though earlier in his career, according to the Almanac of American Politics 1982, he had introduced a constitutional amendment to make the nation explicitly Christian. Not surprisingly, John Anderson worked like gangbusters in the mail.

List Strategy

With the candidate's position set and his financial plan in place, the direct-marketing strategist is now ready to begin working on the real alchemy of direct mail: the selection of mailing lists. It has been said that to understand the world of mailing lists is to understand direct mail. Not surprisingly, almost no one does.

One begins to arrive at an understanding, however, when one stops thinking of a mailing list as a static pile of names and addresses and begins to think of it as an organic creature, a living, breathing, dynamic organism with a past, a present, a future, and even a personality all its own. In the time it takes to print a mailing list into some readable and permanent form—like a membership roster, for example—it has already changed many times. A membership roster is only a snapshot of a mailing list, a picture of how it looked at the moment the decision was made to put it on paper. In fact, if you could see a mailing list the way it really is, it would not look at all like a spool of magnetic tape or a stack of mailing labels but more like something out of a Stephen King novel—a pulsating, breathing blob that sits in the corner, emitting an eerie sound as it constantly changes colors: because mailing lists are not made up of names, they are made up of *people*—millions of real people, each with their own private whims and fancies, their own likes and dislikes, each acting on their own free will . . . and yet, as a whole, capable of behaving in an almost unified, amazingly predictable manner.

There are essentially three different kinds of mailing lists: (1) response lists; (2) compiled lists; and (3) house lists.

Direct marketers believe that the world is divided into two types of people: those who respond to direct mail and those who do not. If an individual isn't accustomed to buying merchandise or contributing to charities by mail, no amount of affection for the candidate, anger about the issues, or interest in the election will induce him to give to a direct-mail solicitation. One is either a "direct-mail respondent" or not. And so the most significant distinction among mailing lists is between "response lists," which are comprised of people who have bought or donated by mail in the past, and "compiled lists," which are lists of people who share some vocational, avocational, or philosophical interest. A list of registered Republicans, for example, is a compiled list. But a list of direct-mail donors to the National Republican Congressional Committee is a response list.

From a fundraising standpoint, response lists almost always work better than compiled lists. Perhaps no more dramatic proof of that fact exists than the experience of the Republican National Committee during the early days of its direct-mail "Sustaining Membership" program. In launching the program, the RNC tested a variety of compiled lists of registered Republicans, businessmen, known conservatives, and various high-income individuals. But in test after test, none of these compiled lists worked as well as a humble response list that apparently had nothing to do with politics at all. Titled "The Carwash Shammy Buyers of America," it was a list of people who had purchased an expensive mail-order rag for polishing their cars. The mere fact that they were used to doing business through the mail (and, of course, that they were suburban families with lots of disposable income) made them better prospects for the RNC's direct-mail program than known conservatives and registered Republicans.

But compiled lists have a role to play in politics, too—especially when it comes to persuasion mail.

Major list-compiling companies own literally millions of names, and they offer the political candidate two important capabilities that are hard to achieve with response lists: *saturation* and *precision*. Using compiled lists, in other words, a candidate can write to *everyone* in his district, or he can write only to precisely targeted groups. For example, he can write only to blacks, to Jews, to people who own their own homes, to people above a certain level of income, to people of a certain age, to only one sex.

Some political candidates, especially at the local level, try to compile their own lists. Starting with the people on the office Rolodex, candidates gradually add party registration lists, donors to previous candidates in the same district, members of friendly civic groups and professional organizations, people who have signed the office guestbook or whose names have been recorded in the telephone log, even the friends and acquaintances of staff members. But no matter whether he needs compiled lists or response lists, the candidate who is really serious about direct mail will eventually have to retain the services of someone called a "list broker."

"I would to God thou and I knew where a commodity of good names could be bought," Falstaff says to Prince Hal in Shakespeare's *King Henry IV*, proving that the need for good lists goes back as far as Elizabethan times, although list brokers probably do not. "Commodity," however, is a very appropriate choice of words. A list broker is someone who deals in the commodity of human names, brokering the transaction between two parties who wish to buy, rent, or exchange mailing lists. It's a kind of high-tech slave trade.

I call it a slave trade because this constant buying and selling of your name takes place largely without your permission and sometimes against your will. Once you have purchased anything by mail, or contributed to any organization, you become part of a multibillion-dollar industry in which everyone involved will make a dollar off your name except you. It's possible actually to watch this process take place by using a trick known to everyone in the direct-mail business but to very few outside it. The next time you buy a mail-order product or contribute to a charity by mail, give your name a code. If your name is really John A. Doe, for example, call yourself John B. Doe. Then sit back and watch as your name is bought, sold, rented, and exchanged by scores of companies and organizations.

Having chosen the lists he wants to test for his prospect mailing, the direct mailer rents the lists from their owners through the offices of the broker, who takes a 20 percent cut.

In most cases the mailer will test small samples of a wide variety of lists in "test cells" of about five thousand names each. When he finds a responsive list, he will return to the broker and order more names from the same list. The mailer is not allowed to keep the rented names and, in most cases, is not even allowed to see them. A magnetic tape will be delivered directly to the service company hired to print the names on labels or computerize the letters. But whenever one of the names on a rented list responds to the mailer's appeal, that name becomes *his* name. It becomes, in short, a part of the "house list."

A good house list is the most valuable commodity in direct mail. Jim Aldige calls the house list the "gold mine" of direct mail. Others have called it "the family jewels." Richard Viguerie keeps his house list in a fireproof room with a round-the-clock security guard posted outside.

House lists are valuable not just because they are the lifeblood of an organization's direct-mail fundraising program but also because they are, in and of themselves, a significant source of income. An organization that has five hundred thousand names on its house list and decides to rent that list ten times a year can expect to clear a two-hundred-thousand-dollar profit annually. For that reason, house lists are jealously guarded by their owners, and while it's common for two organizations to *ex-*

change lists in the hope of finding new members, an organization will never *give* its list to anyone. Republican candidates around the country, for example, seldom understand why the national Republican Party won't let them use the names of contributors in their state. But, in fact, the three major organizations that make up the national GOP won't even share their house lists with each other!

As valuable as house lists are, list owners have several ways of making them worth even more. Foremost among these is a process known as "segmenting" the list. A segmented list is one that has been divided into various groups of names on the basis of personal characteristics, interests, or giving habits that may affect the donors' propensity to respond in the future. A well-segmented house list may be broken down by income, age, sex, mode of payment, frequency of previous gifts, length of time on the file, and special interest. Working with a segmented list, the mailer can select only the names he deems most likely to respond to a particular appeal. Charlie Judd, executive director of The Liberty Federation (the Moral Majority), calls this kind of house mailing "smart mail."

"We segment our list any way you can imagine," says Judd. "Since we're a multi-issue organization, we track all of the hot buttons. We know what each person on our file is most likely to give to and what they're least likely to give to.

"We have several major categories: human life, national defense, humanitarian, school prayer, and religious freedom. So we have the ability to address any particular issue according to their interest. Instead of doing one house file mailing, we'll do five simultaneously."

Another state-of-the-art technique for enhancing the value of the house file, while improving the organization's ability to find new donors, is an analytical process known as a "geodemographic overlay." When the direct mailer runs a geodemographic analysis of his list, he is, in effect, composing a statistical profile of the kind of people who give to his organization. This profile, in turn, will be "overlaid" on prospecting lists like a stencil, enabling him to rent only names that are similar to those already on his own list.

After the lists have been selected and the letter written, a direct-mail project is ready at last to undergo the magic of a man like Bob Harty.

Production

The mysterious craft that Bob Harty performs on a direct-mail piece resembles nothing so much as a kind of high-tech version of the ancient Japanese art of origami, the making of ornamental designs by folding paper. It is still common to make a direct-mail piece the old-fashioned way, by individually printing each component and painstakingly assembling them into one "package" at the end. But now it is possible through modern technology to make an entire direct-mail package out of a single sheet of paper—by printing, folding, cutting, and matching it so it starts out in one piece, fans out into a half-dozen separate pieces, and then all comes back together at the end, wrapped in its own envelope like a tortoise in its shell.

The process begins with the paper itself.

"Are you ready for our tour?" Bob Harty asked me. And before I had a chance to say yes, he was off and running, briskly leading me down narrow, submarinelike corridors, brightly hailing everyone we met along the way in a good-ole-boy accent.

At last we came to a large room at the end of a long corridor. From just outside the door, I could hear a low roar. I thought I recognized the thing in the center of the room. It looked like the stegosaurus in the Museum of Natural History in New York. Except it was bigger. And unlike the stegosaurus, it was alive.

"She can do about a thousand feet a minute," said Harty softly.

A long, thin, skeletal-looking machine, it was a giant offset printing press designed to turn large webs of blank paper into the preprinted "continuous forms" that are the raw material of a personalized direct-mail letter. At one end of the monster, giant spools of plain white paper were being fed to the presses. At the other end—what looked to be about a hundred feet downstream—tinted gray sheets were coming out, fully printed with copy and art, and pierced with the tiny pinholes that later would enable it to be tracked into a computer printer.

"That baby'll cost you about a million and a half," said Harty as we moved to the next room.

We stepped from the age of the dinosaurs into the space age as we walked into an area that looked a lot like the engine room on the starship *Enterprise*. Bright fluorescent lights, clean white walls, and row after row of cool-blue mainframe computers were attended by a smattering of neatly dressed technicians.

"This is our data processing department," said Harty.

"Young lady, what are you working on today?" Harty asked a technician who was standing quietly in a corner punching numbers into a mainframe computer as the spools of magnetic tape rotated back and forth at her command. She explained that she was "making some selects off the RNC master file." In other words, the Republican Party had asked her to pull out some of the segments on its house list for a specialized mailing. The client had supplied her with a series of code numbers only, so she had no idea exactly what kind of people she was extracting. But it could have been anyone: men over fifty years old, women living west of the Mississippi, people who have given more than a hundred dollars in the past year. Perhaps the RNC was considering another mailing to carwash shammy buyers!

In a room adjacent to the mainframe computers stood four large machines representing the latest innovation in direct-mail technology: laser printers. Part laser beam, part photocopier, the laser printer creates an image by flashing powdered toner onto a sheet of paper and thermally affixing it there in a process known as "hot fusion." Although "ink-jet" printers are faster (using a technology that spits ink at the paper at mind-boggling speeds) and "impact" printers create a more realistic image (a technology similar to that of a high-speed typewriter), the laser printer combines both speed and quality in a way that has revolutionized the use of computer personalization in direct mail. The remarkable thing about a laser printer is that it can do just about anything the computer tells it to do. If the computer says, "Print this name in Old English type with letters two inches tall," the laser printer does it. If the computer then says, "Print the same name in fine print and Helvetica lettering," the laser printer does that. There is never a need to make any mechanical adjustment in the printer, since it gets all its instructions electronically. CCA's laser printers have been programmed to print the letters of the alphabet in more than 150 different typestyles—everything from a conventional typewriter font to something that looks like a child's handwriting. The laser can also print words sideways and upside down, a talent that comes in handy when printing a single sheet of paper that will be cut and folded to yield three or four different personalized components of a direct-mail package.

Although some direct mailers like to show off their laser printers with letters that reproduce the recipient's name in a dozen different styles and sizes, the real advantage of this technology is in how it can be used to upgrade gifts. Using a laser printer, it is possible, for example, to circle the twenty-five-dollar box on a reply card and print a little "handwritten" note saying, "Richard: We appreciate your generous gift in April 1987 of fifteen dollars, but we hope you will try to give twenty-five dollars this year." What's more, it's possible to do this at the rate of about six thousand letters per hour. Amazingly, this kind of technology has actually lowered and not increased the overall cost of producing a direct-mail campaign.

Direct-mail production technology, in fact, has become so highly automated that the role of the volunteer in American politics has been greatly diminished. "In the past," says Tim Roper, "campaigns were eager to find volunteers because there was so much drudge work that needed to be done. But nowadays you've got the reverse problem: You have a lot of volunteers sitting around with nothing to do. I can't tell you how many of our mailings have gotten screwed up because we had to send it to be assembled at a headquarters just to give their volunteers something to do."

After the continuous forms have been personalized by laser printers, the forms are carried into another room where they will be "bursted" and "trimmed." It is an impressive exercise in spatial intelligence to cut and trim every fourteen inches of continuous form, separate the different pieces for individual handling and folding, and then bring them all back together again— in sequential order—to be stuffed into the same envelope. One form, for example, may be trimmed to yield a personalized letter, a personalized outer envelope, and a personalized reply card. The letter goes off in one direction to be mated with second sheets and folded. The reply card goes off in another direction for folding. And the portion of the form reserved for the envelope will go off in a third direction, to be manufactured from a flat sheet of paper into an envelope. Then all the pieces are reunited at the automatic inserting machine. The tricky part is keeping them in order as they fan out to various areas of the shop, so that an envelope addressed to John Brown doesn't wind up containing a letter written to Joe Smith. Somehow, with the help of computerized sequential codes, it all comes together perfectly at the end.

The business of finishing, folding, inserting, stamping, and sorting direct mail is known generically as "lettershop" service. And here we glimpse why CCA and companies like it usually are located in the boondocks and not closer to the direct-mail agencies that provide them with most of their work. CCA's Appalachian location gives them access to a large, unskilled, nonunionized, cheap labor force for what is essentially assembly-line work. The lettershop room at CCA looks like a scene from *Norma Rae*, with row after row of plainly dressed women bending over machines that are banging, whirring, and pounding away at a steady, never-ending roar.

Bob Harty couldn't suppress a proud little smile as he led us out of the lettershop department and on to the final stop of our tour. "It took us many, many years to get this," he said as we stepped out of the head-pounding din of the lettershop and walked into a quiet, cool cargo bay, with trucks loading sacks of mail into their trailers.

It was CCA's own post office.

Indeed, the Communications Corporation of America generates so much mail that the U.S. Postal Service has seen fit to open a post office right on the premises. One lone federal employee sits in her tiny office all day with nothing else to do but verify, weigh, and account for the thousands of letters that come tumbling out of the CCA lettershop every hour. It's a full-time job. And as a result of having a post office on the premises, CCA's mailings go directly to the regional postal centers, bypassing the time-consuming process of being handled by a local post office.

It's not unusual for large lettershop firms and mail-order companies to have their own post offices on the premises. The U.S. Postal Service is very accommodating to heavy users of bulk-rate postage . . . and for good reason. Although many Americans think "junk mail" is what drives up the price of a first-class stamp, the truth is exactly the opposite. The tidy profit that the post office makes on third-class mail is the only thing keeping the cost of first-class mail from rising even farther than it has. The post office makes money on bulk mail because the direct mailer takes all the work out of it. Third-class mail is presorted, standardized, weighed, and paid for by the pound. Most important, it is given a deferred priority, meaning that postal workers are allowed to let it sit around until they have time to work on it. As any direct mailer will tell you, sometimes it sits around forever. But since postage is the single biggest expense in direct mail and the only one over which the mailer has no control, the bulk-rate discounts work well for all concerned.

Our tour was over. And with a sweeping gesture that took in not only the private post office but also the enormous warehouse of paper products nearby—a vast, dark, cold warehouse reminiscent of the one in the final scene in *Raiders of the Lost Ark*—Harty concluded his presentation.

"Man," he said, "we've come a long way from when Bob Odell and I used to deliver the Republican Party's mail to the D.C. post office in the back of a borrowed convertible DeSoto."

Bob Odell's partner Tim Roper must have thought his 1982 absentee-ballot mailing was as obsolete as a DeSoto convertible. Because when the time came to try it again in 1984, he pulled out all the stops and created a direct-mail package even Joe Karbo would have to admire.

Now that Deukmejian was governor, the outer envelope looked even more official, embellished with the great seal of the state of California. Of course, the postmaster was warned to expedite the "action-dated legal documents enclosed." Printed on the opposite side of the envelope was a box resembling the surgeon general's cigarette warning: "Notice—This Envelope Contains Important Election Materials Designated For Use By Registered Voters Only." Inside, the letter from Governor Deukmejian generously offered to process your official absentee-ballot application "free of charge." But best of all was the name Roper came up with for the entire package of materials and that he plastered on virtually every piece of paper therein:

"Your 1984 Vote-by-Mail Election Kit."

An election *"kit"*?

"Who taught you how to write direct mail?" I asked Tim Roper.

You did, he replied.

4

Confessions
of a
Junk-Mail
Junkie

I didn't really teach Tim Roper how to write direct mail. He learned how to do it the same way I did: He taught himself. Since we started our careers at the same agency, and since I had worked there slightly longer than he had, I may have given him a pointer or two, just as others had done for me. But nobody goes to school to learn direct-mail copywriting. It's a skill that can be acquired only through experience.

Writing junk mail is not a glamorous profession, but it has its rewards—not the least of which is money. Every year, the direct-marketing newsletter *Who's Mailing What!* publishes a survey of what top free-lance copywriters are charging for a direct-mail package.* To anyone outside the industry, the figures must seem bizarre. Gary Bencivenga charges twenty thousand dollars. Bill Jayme asks for, and gets, eighteen thousand dollars.

* A "package" is the term used to describe all the contents of a direct-mail letter, including (usually) the outer envelope; the letter; the reply card; the return envelope; and one other enclosure, usually a brochure.

Henry Cowen, one of the best-known free-lance copywriters, charges both a flat fee *and* a royalty. He may get, for example, fifteen thousand dollars upfront and ten dollars for every thousand pieces mailed, which, in a multimillion-piece campaign, can come to a substantial sum of money. Clients who balk at paying Cowen's royalty, however, always have the option of paying his flat fee of forty thousand dollars. It's not unusual for the best free-lance copywriters to make six-figure incomes and to do so with surprisingly little effort. Many of them, in fact, are exceedingly proud of how little time they spend at their desks. As Joe Karbo said, "I used to work hard, but I didn't start making real money until I started doing less."

Why are their talents in such demand?

Because writing a direct-mail letter is very different from writing a conventional advertisement, in which one main idea is presented in the most imaginative way possible. Writing a direct-mail letter has less to do with sheer creativity and more to do with manipulating human emotions and playing upon basic human needs. Putting an appealing image in the customer's mind, as the general advertising copywriter does, is one thing. Making that person sit down and write a check, as the direct-mail writer does, is quite another.

The *political* copywriter, in particular, faces a formidable challenge. Using nothing more than words on paper, he must entice people to part with tens, hundreds, sometimes thousands of dollars, offering them nothing in return except good government and a vague sense of accomplishment. It's not easy. And not surprisingly, the people who can do it well command a tidy fee.

The general advertising copywriter never really knows if he's any good at his trade, since the effect of conventional advertising on retail sales is difficult to measure. But the direct-mail copywriter knows exactly how well his last piece of copy worked. If it worked well enough to "beat the control," he knows his services will be even more sought after in the coming months. Some copywriters are so confident of their skills they are willing to tie their compensation directly to results. Richard Viguerie attributes his own success as a copywriter to such a willingness on his part during the early days of his agency.

"It's like the difference between the rabbit and the fox," says

Viguerie. "Ninety-nine times out of a hundred, the rabbit will outrun the fox. That's because the fox is running for supper, but the rabbit is running for his life. And when I started writing direct-mail copy, I was writing for my life. We had contracts with our clients that were based on performance. If we didn't perform, we didn't get paid."

Perhaps because of the life-and-death significance of the task, Viguerie approaches writing a direct-mail letter with the solemnity of a monk:

"I hide. I isolate myself. I don't talk to anybody. I don't take any phone calls. I don't eat. I don't put anything in my stomach. I might go all day without eating.

"I write on a legal pad in longhand. I don't believe you can write on a word processor. No, it's word by word. Point by point. It's agonizing. Painstaking.

"When I'm finished writing, I'm exhausted. I'm tired. It's almost hard to stand up."

Indeed, just reading a Richard Viguerie-composed direct-mail letter can be exhausting. During the course of one Viguerie letter, it is not unusual for the reader to be asked to: (1) sign a petition; (2) move a "Yes" token from the letter to the reply card; (3) fill out an opinion poll; (4) mail one postcard to his congressman and two postcards to each of his senators; (5) place commemorative stamps on all his personal correspondence; and, of course, (6) make a contribution. In some households, the arrival of a Richard Viguerie direct-mail letter may put an end to all other useful work for the rest of the day.

Of course, most people claim they throw away their "junk mail" unopened. But if we trusted what we hear from our friends, we would have to believe that no one in America watches television or reads direct mail. Actually, research shows that approximately 75 percent of the American people open and glance at every piece of mail they receive. When it comes to fundraising mail, including political, over four of five survey respondents (81 percent) say they open it and at least glance at the contents.

The pejorative term "junk mail," in fact, is not a phrase that arose spontaneously among the American people but one that has been deliberately foisted upon the public and kept alive by newspaper publishers. The newspaper industry, suffering from many problems of its own, has watched with growing alarm as direct mail pursued, drew even with, and finally surpassed newspapers as the nation's number-two advertising medium (after television). Despite newspaper editorials and despite what people themselves often say, the evidence suggests that most people actually *like* direct mail. And the billions of dollars worth of goods sold every year by direct mail certainly proves that it works. The question is, *how* does it work? And *why*?

"The first time I saw a direct-mail letter," says Tim Roper, "I said to myself I would never read that thing or respond to it." Some people keep telling themselves the same thing right up to the moment when they mail in their check. Direct mail is the most unabashedly manipulative advertising medium ever invented. It is both overtly manipulative and, quite often, deceptively manipulative.

The essence of direct-mail manipulation is based on a formula that is used consciously or unconsciously by virtually every direct-mail copywriter. It is symbolized by an acronym that sounds like a famous opera, "AIDA." It stands for: (1) Attention; (2) Involvement (or Interest); (3) Desire; and (4) Action. The object is to capture the prospect's attention, gather his involvement with the direct-mail piece, whet his desire for the product (or the cause), and spur him into action. A typical direct-mail package consists of five components: an outer envelope; a letter; a reply card; a return envelope; and one other enclosure (which in commercial direct mail usually is a brochure and in political direct mail usually is an "involvement device," such as an opinion poll or a petition). Each piece has a part to play in the AIDA orchestration. The outer envelope grabs the donor's attention with an enticing (and often deceptive) "teaser" line. The opinion poll, petition, or membership card serves to get the donor physically involved with the package and intellectually interested in it. The letter, usually couched in the most emotional and strident language, brings the donor's desire to a fever pitch. And the reply card and reply envelope offer the donor a ready-made opportunity to leap into action.

The Envelope

The outer envelope captures the prospect's attention in two ways: first, by adhering to certain conventions or expectations we have about the size, the look, and the texture of our mail; second, by arousing the reader's curiosity with a compelling "teaser."

Convention plays an important role in making direct mail conform to the reader's expectations about what kind of mail comes in what kind of envelopes. We generally expect invitations, for example, to arrive in tiny baronial envelopes made from heavy, highly textured, colored paper. Bills are likely to arrive in a No. 9 window envelope, important business correspondence in a No. 10. Personal letters often come in a "Monarch size," $3\frac{7}{8} \times 7\frac{1}{2}$". The clever direct mailer will use all these assumptions in posing his envelope as something of more interest to the prospect than just another junk-mail letter. Political mailers in particular are fond of creating a sense of urgency by imitating telegrams and, more recently, overnight express letters.

"I think we were the first to try this," says Roper. "We'd already done a bunch of telegrams for this client, and we had to do yet another 'urgent' package, so we came up with"—he imitates the voice of a television announcer—"TRANSCONTINENTAL PRIORITY EXPRESS—SERVICES ALL ACROSS AMERICA, DELIVERED TO YOU BY THE U.S. POSTAL SERVICE.

"We had an airplane and a little truck on it, and all that stuff. We mailed that baby out just before the election, and boatloads of money came back in.

"Not long after we sent it out, the executive director of the California Republican Party got a call from one of their contributors. The party is located in Burbank, and this guy lived over in West Hollywood, and he was outraged. 'I don't understand why the party is spending so much money sending me overnight express letters when I live right down the street!' "

On a similar piece, also conceived by Roper, one can see how teaser lines are cleverly used to enhance the image created by the envelope itself. "AERO JET EXPRESS," it says, "WHEN YOUR MESSAGE IS ABSOLUTELY IMPORTANT!" Underneath the back flap, emblazoned over a global view of the world, are the words "Aero Jet Express's New Correspondence Delivery Service Can Reach Anyone, Anywhere, Throughout the United States and the Free World." All of this is true, of course, except perhaps the word "new," since the U.S. Postal Service has been around for some time.

But the usual teaser is more straightforward. Generally, teaser copy seeks to appeal to the reader's self-interest or pique his curiosity about what's inside the envelope. A devilishly clever teaser written by Roper for the National Taxpayers Union manages to do both. "FREE GIFT ENCLOSED!" says the teaser in large red type. "Yours to keep. Free merchandise valued by the federal government at $91.00!" Inside, the recipient finds an ordinary washer, such as one might use to fix a leaky faucet. Upon reading the accompanying letter, the donor learns that the Pentagon has indeed paid as much as ninety-one dollars for washers like the one enclosed.

Involvement Devices

The washer itself in this particular letter plays a different role from the outer envelope. It is the "involvement device," the component designed to pique the donor's interest and encourage him to become physically involved with the package. Surveys, opinion polls, petitions, postcards to congressmen, coins, dollar bills, checks, packages of seeds, recipes, perforated stamps, Yes/No stickers, carbon copies of earlier letters, and snapshots of the candidate's family are all examples of involvement devices that have been used effectively in political direct mail.

The three most common kinds of involvement devices in political direct mail are opinion surveys; petitions or postcards to members of Congress; and various kinds of "status gifts" designed to flatter the donor and give him an inflated view of his own importance to the campaign.

Opinion surveys, in particular, are the mother's milk of political direct mail. GOP consultant Stephen Winchell calls them "the single most effective"[1] form of involvement device. But the Direct Marketing Association—the industry's top trade association—calls them unethical. "No one should make offers or solicitations," says the DMA code of ethics, "in the guise of research or a survey when the real intent is to sell products or services or to raise funds."[2] As the author of literally hundreds of direct-mail opinion surveys, I can state unequivocally that they never serve any purpose *other* than to raise funds. Such surveys have absolutely no value as research, since the questions are unscientifically formulated, the results are haphazardly tabulated (if at all), and—most important—the audience is politically and demographically skewed.

In his "how-to" manual on political direct mail, conservative consultant Bruce Eberle offers some insight into the *real* reason why opinion surveys are included in many political direct-mail packages.

"First you commit your prospect to respond [to the survey]. He agrees that it's important for him to return his poll. . . . Then he says, 'Oh, my, if I send this poll without sending in a contribution, I'm not really being fair.' And that is the reason why polls, if created properly . . . work."[3]

Petitions and ready-made postcards to the donor's congressman operate on essentially the same principle. The donor is first encouraged to believe that his signature on the enclosed petition is vital to the future of the country, and then he is made to feel *guilty* about mailing in the postcard or petition without enclosing a contribution "to help defray the cost of our massive lobbying campaign." The more urgent and official the petition looks, the better.

Status gifts are also fundamentally based on guilt. If you give people something—flags, autographed pictures, commemorative stamps, etc.—usually it makes them feel guilty enough to give something back. It's rather like those occasions when you receive a Christmas present from someone you're not particularly close to and feel honorbound to send one in return.

Status gifts usually are no more authentic than the opinion

surveys and "official" petitions. Your personally signed photo-graph of the president probably was done by laser printer or, at best, "auto-pen." Your limited edition of the commemorative coin is "limited" only to the number of donors who are willing to spring for it. The vital "Committee of 1000" you have been "carefully selected to join" may also include a number of people who were not so carefully selected. In a 1976 Montana U.S. Senate race, for example, Republican Stanley Burger discovered to his chagrin that he had invited his opponent, Senator John Melcher, to serve on a "special advisory committee." He also had invited several members of Melcher's family and staff.

Tim Roper is fond of telling an (unconfirmed) story about one of the National Republican Senatorial Committee's status gifts, American flags:

"They launched this program called the 'Presidential Task Force,' and if you contributed to the Task Force, you'd get a box full of goodies, including a flag 'flown over the U.S. Capitol.' Well, they did the mailing, and they got a bigger response than they expected. They didn't have time to run each flag up the flagpole. So they took the flags, they put 'em on an airplane, and they flew 'em over the Capitol."

Perhaps because the typical direct-mail donor deeply wants to believe he is more important to the campaign than he really is, the reaction to involvement devices is often surprisingly sincere. I once sat next to a man on an airplane who, upon learning that one of my clients was the Ohio Republican Party, proudly reached into his wallet and pulled out the ORP membership card I had written and designed. He had properly endorsed the card on the back with his signature to "validate" it, as I'd suggested in my copy. I didn't have the heart to tell him that his validated membership card, plus fifty cents, would entitle him to a cup of coffee in any diner in Ohio.

It is this very sincere reaction among otherwise intelligent people that gives one pause when involvement devices cross the fine line from manipulation to deception, as they frequently do. For a while it was very common to send out renewal letters that looked exactly like invoices to members of political and charitable organizations. The donor was deliberately left with the impression that he had no choice but to remit his "membership dues" for the current year. "Official information" about taxes or Social Security, wrapped in plain brown envelopes, also is common in political direct mail. Even mock telegrams base their impact on tricking the donor into thinking he has received something other than just another fundraising appeal. "Their first thought," advises Eberle in his how-to manual, "may be that someone is sick or dying."[4]

"We're mailing to adults," says Richard Parker somewhat testily. But being an adult is no guarantee against being gullible, and even direct-mail professionals have been known to fall for some of the gimmicks in their own mailboxes. I once received a letter from the National Taxpayers Union that looked so much like a notice from the Internal Revenue Service that I could almost hear the prison doors clanging in my ears as I tore it open. "IMPORTANT: CONTAINS YOUR 1984 STATEMENT," said the plain brown No. 10 envelope, postmarked Washington, D.C. "Great," I thought, "1984 was the year I listed my VCR as a business expense." Inside the window on the envelope, above the label bearing my name, were the words, "TAXPAYER NAME AND ADDRESS." When I discovered the letter only wanted to talk to me about lowering taxes, I was so relieved, and so sympathetic to the argument, that I was sorely tempted to contribute. Direct-mail copywriters are, in fact, highly "mail-respondent" people. We are junk-mail junkies in the truest sense of the word, both pushers and users of the stuff. And perhaps, like junkies, our actions are beyond our control.

"It's like the arms race," says Richard Parker. "You see somebody else doing it, and you discover they're getting a three percent response rate, and you say, 'Well, shit, I've got to get out there and do that, too.'"

The Letter

Interestingly, though, the most important and most persuasive component of a direct-mail package is not the involvement device. It's the letter. The involvement device serves only to pique the prospect's interest. But the letter systematically stokes the donor's emotional furnace to the point where he is ready to part with his hard-earned cash.

Like the direct-mail package as a whole, the letter operates basically on the formula of attention, interest, desire, and action. The first line is exceedingly important, and, like Viguerie, many copywriters will spend more than half of their time trying to come up with a line that will capture the prospect's attention. The best opening line is one that genuinely shocks the reader. "If your opponent took off all his clothes in public," writes Bruce Eberle, "then be sure and put that in your first line."[5] A sense of urgency is important, as is timeliness. A typical political letter, for example, may have the words "Monday morning" printed on the dateline to convey immediacy (even though the letter may have been written and mailed weeks earlier) and begin with a breathless line like, "this is the most important letter you will receive this year." One direct-mail consultant confided to Larry Sabato that "we usually write about ten 'most important letters ever written' letters a year."[6]

After he has captured the reader's attention, the skilled copywriter uses a variety of techniques for maintaining interest. Foremost among them is personalization, both the kind manufactured by a computer and the kind that naturally arises from good copywriting.

Computer personalization is useful not so much for its ability to reproduce the donor's name in the salutation and elsewhere throughout the letter as it is for its capacity to make specific references to the donor's prior giving history, plus a few pertinent facts about his life. "I thank you, Mr. Jones, for your recent gift of a hundred dollars. It was probably the most generous contribution we received from anyone in the Middletown area. I've always been able to count on you since you first joined our team in April 1986." Too much computerization can backfire, though, and every direct-mail professional has a story about their favorite computer mistakes. One National Republican Senatorial Committee letter, for example, was sent to an Oakland insurance firm named Dealy, Renton and Associates. When a careless keypuncher abbreviated the name as "Dealy, Renton Ass.," the letter began by saying, "Dear Mr. Ass."

Even more important than computerization, however, is the need to maintain a highly personal, me-to-you writing style throughout the letter. Tom Collins, for example, creates a kind of inner dialogue between himself and the reader.

"I write a sentence, and then I ask myself how the reader

will respond to that sentence. Maybe I think he will say, 'Yeah, but you're forgetting about such-and-such.' So I write, 'You're probably wondering about such-and-such.' Then after the next sentence, I imagine the reader might say, 'Well, it's not that simple.' So I write, 'You're probably thinking it's not that simple.' And so on."

This highly conversational approach makes for short, simple, easy-to-read sentences and paragraphs that are rarely more than six lines in length. When it comes to direct-mail copywriting, the conventional rules of English composition are thrown away in favor of a style wherein the most important qualities are readability, informality, and sincerity.

The visual aspect of a direct-mail letter, the actual arrangement of the words on the page, is almost as important as the letter's content. Almost nothing is left to chance. The last sentence of each page, for example, is deliberately broken in the middle so the reader will have to turn the page to see how it ends. A direct-mail letter always is typewritten, not typeset, so it will look as if the letter came directly from the candidate's own Smith-Corona. In fact, before black carbon ribbons became common, direct mailers often used halftone screens (the same process used to print photographs) to reproduce the faded and broken look of ink-ribbon typewriters.

Master copywriter Ed McClean talks about what he calls a "friendly page." Wide margins, short sentences, short paragraphs, lots of underlining, and visual effects like bullets, indented paragraphs, and even "handwritten" notes in the margins are all designed to make the reader think, "Gee, this thing won't be so bad" and to keep him reading until he is hooked on the content.

And the way to hook the reader on the content of a direct-mail letter is to lavish him with benefits. Writing benefit-oriented copy, as it's known in the trade, is much harder in fundraising than in commercial direct mail. "What are you going to say?" asks Richard Parker with a laugh. "Buy one Teddy Kennedy, and get one free?"

Failing that, the copywriter must concentrate instead on the problems facing the donor and suggest that the candidate can solve them. This can be very difficult on the copywriter since he or she often is close enough to the real world of politics to know that the power of one congressman to alter the direction of the federal government is roughly equal to the gravitational pull on earth of the moon. Nevertheless, every attempt is made to make it look like the problem is: (a) solvable and (b) solvable by the candidate.

"You want to explain exactly and precisely how [the problem] is going to affect your prospective donor," writes Eberle. "But frankly, it is of little value to talk about a national debt of six hundred billion dollars. . . . You've got to bring down the language to their level. Talk about what this is going to cost them individually."[7]

Love of money is, however, not the only weapon in the copywriter's arsenal of deep-seated human motivations. Fear also is important. So is guilt. And exclusivity—the need to feel unique, special, and important—is something the political copywriter relies on heavily.

The Inner Circle, an offshoot of the National Republican Senatorial Committee, uses a two-step prospect mailing that literally screams exclusivity. In the first step, the donor receives a gold-embossed, ivory stock letter that quietly informs him that "at the last membership meeting of the Republican Senatorial Inner Circle, your name was placed in nomination by Senator Baker, and you were accepted for membership." The Inner Circle, the letter goes on, is comprised of only twenty-seven hundred members nationwide, including such celebrated people as Gene Autry, Ted Turner, and John Connally. The donor learns in this mailing that the purpose of the Inner Circle is to get together a few times a year and schmooze with these celebrities, discussing the pressing problems of the day at small dinner parties hosted by important Washington officials. A formal invitation will follow, says the copy.

The second mailing arrives in a small baronial envelope and contains a hand-calligraphed invitation to join the Inner Circle. Also included is a "Dinner Reservation Register" on which the recipient is asked to place a checkmark by the name of the Washington dignitary next to whom he would most like to be seated at dinner. Finally, the reply card asks for the Social Security number and birth date of the donor, which seems a little peculiar until one reads the explanation next to it: "Needed for Secret Service clearance for Presidential and Vice Presidential events."[8]

Asking for the contribution is the moment of truth in a direct-mail letter, and it helps if the request is phrased in a specific amount for a specific need, especially an urgent need. "You must make a clear relationship between the contribution and how it will be used," says one direct-mail consultant. And the way to do that is to talk in terms of specifics: "I must have your contribution of $219.86 by September 1, or I will not be able to reserve sixty seconds of important radio time in Des Moines." Broadcast time, in fact, is the most frequently cited reason for asking for a campaign contribution. Eberle explains why:

"People like, as they say, to buy bricks and mortar. . . . They don't want to pay for salaries, they don't want to pay for overhead, but rather they want to pay for items like telephones, printing, postage, TV ads, radio ads, or newspaper ads. In other words, they want to pay for action items."[9]

But these specific needs and specific amounts usually are the figments of a copywriter's fertile imagination. A copywriter in a political direct-mail agency rarely works closely enough with the client to have any idea what the campaign really needs or what the donor's money will be used for. Sometimes even the campaign staff doesn't know. Often, in fact, there *is* no need. Many candidates are so well heeled from PAC contributions that the direct-mail letters will blithely talk about the "urgent need" for radio time or newspaper ads when all those things have been paid for long ago, with money to spare. One day, while composing a direct-mail package for the Republican state committee of a large northeastern state, I found myself at a place in the letter where I needed to talk about how the donor's gift would be used. I placed a call to my client and asked him what the party was planning to do with the revenue from the mailing.

"Well," he replied, "we're taking the whole office to Bermuda in September."

It's hard to tell donors their contributions will be used to perpetuate a do-nothing organization by paying the salaries of people who will devote roughly 80 percent of their time to figuring out how to raise more money. That's why such stock items as radio and TV time come in very handy.

All of this fabrication raises the question of credibility, which, as it happens, is very important in direct mail. But again, credibility can be created through technique. The most common way for lending your direct-mail letter an air of believability is to convince someone other than the candidate—especially a celebrated politician—to sign it. The signing of direct-mail letters is to politicians what the conferring of honorary degrees is to college presidents—a professional courtesy. This is not to say that a famous politician will sign your candidate's letter for no reason. Usually there is a *quid pro quo*. Quite often it involves sharing names to be generated by the mailing. Perhaps the signer is returning a favor, or expects to have his own favor returned. Many deals are cut in the creation of what appears to the donor to be an unqualified endorsement. Once the important matters are out of the way, however, the politician experienced with direct mail cares little about the content of the letter. In many cases he won't even bother to read it.

Every direct-mail letter concludes with a P.S. Notice I didn't say most letters do, or a lot of letters do. I said *every* letter does. And the reason is simple. Direct mailers learned long ago the postcript is among the most carefully read portions of the letter. The average direct-mail respondent looks first at his own name in the salutation, turns the pages to the end and reads the P.S., returns to the beginning, and glances at the opening line. If he hasn't been "caught" by then, he probably is lost forever. So direct-mail copywriters expend a lot of time and ingenuity devising intriguing postscripts.

It's probably a good thing respondents look first at the P.S., because if they waited until they'd finished the whole letter, they might be too old to act upon it. Political direct-mail letters are long. Very long. George McGovern's original announcement letter, for example, set the precedent for lengthy letters by running seven pages. Nowadays it's not unusual to see them go to twelve pages or more. Candidates and their campaign staffers rarely understand why their letters have to be so long. Even the donors themselves balk at them. On several occasions our agency received notes from donors who were trying to be helpful, saying, "People don't read such long letters."

In fact, people *don't* read them. But they do respond to them.

Even the best direct-mail prospect letter will only get about a 2 or 3 percent response. That means ninety-seven of a hundred people who receive a given letter pay little or no attention to it. The direct-mail copywriter knows this, so he forgets about the ninety-seven who don't give a damn about the letter and focuses his efforts on the 2 or 3 percent who do. These "happy few" who are genuinely interested in the candidate aren't put off by

a twelve-page letter at all. They would read a hundred-page letter from the candidate if only he could afford to send them one.
They *want* to learn about the issues. They *want* to hear about
how important they are to the campaign. They *want* to find out
exactly how their contribution will make a difference. Every additional sentence, every additional paragraph, every additional
page brings them one step closer to reaching for their checkbook.

It's true the donor may not read every word. He may, in fact,
merely skim a long letter. But he will read as much of it as
necessary to make a decision about whether to give. "A direct-
mail letter is like a smorgasbord," says Tom Collins. "People
will go through it and take out what they want and need."

"When you're selling anything that's complicated," says Roger
Craver, "making it too short is showing contempt for the mind
of the reader. It isn't very believable that you can solve the
problem of nuclear war, for example, in two paragraphs."

But no matter how complex the topic is, what you say in
those twelve pages is not as important as how you say it.

And the way to say it is *emotionally*.

"When emotion and intellect come into conflict," writes Herschell Gordon Lewis in his book *Direct Mail Copy That Sells*,
"emotion always wins."[10] And since Lewis is thinking primarily
of the practical world of commercial direct mail, one can only
assume his rule is magnified many times in the intangible realm
of political fundraising.

"When you stop and think about it," writes Bruce Eberle, "it
is very tough to get someone to contribute after reading a piece
of literature they received through the mail."[11]

In fact, it is virtually impossible to present a logical, well-
reasoned argument asking someone to put twenty-five dollars
into an envelope and send it away to a distant address, expect-
ing nothing in return. Logical direct mail always fails because as
soon as the prospect starts to *think* about the direct mail piece
at all, he is bound to see the absurdity of what he is being asked
to do. Mr. Spock on the television program *Star Trek* would
probably never respond to political direct mail. "It's not logical,
Captain." But "Bones," the high-strung ship's doctor, would likely
be on every mailing list in the universe. The copywriter's job is
not to make people think but to make them react. And to do
that, he deals not in the realm of ideas but in the realm of feel-

ings. That's why it's not unusual in direct mail to find lines like this one, taken from a letter signed by Jesse Helms for the National Conservative Political Action Committee:

"Your tax dollars are being used to pay for grade school classes that teach our children that CANNIBALISM, WIFE-SWAPPING, and the MURDER of infants and the elderly are acceptable behavior."

Much of this emotionalism arises from the underlying direct-mail strategy of mailing only to those who are predisposed to support the cause. Just as Hitler could work himself into a frenzy when speaking at the Chancellery, so the direct-mail copywriter is not afraid to pull out all the stops when communicating with people he knows already agree with him. One anti-abortion letter, for example, attacked Senators Birch Bayh and George McGovern as "baby killers." The letter used the words "baby killers" and "murder" no less than forty-one times and included some grisly passages describing how an abortion is performed. No time is wasted on convincing the uncommitted, persuading the doubtful, or arguing fine points of logic. The idea is to take a list of people who are already inclined to make a contribution and inflame their emotions to the point where they cannot resist doing so.

Unfortunately, not every political issue can engender enough emotion to be useful in direct mail. It's not unusual for a direct-mail consultant to skim through his client's position papers looking for the one issue emotional enough to work in the mail—regardless of whether that issue is a significant part of the candidate's agenda. Once he has found it, a direct-mail consultant like Roger Craver will encourage the candidate to write about the issue in the strongest possible language:

"I usually say to my clients, 'Look, if you don't feel this way, then don't say it. But if you do feel this way and you're afraid the words are too strong, that's different. As a last resort, we can always test it.' "

We can always test it—the direct mailer's final solution to every creative problem. Blessed with an effective control letter, the direct-mail consultant will conduct test after test to determine what elements can be changed to lift the response rate even the tiniest amount. He may try a real stamp on the envelope instead of a bulk-rate indicia, or a commemorative stamp instead of a regular one. He may try condensing his letter to one page, or expanding it to four. He'll print the signature in blue instead of black. He'll try it with a teaser line on the outside envelope, or try it without. Almost nothing is too trivial to test, because even the most innocuous changes have been shown to have measurable effects.

Another important factor when choosing an issue on which to focus the direct-mail appeal is to pick one that the donor perceives as solvable. Terrorism, for example, is not a good direct-mail issue, even though it is an emotional one, because most people are skeptical of the government's ability to do anything about it.

Having made that one small concession to credibility, though, the political direct-mail copywriter often goes on to play rather fast and loose with the facts.

"There's too much looseness with the facts," says Richard Viguerie, "too much poetic license." The Viguerie Company is rare among political direct-mail agencies in that it has a policy of checking the copy of direct-mail letters to make sure all the facts are scrupulously accurate. At some agencies, it is more common to make up a good story first and find the facts later. "Factualization," I like to call it.

Unlike media consultants, who stop just short of sleeping with their clients, direct-mail agencies tend to be somewhat insulated from the campaign. They also are under a great deal of pressure to keep coming up with new concepts and themes for mailings scheduled as frequently as six weeks apart. As a result, agency copywriters often sit back and dream up dramatic stories based on whatever scraps of information they have about the campaign. If an account executive pops his head in the copywriter's office and says something like, "The John Doe campaign needs money for radio," it may come out of the copywriter's typewriter a few hours later looking something like this:

Dear Friend,

It's 1:00 A.M. I have just put my kids to bed and kissed my wife good night after another long day on the campaign trail.

She has worked so hard. And given so much. I think the hardest part about losing this race—*if* I lose—will be to tell Jane and the kids that we didn't succeed.

The news from the most recent opinion poll is not good. We

are trailing by a solid two to three points, especially in the key St. Paul and Bloomington areas.

My advisers tell me that one or two well-chosen radio spots may be all we need to make up the difference. If only we had the money . . .

But if the writer is not feeling particularly creative on a given day, he may choose instead to plagiarize a letter from a competitor. Since direct mail is rarely copyrighted, it's not unusual to see wholesale borrowing take place, not just of ideas and formats but also of actual wording. In 1979, Ronald Reagan's presidential committee mailed a letter in which ten out of the first eleven paragraphs were lifted intact from a letter originally produced by Phil Crane's presidential campaign fifteen months earlier.

As one can see from the hypothetical example just given, direct-mail copy doesn't always have to be politically strident to be emotional. At least once during the course of a campaign, both Richard Viguerie and Bruce Eberle insist that their clients use something known generically as "the wife letter."

Larry Sabato provides an apt description of a typical one:

> Written in longhand by the candidate's wife on personal, pastel stationery, the letter is an expensive, photo-offset production that is mailed in a ladylike envelope with full postage (no bulk reduction, and using live stamps). It is even shipped back to the candidate's hometown for a local postmark! In the four-page letter, the wife gives a chatty rendition of her family history, children, and marriage, lightly connecting it all to her husband-candidate's concerns about inflation, taxes, energy, and other problems. The text is opened and closed with references to housewifely and childbearing duties ("The baby's crying so I must close for now," ended one), and a photo of the happy family, pets included, is enclosed with a hand scrawled inscription.[12]

Eberle explains the rationale behind the wife letter by suggesting that the candidate's wife can say things about her husband that he can't say himself. And she can talk in straightforward, emotional terms about common, everyday problems.

But in some cases those problems are not so common. In some cases they are quite dramatic. And on those occasions one wonders if the reader's emotional response is being exploited.

Take the Republican National Committee's use of a letter signed by Sarah Brady, for example. The wife of former Reagan press secretary Jim Brady, who was gravely injured in the attempt on Reagan's life, offers GOP donors a book edited by her husband about Ronald Reagan as a premium for a contribution to the RNC.

"In those dark days," says the copy, "who would have dared to dream that Jim would even survive, much less recover to edit a book like the one I've sent you?" The pitch, it turns out, is that the donor's contribution will be used to mail the book to millions of other Americans, "people not as knowledgeable, perhaps, as you." It's missionary work, sort of. But one wonders if the letter's appeal is not based primarily on the public's sympathy for Brady and the desire to see him lead a productive life.

Or consider this postscript from a letter from George Wallace's 1976 presidential campaign:

> P.S. I still have a little pain at various times during the day. But the doctors say the pain will get less and less as time goes by.

Yet while people like Wallace and Brady naturally evoke a sympathetic response because of the tragedies they've endured in their lives, other names evoke a knee-jerk reaction of hatred and anger. They are the "direct-mail devils," and most consultants could not stay in business without them. The mere mention of their names is enough to make some people's blood boil. And when the blood begins to boil, a contribution is close at hand.

One rarely sees a direct-mail letter from a Republican or conservative organization in which Ted Kennedy doesn't make at least a cameo appearance. His name will be invoked on the slightest excuse, because it carries its own baggage of built-in animosity and anger. Until his retirement, this was also true of Tip O'Neill. As the leader of his party in the House, O'Neill could be tied to virtually any bill that the Democratic Party came up with. If some crackpot congressman from California proposed legislation to legalize wife-beating, the GOP direct-mail letter inevitably would begin: "Tip O'Neill and his cronies in Congress have decided it's okay to beat your wife." Tom Hayden and his wife, Jane, also are good for an occasional reference. Ms. Fonda is particularly useful when the topic has anything to do with national security, since many Americans will carry the image of her in North Vietnam to their graves and *still* be angry about it.

The political left is somewhat disadvantaged when it comes to direct-mail devils because there seems to be so much personal affection for President Reagan, even among his enemies. But Jesse Helms is always handy. Attorney General Ed Meese shows some promise. And James Watt probably was the most significant contribution that the Reagan administration made to the environmental movement. Some direct-mail staffers and consultants at environmental organizations were actually *sad* to see Watt resign. "Hooray, he's gone," Kay Lautman of The Oram Group remembers saying when she heard of Watt's demise. "Boo-hoo, he's gone."

Does all this emotional manipulation really work?

Clearly, the response rates and contributions prove that it works well enough to be profitable. But one cannot develop a real sense of the impact of direct mail on the public without getting one's hands dirty in the mailroom, opening the incoming sacks of business return envelopes, and reading the reply cards. This process of opening envelopes, removing checks, and batching reply cards into small groups for keypunching is called "caging." And my first job in direct mail was caging checks for the Republican National Committee.

In addition to generating contributions, every direct-mail campaign produces a flurry of what is known in the business as "white mail," presumably so-named because it arrives on the recipient's plain white stationery and not in the gaudy reply cards the mailer is anticipating. In my job at the RNC, I was in a position to see a great deal of white mail, and reading it gave me precious insight into the nature of the political direct-mail audience.

Religious literature, of course, was a major motif. After reading our letters, many people evidently felt we were in need of a good dose of God. So they packed our business return envelope with religious pamphlets and jotted notes on the reply card suggesting that it was, perhaps, not too late for the Republican Party to receive salvation. Every now and then our letters would scare up a few Democrats, and this would invariably provoke an emotional reaction. "I'm a Democrat, you stupid bastards," screamed the angry scrawl on the reply card. "I have been since Roosevelt, for Chrissakes."

This was during the Nixon administration, and since Nixon was guaranteed to provoke strong feelings, even among Republicans, the morning was not complete without at least two dozen "FUCK NIXON's" and several variations on that theme. Placing a pithy note in the business return envelope (BRE) and mailing it back to the sender is actually a very effective way to register your disagreement with a direct-mail organization, since the mailer will pay for the privilege of hearing you sound off. It is not advisable, however, to paste the BRE on a brick—as people occasionally do—since the post office will not only refuse to deliver it, but they also may seek to fine you.

Political direct mail, as we've already seen, has a way of getting into the homes of people who are suffering from feelings of isolation, alienation, and frustration. In some people these feelings are no longer just minor insecurities but evidence of far more serious disorders. "What is the Republican Party planning to do about the forthcoming invasion from the Planet Xenon?" a carefully typewritten letter might inquire. Complaints about NASA's space program causing too much rain or daylight saving time causing too much sun also were common.

But the most important thing I learned from reading white mail is simply how sincere, how patriotic, and how just plain *old* most direct-mail respondents are. "Social Security" is the most common phrase one finds on white mail, edging out "fuck you" by a wide margin.

"I'd love to give to you, but I can't because I am old and I am on Social Security."

That one sentence exemplifies the single most common message to be found in white mail—although people may take several pages of a handwritten letter to get there, touching along the way on everything from tomato gardening to the Shroud of Turin.

Most poignant of all were the letters from people who said they were old, they had no money, they were on Social Security, but they wanted to make a contribution anyway! Often it would only be two or three dollars, and invariably it would be accompanied by an apologetic note: "Here is $2. I wish it could be more. But I am old and I am living on Social . . ."

On those occasions I couldn't help but wonder if this individual didn't need those two dollars more than the Republican Party did.

Perhaps Ronald Reagan was wondering the same thing when he mailed a personal check for $215 to one Gerald Colf. A lifelong Republican, the eighty-four-year-old Colf was on the mailing lists of no fewer than twenty-seven Republican and conservative organizations. When those groups began to gear up their donor resolicitation and donor upgrading efforts for the 1984 election, Mr. Colf gave, and gave, and gave . . . until his checkbook ran dry. Mr. Colf went bankrupt.

Reagan sent a check to Colf to cover his contributions to those committees using letters that actually bore the president's signature. He also enclosed a note to Colf suggesting that he not respond to any more fundraising appeals. Excellent advice. But how many more Gerald Colfs are out there?

Professor Sabato draws an analogy between direct-mail fundraising and hypnosis. "You can't hypnotize someone who is not open to hypnosis. And once under hypnosis, you can't make him do anything that he wouldn't otherwise be predisposed to to anyway. I think direct mail is similar. Direct mail can't induce a contribution from a person not predisposed in some way to support the organization. But it can push someone over the edge." And clearly older Americans are most likely to be pushed.

Perhaps that's why the Republican Party raised such a fuss when Roger Craver designed a direct-mail package for the Democratic National Committee that looked suspiciously like correspondence from the Social Security Administration.

"We used a brown kraft envelope and made it look just like a Social Security envelope," Craver recalls. "We put a teaser on it that said, 'Your Social Security Information Enclosed.' And we mailed twenty million of them. When the Republicans saw it, they said, 'Bull!' But that was a lot less deceptive than what [the Republicans] were trying to do to the American public at the time, so I didn't feel bad about it."

No qualms about it at all? I wondered.

"Look," said Craver, "I mailed it only to people who were in an age range where they might be *thinking* about Social Security but who were not yet receiving it. I didn't want to scare people who were already getting Social Security."

I believe him.

But not everybody has Roger's scruples.

5

The Goose
That Laid
The
Golden Egg

By now the gentle reader knows enough about political direct mail to know, upon receiving a letter from a group calling itself The National Committee to Preserve Social Security and Medicare, that something is rotten in the state of Denmark.

"URGENT! IMPORTANT SOCIAL SECURITY AND MEDICARE INFORMATION ENCLOSED" shouts the large manila envelope.

"Attention New York Postmaster: Time-Dated Official National Committee Documents Enclosed. Expedite for Immediate Delivery."

What kind of documents?

"National Committee Social Security and Medicare Documents," another teaser explains.

From whom?

"The National Committee to Preserve Social Security and Medicare, National Administration Office, 1300 19th Street, NW, Washington, DC 20036."

National *Administration* Office?

Yes, just like the Social Security *Administration*. And here's a coincidence: The organization's logo—a Greek column printed in blue—happens to be identical to the one on a Social Security card.

Inside there's a letter from a big name in the history of Social Security—Roosevelt. Not Eleanor's husband, though. This is from their son James Roosevelt, a former congressman from California.

"Never in the 50 years since my father, Franklin Delano Roosevelt, started the Social Security system has there been such a threat to our Social Security and Medicare benefits as the decade of the 80's. Just consider these facts."

What follows is a rather distorted list of the various proposals to reform the Social Security and Medicare systems, portrayed in the most frightening terms possible.

"Deep cuts," Roosevelt concludes, "will mean a <u>dreary existence</u> for present and future Social Security and Medicare recipients, and will create a terrible hardship on their children and grandchildren who will somehow have to support retired family members."

But wait! Don't despair. There's something we can do. Two things, in fact. First, we can sign the enclosed petition so Mr. Roosevelt can haul it over to the Capitol and hold a press conference. And second, we should send ten dollars to join the National Committee to Preserve Social Security and Medicare.

What do we get in return?

A gold-embossed membership card and a subscription to "our regular newspaper, *Saving Social Security*." And, of course, we get the warmth of knowing we are "helping to make it possible to continue [the National Committee's] work here in the Capital with many leaders in Congress to protect, defend, and improve the Social Security and Medicare programs."

As it happens, this letter did raise quite a fuss in Congress, but not the kind Mr. Roosevelt was hoping for. Representative Sherwood Boehlert (Republican of New York) and Representative Robert Matsui (Democrat of California) charged that the letter was deceptive in appearance and misleading in content.

"The basic problem with the letter," said Boehlert, "is that it purposely and inaccurately gives the impression that Social Security and Medicare are on the brink of collapse."[1]

Indeed, the scare tactics used in the letter were so effective that James Brown, a Social Security Administration spokesman, said elderly people were coming into Social Security field offices and offering to pay their ten dollars in person to save their benefits. "He [Roosevelt] is scaring the wits out of people,"[2] said Brown.

As a result of this flak, Roosevelt had a meeting in Washington with Boehlert and Jake Pickle, chairman of the House Ways and Means Subcommittee on Social Security. Roosevelt agreed to make some minor changes in the letter, and everybody walked away happy. But the big questions never got answered. Namely, what exactly *is* the National Committee to Preserve Social Security and Medicare, and what the hell are they doing with the donor's ten bucks?

After all, as we've already seen, scare tactics, deceptive teasers, and misleading statements are not unusual in political direct mail. One might go so far as to suggest that they are the essence of political direct mail. Yet not every direct-mail letter gets hauled into the congressional woodshed. Matsui put his finger on the real problem with the letter when he wondered why he had never had any contact with the National Committee before. "The truth is," said Matsui, "[Roosevelt's organization] has done virtually no lobbying."[3] And he should know, since he sits on the subcommittee that oversees the Social Security Administration.

That's not true, replied Roosevelt. "I'm proud of the beginning we've made."[4]

And indeed, by the first quarter of 1985, Roosevelt could point to the fact that his organization was on file with the clerk of the House and the clerk of the Senate as having spent $781,883 on lobbying in the first three months of the year, more than any of the other seven thousand registered lobbyists.

But isn't that strange? Here's an organization that is the number-one lobby in the country, and a congressman who sits on the most important committee in that lobby's area of interest says that, in his opinion, they are doing virtually no lobbying.

When an AP reporter asked Bill Lessard, the National Committee's director of policy and research, what those $781,883 were being used for, here's what he said:

"Lessard . . . said that money poured into a direct-mail, grass-roots campaign resulted in 1.8 million letters and telegrams being sent to the White House and members of Congress."[5]

In short, Lessard said the money the National Committee spent mailing fundraising letters was actually money it spent lobbying Congress! By calling their fundraising expense a lobbying expenditure, they guaranteed themselves the number-one position on Congress's list of big-spending lobbyists. And that in itself is ironic, because most lobbyists try like mad to stay off the top of that list. The list of registered lobbyists is probably the only list in status-conscious Washington that people are fighting to have their names removed from. But not the National Committee to Preserve Social Security and Medicare! No, they're clawing their way to the top of it, and why else but to prove to their critics that they are a legitimate organization?

Although it certainly would not be noticeable to the millions of elderly Americans who received this letter and probably not even to political sophisticates like Congressmen Matsui and Boehlert, any direct-mail professional would recognize immediately that there was something strange about the mail-order mathematics of this fundraising campaign.

First of all, the direct-mail package is too expensive. A $13'' \times 6''$ envelope with computer personalization on the envelope and on two other components (the letter and the reply card), a four-page letter, an additional one-page letter from Congressman Claude Pepper, a petition, a response device, and a business return envelope all combine to make this the kind of letter most direct mailers would send only to current donors, rarely to cold prospects. To make money on a letter of this kind, the mailer would have to anticipate a response rate of over 5 percent and an average gift of at least twenty dollars, neither of which he is likely to get by mailing to strangers. Indeed, the letter does not even ask for a contribution larger than ten dollars, nor does it give the donor an *opportunity* to make such a donation. The response form contains only one box: "[] Enclosed is my check for $10."

Although it's common, as we've seen, to break even or take a small loss on prospecting, no direct mailer in complete control of his faculties tries to go bankrupt on a mailing unless, of course, he has something on his mind besides fundraising.

Obviously, the National Committee is interested in building

a responsive list, and apparently they are willing to do so at no better than the break-even point. Clearly they are hoping to "milk" that list. But to what end? And how?

Part of the answer is in the letter itself. Among the "benefits" one receives upon joining the National Committee to Preserve Social Security and Medicare is automatic enrollment in something called the "Legislative Alert Service."

Here's how Roosevelt explains it:

> In addition, as a Member, you will be enrolled in our Legislative Alert Service which will immediately advise you, by telegram or letter, of fast-breaking developments in Washington, involving Social Security and Medicare benefits.

In short, one of the benefits of being a member of the National Committee is the privilege of being on its mailing list and the honor of receiving many urgent letters threatening the demise of Social Security and Medicare. Presumably some of these letters will ask for an additional contribution.

But there's more.

From Congressman Boehlert's office I obtained a second direct-mail package produced by the National Committee to Preserve Social Security and Medicare. Similar to the original in all respects, the new letter again calls upon the recipient to sign a petition and join the National Committee. But the price of membership has dropped. Drastically.

"Our Board of Directors has authorized me to offer you a Special first year Membership for only $1," said the letter.

A one-dollar membership? How can the National Committee be raising money on this?

The answer to that question comes a few paragraphs later.

"You will also receive as part of your Special Membership a valuable insurance certificate at no cost to you! Up to $10,000 Reducing Term Life coverage at no cost to you during the three month trial period is guaranteed to be issued to you if you decide to enroll (only benefits for accidental death paid for the first 30 months). You absolutely cannot be turned down for this coverage, for any reason, if you are a member of the National Committee to Preserve Social Security and Medicare and are under the age of 80. After three months, you can continue this term life insurance at low group rates."

And so the National Committee to Preserve Social Security and Medicare wasn't going broke after all. Far from it. With list rental, life insurance marketing, renewal mailings, and even by accepting outside advertising in their monthly newsletter, this massive direct-mail program was generating lots of income, not just for the National Committee itself but also for its direct-mail agency.

Yet there's another side to the National Committee's story, one that I would be remiss if I did not mention.

When I received my first direct-mail letter from the National Committee to Preserve Social Security, I confess that I thought it was a completely fraudulent organization, a paper empire that made money by scaring old people into mailing ten-dollar checks and walking away with the money without doing what it promised to do. The National Committee looked to me like a stepchild of the imagination of its own direct-mail agency, a moneymaking scheme designed to break even as a political organization while generating millions in fees and production commissions for its consultants. During the first few years I was keeping my eye on the National Committee, I encountered nothing in the press, in my own mailbox (where, after joining the organization, I received dozens of fundraising letters at the rate of almost one a month), or in my conversations with other direct-mail consultants to dissuade me from that point of view.

Nevertheless, as time went on, the National Committee underwent a kind of metamorphosis. Where once it had been, according to the *Los Angeles Times*, "essentially a mailing operation with a small Washington staff,"[6] it now has a staff of some thirty-three people, including the former head of the Social Security Administration herself! Where once Congressman Matsui could wonder out loud why he had never had any contact with an organization that purported to be a major lobbyist in his own area of interest, the National Committee now has attained a reputation for effectiveness in Congress. "They're certainly making a presence on the Hill,"[7] said the staff director for the House Committee on Aging. In James Roosevelt's own words:

"The National Committee is evolving. While our original concept was to use our membership as direct lobbyists, we began to recognize the need to supplement this great and vital force with a Capitol Hill presence. During the last year, we have enlarged our staff to include some of the most professional advocates working in this town. And that process will continue."*[8]

So what are we to make of the National Committee to Preserve Social Security and Medicare? And what are we to make of political direct mail?

Is it good politics?

Or just good business?

No matter what we may think of the National Committee to Preserve Social Security and Medicare, one thing is certain: It couldn't exist without a hot issue.

In political direct mail, a hot issue is the goose that lays the golden egg. It doesn't matter what side of the issue you happen to be on. And it doesn't matter whether your organization is capable of doing anything about the issue. Nor does it matter if the issue is significant. All that matters is that the issue is emotional.

Take the Panama Canal, for example. Exactly how important is the Panama Canal to the security of the United States? In a thermonuclear war, the Canal is not likely to play a significant role, and even if it did, the U.S. military shouldn't have any trouble recapturing it. Is a treaty calling for the gradual return of the Canal to Panama an important enough issue on which to launch the single most significant political movement in American politics since Vietnam?

It wouldn't seem so.

But without the Panama Canal Treaties and without the millions of dollars raised and the millions of letters mailed in the unsuccessful effort to keep it from being ratified, there never would have been a "New Right."

Although virtually every responsible politician and pundit across the political spectrum supported the treaty, Richard Viguerie realized early on that the issue of whether or not to "surrender" the Canal to Panama was one that could be simplified and dramatized to the point where patriotic conservatives could be driven to a fever pitch. The New Right's oversimplified and emotional view of the Canal Treaties was summed up by none other than Ronald Reagan, who coined the slogan "We built it, we paid for it, it's ours, and we're going to keep it."

*In addition to these welcome developments, the National Committee also seems to have abandoned its involvement with life insurance. Recent mailings have not mentioned insurance at all.

Operating at that level of intellectual discourse, Viguerie and his companions in the conservative movement proceeded to flood the U.S. Postal Service with letters aimed at conservatives around the country; many of these letters contained petitions to Congress similar to the one in the National Committee letter. And the idea was the same. Send us money so we can mail *more* letters and *more* petitions. The Conservative Caucus mailed three million letters. The National Conservative Political Action Committee mailed half a million. John Fisher's American Security Council mailed two million letters. The Council on Inter-American Security mailed two million. The American Conservative Union mailed two million. The Viguerie Company raised enough money for a "Truth Squad" of senators and congressmen to fly around the country in a chartered Boeing 737, holding press conferences during which they spoke out against the treaty. The Viguerie Company also published a book on the Panama Canal by Congressman Phil Crane with the thoughtful and objective title of *Surrender in Panama.*

As it turned out, the New Right lost the battle, but they won the war. Although the Panama Canal Treaties passed the Senate by two votes, the hodgepodge of fledgling conservative organizations who opposed it came away from the experience with at least four things they didn't have before: (1) a sense of cohesiveness on the issues; (2) a feeling that they could wield real political power by forming coalitions instead of arguing among themselves; (3) much more money; and (4) many new donors. Indeed, Viguerie estimates that the campaign against the Panama Canal Treaties enlisted as many as four hundred thousand new donors to the various groups that comprise the New Right.

Armed with these new donors and this newfound sense of confidence, the New Right turned its attention to hot issue after hot issue, each one generating more money and more contributors. Some of these issues were even less substantive than the Panama Canal Treaties. For example, common situs picketing, an obscure labor rule calling for different trade unions to honor each other's picket lines at a given construction site, raised millions for the New Right. Phyllis Schlafly chimed in with her quixotic opposition to the ERA, and the New Right jumped on the bandwagon. Opposition to the ratification of SALT II (even though both sides were abiding by it anyway), instant voter registration, public financing of elections, right-to-work, and, of course, abortion fueled the growth of the New Right throughout the late 1970s. By 1980, New Right groups like NCPAC had grown so financially strong and politically well organized that they made a significant impact in the U.S. Senate elections that year.

But while the right has used direct mail primarily to finance election campaigns and multicandidate political action committees, the left has used it to assemble a bureaucracy of single-issue advocacy groups.

"The whole concept of citizen involvement with issue politics emerged out of the medium of direct mail," says Roger Craver. And the first public-interest group to emerge was the one that Craver himself helped to launch, Common Cause. A startling example of the power of direct mail to create a political organization out of thin air, Common Cause went from zero members to three hundred thousand in one year.

"In the past," Craver observes, "there have been large grass-roots political movements—the progressive movement, labor movements, and so on—but it wasn't easy to start those things. You had to have foot soldiers. Shop stewards. Doorbell ringers. Canvassers. You had to have thousands of people talking to each other one-to-one." But nowadays all it takes to launch such an organization is the telephone number of a good direct-mail agency.

Direct-mail consultants like to work with advocacy groups and multicandidate PACs much more than they do political candidates. Political campaigning is seasonal work, and it doesn't pay very well. Sometimes it doesn't pay at all. It's hard to raise large sums of money by direct mail in a short time, and it's especially hard when the candidate keeps borrowing the money earmarked for reinvestment in the direct-mail program to pay for television commercials. For all these reasons, most political direct-mail consultants will jump at the chance to work for an organization that's willing to make the commitment of time and money necessary to succeed in direct mail. It's not an exaggeration to suggest that the growing cadre of political direct-mail consultants in Washington, looking for steady work to tide them over between election years, played a key role in the burgeoning public-interest industry and in the explosive growth of ideological PACs. The direct-mail agencies were partially responsible for this growth not just because they provided a ready means of funding but also, in some cases, because they provided the seed money for advocacy groups to get off the ground.

Many organizations in the New Right, for example, got their start because Richard Viguerie was willing to conduct the early mailings at his own expense and defer his agency's fees until the fledgling organization had raised enough money to repay him. This occasionally put Viguerie in the somewhat embarrassing position of taking virtually every penny his clients raised. If these incidents came to light, the press would have a field day. But reporters inevitably missed the real story. Financially, Viguerie was only getting his due. But in every other respect he was assuming an unprecedented level of control over his clients' affairs. Indeed, he could create an organization out of thin air. Armed with his powerful in-house mailing list (which he built by asking that his clients share their donors' names with him), it was theoretically possible for Viguerie to read about a hot issue in the newspaper on Monday morning, make a few calls to form a board of directors that afternoon, set his creative team to work on a mailing by Tuesday, drop it in the mail by the end of the week, and have a bouncing baby political action committee in his arms within a month.

"We have built a movement through direct mail," says Viguerie quietly.

In the meantime, however, a movement was being built on the other side of the fence as well. Common Cause, The Sierra Club, SANE, NOW, Planned Parenthood, Public Citizen, and scores of other special-interest groups all owe their existence in one way or another to direct mail.

But what do these organizations *do*? What do political advocacy groups, on both the right and the left, actually accomplish?

It varies. Some—the good ones—become effective lobbyists for their cause. Others become rapidly expanding bureaucracies primarily dedicated to their own survival and prosperity. They pay their employees good salaries and benefits. Apparently they spend a lot of time thinking, since "research" is always listed as a major activity. When they're finished thinking, they publish whatever they thought about. Some groups, in fact, have become so good at the publishing business that they've all but left politics behind, doing just enough advocacy to make sure they can continue to mail their subscription promotions at the low postage rates reserved for nonprofit organizations. And, of course, they raise more money. One Washington observer estimates that the typical public-interest-group director spends from 50 to 80 percent of his time raising money, whether by direct mail or other means. Meanwhile, the remaining 20 to 50 percent of the time may be spent doing the group's business so it will have the maximum impact on fundraising. While the corporate lobbyist still likes to influence Congress the old-fashioned way (arm-twisting, campaign contributions, fancy lunches, and an occasional call girl), the so-called public-interest lobbyist prefers to lobby by using PR stunts, press releases, and (this should come as no surprise) direct mail.

Nowadays, in fact, lobbyists use computerized direct mail to stimulate "grass-roots" letter-writing campaigns, and congressmen use computerized direct mail to answer the letters. So we have a singular situation, gleefully noted by some Washington pundits, in which public policy is formed by computers talking to computers.

But nobody uses direct mail to greater effect than the national political parties themselves.

Ever since *Washington Post* reporter David Broder published a widely publicized book titled *The Party's Over*, the conventional wisdom in Washington and throughout the country has been that the two great American political parties were dead. But nothing could be farther from the truth. In fact, the two national parties—especially the Republican Party—are stronger now than they have been at any time since television gave individual candidates direct access to the voter. And the reason for this newfound strength is nothing other than direct mail.

Direct-mail fundraising has enabled the political parties to make the difficult but necessary transition from being *instrumental* political leaders to becoming *facilitative* ones. In the old days, political parties enjoyed considerable influence over which candidates would be nominated and, once elected, how they would vote. But since today's technology allows direct and instantaneous communication between the candidate and voter, it's no longer possible for the party to exert that kind of power. Instead, direct-mail fundraising has given the political parties the power of the purse strings and the power of knowledge, specifically the knowledge of how to use technology.

Sociologists say that every group of human beings has at least two leaders. One leader decides what the group will do.

The other decides how they'll do it. In the traditional nuclear family, for example, Daddy decided that the family was going to move to Denver, but it was up to Mommy to explain the move to the children, solicit their help with packing boxes, hire the moving company, pick out the new house, and so on. You could say that the national parties used to act like Daddy, and now they act like Mommy. Yet they are just as strong, if not stronger, than they've ever been.

The key to the change has been direct mail.

Thanks to its massive direct-mail operation, the national Republican Party in 1982, for example, contributed nearly twenty million dollars to GOP House and Senate candidates, which was more than those candidates received from any other source. Meanwhile, the party was able to finance a wide variety of centralized resources for the benefit of its candidates, including polling, opposition research, candidate training seminars, publicity, precinct analysis, computerized phone banks, voter registration, and get-out-the-vote drives.

Much has been made of the fact that the Democratic Party raises considerably less money by direct mail than the Republicans do. And they do. In 1983, for example, the RNC's bill for stamps alone was equal to half of the DNC's entire operating budget. Democrats are fond of attributing the disparity to the fact that they are the party of the poor and downtrodden. But that explanation doesn't quite cut it in a number of respects. Indeed, all the evidence suggests that the exact opposite is closer to the truth. The Republican Party is the party of the modest but deeply committed donor. The Democratic Party is the party of the fat cat and the labor boss. The real reasons why Democrats lag behind in direct mail are far more subtle, and some of them have to do with the historical attitude of each party toward new technology.

The story of Democratic and Republican use of direct mail is, in fact, a tale of two mailing lists.

Having been involved with direct mail to some degree since 1952, the GOP immediately recognized the value of the infusion of conservative names it got from the Goldwater campaign of 1964. Many of those names flew in the window of Republican headquarters as a result of a televised speech delivered on behalf of Goldwater by a former movie actor named Ronald Reagan. The Republican Party proceeded to cultivate and nurture this list with tender, loving care. The RNC created a never-ending series of special appeals; they started a sustaining membership program; they mailed out plastic membership cards; they offered premiums (like Eisenhower dollars or life-size posters of Richard Nixon); and they pursued a carefully designed strategy of donor upgrading. By 1972 the Republican Party house list was a golden goose capable of laying eggs to the tune of several million dollars a year.

But in that same year, the Democrats were given a list that was quite possibly the most valuable political mailing list of all time. After he lost the election, George McGovern handed his twelve-million-dollar in-house mailing list to Bob Strauss, chairman of the Democratic National Committee. According to Richard Parker, Strauss took the list and proceeded to do something very peculiar with it:

"He put it in a desk drawer and did not touch it for years."

The threat that McGovern posed to the traditional Democratic Party was not only ideological, it was also structural. The ward bosses and old-time party leaders saw direct mail as a threat to their own power. After McGovern lost the election, Strauss wanted to rebuild the traditional structure. He didn't want to concede the essential realignment that McGovern had created. "So the last thing [the oldtime party bosses] wanted to do was to become financially dependent on McGovern donors," says Richard Parker. To rebuild the old Democratic Party they had to return to the traditional sources of money.

Strauss was able to treat a twelve-million-dollar asset so cavalierly for two reasons: (1) He probably was unaware of its real value; and (2) at the time, he didn't really need it anyway. Even though McGovern went down in flames in the presidential election, the Democratic Party was not as devastated then as the GOP was after 1964. The Democrats still had a hammerlock on both houses of Congress, a secure grip on the majority of gubernatorial seats, and a strong position in state legislatures around the country.

"If you're fat and happy," says Larry Sabato, "you say, 'Well, we must be doing something right.' But if you've just had two disasters like Goldwater and Watergate, you're forced to try something new."

Another reason Sabato gives for why the Republicans have outgunned the Democrats in direct mail is that "the Republicans draw their talent from the managerial class. Republicans are more attuned to new technologies and more familiar with how to use them because they have encountered them in business."

The remark is certainly a generalization, but it contains more than a little truth, especially when you consider two key facts: (1) The Democrats have never understood the importance of *reinvesting* in their direct-mail program; and (2) the Democrats have never really understood the real meaning of "marketing" as it is applied to political direct mail.

"When my agency started working for the Democratic National Committee," says Roger Craver, "they had sixty thousand donors; when we left, they had 750,000. When we started, they were raising 1.2 million dollars in direct mail; when we left, they were raising eighteen million dollars. But they spend it all! They don't plow it back into the program. In the GOP, the political managers have also been good investment managers."

But Rod Smith, formerly the executive finance director of the National Republican Senatorial Committee, thinks the Democratic Party's biggest handicap in making direct mail work for them is that they just don't know what they want to sell.

When the Republicans have success with an opinion poll, the Democrats try an opinion poll. When the Republicans mail a certificate of appreciation, the Democrats try a certificate of appreciation. "But these [involvement devices]," says Smith, "are just sales techniques. They are not marketing techniques."

"Marketing," Smith continues, "means creating a product. And the Democrats have yet to develop a product that is uniquely theirs."

Smith knows what he's talking about. Not only is he a C.P.A. and an M.B.A. (giving some credence to Sabato's theory), but he also runs an organization that is the political equivalent of Procter & Gamble. The National Republican Senatorial Committee has more subcommittees, clubs, task forces, and advisory boards than P&G has brands of soap.

"You take the National Republican Senatorial Committee," says Smith, "and you've got something that sounds like a monolithic institution. Not too sexy. But if you take that committee and you break it down into its parts, then you have things like the Republican Senatorial Trust, which is a very exclusive group of two hundred people who give ten thousand dollars a year. Or the Republican Inner Circle, thousand-dollar contributors who get to have dinner with cabinet members and senators. Or the Republican Business Advisory Board. Or the Presidential Task Force.

"[This is] product development, product strategy. Commercial strategic thinking applies just as much to fundraising as it does to selling a product."

When I told Smith that his organization reminded me of Procter & Gamble, he smiled and said, "That's exactly right. It's something for everybody. But the big difference between us and Procter & Gamble is that we don't have any kind of training ground to bring people in to run these programs . . .

"The only stability there is in politics is in the consulting corps."

Indeed, some have suggested that the consultants—specifically the major direct-mail agencies—are the only parties who really have benefited from political direct mail at all.

The most common agency fee structure in the political direct-mail business calls for a flat monthly retainer plus a commission on production. A typical contract between a direct-mail agency and a political candidate, therefore, might be two thousand dollars per month plus 15 percent of all the money spent on printing, data processing, lettershop services, artwork, and so on. The agency gets paid whether the client makes any money on the mailing or not. And the more letters the client mails, the more money the agency makes.

This arrangement is basically a fair one, but it provides the agency with a strong incentive to urge the client to mail in large quantities, even when it isn't in the client's best interest to do so. As already noted, direct-mail agencies occasionally will front the money to a fledgling organization by delaying bills until the client has raised enough money in the mail to pay them. Some agencies will go so far as to create a client out of thin air if they spot an opportunity to cash in on a hot issue. And agencies have also been known to support a foundering organization in the mail as long as it is making enough money to pay its bills, but not enough to do the political or charitable work it claims to be doing.

Since he who pays the piper also calls the tune, agencies that are involved in fronting money or loaning services to their clients usually demand, in return for their generosity, joint ownership of the donors' names. When an agency has a responsive in-house list to call its own, it's easier for the agency to launch new clients into the mail. It also gives the agency the opportunity, should it choose to pursue it, to diversify into the list business by renting its own list and brokering others.

Clients may come and go, but the agencies stay and prosper. As a result, many people who are knowledgeable about direct-mail technology have grown cynical altogether about its role in politics. When Richard Viguerie organized several of his clients into a campaign to "defund the left" by depriving them of federal grant support for their think tanks, and Roger Craver rallied his own clients to cry "unfair," a weary *Village Voice* reporter concluded his story by suggesting that the whole thing was a case of Richard Viguerie vs. Roger Craver "staging a fake war of words through which only they grow rich."[9]

As cynical as one can easily become about political direct mail, however, it's hard to deny that it's had an effect on American politics—although not quite the effect that direct-mail experts believe it's had.

There is little doubt, for example, that direct mail has played a role in the "conservatization" of the Republican Party. Partly because the GOP's mailing list traces its roots to the Barry Goldwater campaign, partly because Viguerie and the New Right have been so successful in setting the national agenda of political issues, the Republican Party is a far more conservative organization today than it was twenty-five years ago. With a few notable exceptions, like Senator Lowell Weicker, the moderate-to-liberal Republican politician no longer exists. Virtually everyone in the Republican Party today is a conservative or talks like one. Even lifelong moderates like George Bush have to spend a lot of time *pretending* to be conservative if they want to run on the Republican ticket. Direct-mail donors don't respond to moderation. They respond to emotion, to extremism, to fire and brimstone. And if a political party wants to base its entire financial structure on direct mail—as the GOP evidently does—it can't afford to pussyfoot around with moderate positions on the issues.

Meanwhile, on the other side of the fence, the Democratic Party's lack of sophistication in direct mail created a power vacuum that was quickly filled by special-interest groups. McGovern disrupted the traditional power structure of the

Democratic Party and left it in a shambles. He also left the DNC a valuable mailing list. But the party bureaucrats were too short-sighted to make use of it. As a result, the Democratic Party's ability to influence events was severely diminished. The DNC never got the hang of direct mail. But SANE, Planned Parenthood, Common Cause, NOW, the Sierra Club, and the rest of what is sometimes known as "the K Street Mafia" most certainly did. As a result, it is these organizations—not the Democratic Party—who now set the issue agenda for Democratic candidates. By 1976, the Democratic National Convention nominated a man who literally had no ties to the traditional party structure but who, instead, was inextricably tied to every special-interest group under the sun. Part of the reason Jimmy Carter's presidency was so flawed was that he owed his power not to a strong, centralized party structure but to a coalition of disparate interest groups, each one exerting pressure in a different direction. Carter behaved at times like a marionette whose every string was held by a different puppeteer.

And if that was true of Jimmy Carter, it was a hundred times more true of the Democratic Party's *next* presidential nominee, Walter Mondale. The 1984 presidential election campaign between Walter Mondale and Ronald Reagan may have been the apex of direct-mail-inspired politics in America. It's hard to imagine either of these men rising to power without it. The Republicans renominated a man who in 1968 and 1976 had been rejected by his party for being too conservative. But after twenty years of direct mail working its evolutionary changes on GOP ideology, he became the right man at the right time. The Democrats, on the other hand, nominated a man who, it seems, almost no one really liked but who had systematically assembled a labyrinthine web of endorsements from special-interest groups so intricate that it made his nomination a foregone conclusion. It was a battle of two Frankensteins, each created by a technology gone wildly out of control.

So far, the Republican Party has been able to avoid the splintering effect that direct mail has had on the Democrats. Perhaps as the perennial number-two party, Republicans have, like Avis Rent-a-Car, remembered the importance of trying harder and sticking together. But it's only a matter of time before the glue that holds together the coalition of direct-mail-funded organizations on the right starts to melt. Internecine arguments on the right about which issues should be placed on the national agenda will get more and more heated. The eventual rift is likely to form around the so-called religious right. The coalition between fiscal conservatives and religious fundamentalists always has been more a marriage of convenience than of love. When a man like Pat Robertson can make a serious run for the Republican presidential nomination, there's no question that some traditional GOP toes will get stepped on and some intramural feuds begun. There always has been a core of Barry Goldwater-style conservatives in the Republican Party who have never fully bought into the New Right morality anyway. You may recall that when Jerry Falwell said that every good Christian should oppose the nomination of Sandra Day O'Connor to the U.S. Supreme Court, it was none other than Barry Goldwater who said, "every good Christian ought to kick Jerry Falwell right in the ass."

Direct mail has a tendency to put a premium on ass-kicking and set little stock by thoughtful negotiation. Politics in America used to be the art of compromise. Now it's the art of confrontation. Extremists always prefer to go down fighting for a cause rather than compromise their principles. And since direct mail has a tendency to elect extremists, some critics have charged that direct mail has served to rigidify American politics by making our politicians more inflexible and making the electorate more concerned about individual issues than about good government. Congressman Jim Leach, Republican of Iowa, has said, "America, as a society, with all its diversity, functions by exercising tolerance. The fundraising mail can be classified as intolerant, stressing divisions, not healing them."[10]

Direct mail encourages voters to walk inside the polling booth armed with a black-and-white view of the world. To work as a fundraising medium, direct mail must offer a highly oversimplified view of complex issues. So, for example, the entire range of cultural, historical, economic, diplomatic, and strategic considerations involved in the decision to return the Panama Canal to the Panamanians gets boiled down in Ronald Reagan's mind—and in the minds of those who received direct-mail letters from him—to: "We built it, we paid for it, it's ours, and we're going to keep it."

One wonders if we should be deciding questions of foreign policy by means of direct mail at all. Foreign policy is one area of government where the public interest is best served when all patriotic Americans make an effort to speak with one tongue and to present a united front to the outside world. Whenever the American people appear to be seriously divided on issues of foreign policy, it works to our enemies' advantage and not to our own (as it most surely did, for example, during Vietnam). Fortunately, the American people show a natural tendency to rally around the president when it comes to matters of national security. But direct mail only subverts this tendency, creating division and disagreement where none needs to exist. Throughout the Reagan presidency, for example, Richard Viguerie has waged a campaign against Reagan's foreign policy. At one point, Viguerie even mailed a letter containing a "pink slip" for Secretary of State George Shultz.

Opposition to Reagan's foreign policy certainly is a minority view among Republicans and conservatives. Yet if one looks at the world from the vantage point of a corner office at The Viguerie Company, it would seem like Republicans and conservatives all across America are steaming mad about Reagan and ready to storm the White House to lynch him for crimes against humanity. In the world of political direct mail, the views of the majority are unimportant. Only the views of the extreme minority—the 1 or 2 percent who will respond to the letter—are worthy of consideration. You might call this "The 1 Percent Solution," and it's a formula with frightening implications for American politics. Increasingly, our national agenda is being determined by crackpots, extremists, fanatics, and lunatics. And not surprisingly, these people are deciding which issues will become part of the national political debate *not* on the basis of which ones are important to the future of this country but on the basis of which ones really make their blood boil. Is school prayer, for example, really the most important issue we should be focusing on at this point in our nation's history? Is abortion, for that matter? What about the balance of trade, the national debt, the decline of our manufacturing base, the depletion of our energy resources, the decay of the infrastructure? When are we going to see some direct mail on those vastly important but complex and, for the most part, unemotional issues? It seems to me that, thanks in part to the influence of direct-mail-funded political organizations, Americans are in danger of fiddling around with issues like the Panama Canal Treaties while the more serious issues go completely unattended.

As long as direct mail continues to play an important role in politics, Congress and the White House are going to be paying more attention to "hot" issues than to important ones. Perhaps to a certain extent they always have. But there's little doubt that direct mail makes the situation considerably worse.

Can anything *good* be said about direct mail?

Yes. A lot.

Thanks to direct mail, more people are involved in the political process, and involved in a meaningful way, than ever before in the history of this country. Although it tends to simplify issues and tends to choose issues solely on the basis of emotion, it is, at least, an *issue-based* medium, not an image-based medium like television. When it works, direct mail is a marvelous way to finance political campaigns, much better for the overall health of democracy than the old system of fat cats or the newer system of political action committees. Direct mail also is better than public financing—the only other alternative—because public financing would give an enormous advantage to incumbents. Direct mail probably is the only form of campaign financing that offers no built-in advantage to the incumbent. If anything, it works slightly to the advantage of the challenger. Fat cats and political action committees usually like to be on the side of the winner, so their money flows heavily to candidates who are already in office. The direct-mail donor is the only political donor who instinctively prefers the underdog, and that's probably a good thing for American politics. Direct mail, as we've seen, also has played a role in revitalizing the national political parties. And that's probably a good thing, too.

But for all its strong points, direct mail has no shortage of critics. And the nicest thing most of them have had to say about direct mail recently is this:

It may be dying.

On the day I met with Richard Viguerie in the spring of 1986 to interview him for this book, his empire was crumbling around him and the national press was trumpeting his imminent demise. "From Money Magic to Money Misery" said one story in *The New York Times*. "Trouble on the Far Right," wrote *Newsweek. Time* called him "The New Right's Loss Leader." And *The Washington Post* wrote an editorial on Viguerie's problems headlined "The Decline of Direct Mail." Typically, the *Post* couldn't resist adding in the text that "a great many people, including us, find this no tragedy."

Yet Viguerie looked no worse for the wear. He came bounding into his outer office and shook my hand vigorously, obviously approaching the interview with enthusiasm. His secretary had told me that Mr. Viguerie was swearing off reporters because he felt the need to pay more attention to his business. But he made an exception in my case. And after spending about an hour in his office and outer office, it became clear that he had made an exception in several other cases as well. As I was leaving, Viguerie was preparing to take a phone call from a *USA Today* reporter to assure him that Lyndon LaRouche was a left-winger and not, as had been widely reported, a conservative.

Viguerie is a short and slight man. Mostly bald. Impeccably well dressed in a three-piece suit, and—for a man who has made his living by ranting and raving in print—disarmingly soft-spoken and thoughtful. I found it amusingly appropriate that for a man who once said he tried to be as much like Jesus Christ as possible, he spoke almost entirely in parables. During my short visit he told me stories about the rabbit and the fox, the man stuck in the ditch, the Russian worker stealing wheelbarrows, and Jack Nicklaus on the PGA tour. In this respect he was reminiscent of Ronald Reagan, but the overall impression Viguerie gives is a very different one.

Reagan is the handsome, wholesome, affable, maybe a little slow-witted, hometown hero. It must have been a simple matter to cast Reagan as the Notre Dame football star George Gipp. But Viguerie would more likely be cast as a radical, bespectacled intellectual plotting a revolution from his basement apartment, constantly reading books whenever he wasn't tinkering with a homemade bomb. In researching Viguerie's life, the most unusual, yet somehow the most revealing, item I found was that when he was living in New York and working for Young Americans for Freedom, he chose to live in Greenwich Village. His favorite bar was The White Horse Tavern (where Dylan Thomas drank himself to death), and his closest friends were drawn from among the young socialists and beatniks who populated the Village coffeehouses in the early 1960s. It's hard to picture Viguerie wearing sandals and playing bongos, but in some ways it fits.

Indeed, Viguerie may be wearing sandals again sometime soon. After a disastrously unsuccessful run for the lieutenant governorship of Virginia in 1985, his first experience as a political candidate, Viguerie returned to find his business affairs in a shambles. Altogether, at least seven conservative political action committees in Viguerie's fold of clients were balking at paying nearly four million dollars' worth of invoices. As a result, Viguerie was unable to pay his own debts, and his attorneys spent the early part of 1986 defending The Viguerie Company in court against lawsuits for unpaid office bills. To raise money, Viguerie sold his precious magazine, *The Conservative Digest*. He put his huge suburban office building up for sale. He reduced his staff dramatically. Worst of all, he started to sell off parts of his house mailing list. The great political power base that began when Richard Viguerie transcribed the names of Goldwater donors onto his yellow pad was about to be pawned for cash.

What happened?

Almost to the man, newspaper and magazine reporters who covered Viguerie's financial woes attributed them to his political success. Essentially, the prevailing theory went that since Reagan was in the White House and all was right with the world, Viguerie and his clients were having trouble raising money using the gloom-and-doom appeals that had always worked in the past.

The theory is correct so far as it goes. There's no question that it's more difficult to raise money in political direct mail when the donor is content than when he is angry. But the problems Richard Viguerie is facing are much more serious than that . . . and much more deeply rooted. Indeed, they are problems faced by everyone who makes a living by political direct mail, no matter where they fall on the ideological spectrum.

The first problem is one of sheer overpopulation. The number of political, quasi-political, and charitable organizations using direct-mail fundraising has grown tremendously in the past fifteen years. But the number of people who *respond* to such appeals is now, always has been, and always will be limited. As a result, some avid direct-mail donors need a machete to hack their way into their own mailboxes. Table 3 shows a list of the direct-mail fundraising appeals collected by one liberal-minded individual after just one month of saving what he found in his mailbox. Anyone capable of giving to this many requests for money, or even a portion of them, is no longer a direct-mail donor but has become, instead, a small foundation.

Meanwhile, the cost of burying this lonely donor in an ava-

Table 3

Please, please, Mister Postman

During the month of March [1983], Howard H. Cammack of Delray Beach, Florida, received direct-mail solicitations (128 in all) from the following groups and causes.

Democratic House and Senate campaigns (5)
Democratic National Committee (1)
Walter Mondale (7)
Sen. Teddy Kennedy (1)
Karen Silkwood Defense Fund (1)
North Carolina Campaign (2)
Association for Humanistic Psychology (1)
Mental Health Law Project (1)
National Cancer Foundation (1)
American Lung Association (1)
American Kidney Fund (3)
Hope (1)
National Council for the Aging (2)
American Parkinson's Disease Foundation (4)
National Women's Health Network (1)
Population Institute (3)
Planned Parenthood (1)
National Abortion Rights Action League (1)
Blinded Veterans Association (1)
Epilepsy Foundation (1)
Braille and Recorded Editions (1)
Eleanor Smeal Report (1)
World Rehabilitation (1)
Berea College (1)
Gallaudet College (2)

Smithsonian Institution (1)
United Negro College Fund (4)
Anti-Nuclear Coalition (2)
Nuclear Weapons Freeze (1)
U.S. Committee Against Nuclear War (2)
International Physicians Against Nuclear Weapons (2)
SANE (1)
National Mobilization for Survival (2)
Peace PAC (1)
Southern Poverty Law Center (1)
Center for Defense Information (1)
American Friends Service Committee (1)
Environment Defense Fund (1)
Nature Conservancy (1)
New Forests Fund (1)
Environmental Task Force (1)
The Wilderness Society (3)
Sierra Club (1)
International Fund for Animal Welfare (1)
Friends of the Earth (1)
Meals for Millions (5)
Urban League (2)
American Civil Liberties Union (5)
Covenant House for Under 21 (2)

World Relief (1)
NOW Legal Defense and Education (1)
USO (1)
United States Golf Association (1)
Fortune Society (1)
Zero Population Growth (1)
International Church Relief Fund (1)
Foundation for Christian Living (1)
Guideposts (1)
Holy Land Christian Mission (1)
Maryknoll Sisters (1)
Recordings for the Blind (2)
NAACP (3)
World Federalists (3)
Clergy and Laity Concerned (2)
Council for a Livable World (2)
Women's International League for Peace and Freedom (1)
Physicians for Social Responsibility (1)
Union of Concerned Scientists (1)
American Cancer Society (2)
Amnesty International (1)
UNICEF (2)
League of Women Voters (1)
FARAL (1)

Meharry Medical College (3)	Nutrition Action (1)	Handgun Control (1)
St. Labre Indian School (1)	Direct Relief International (1)	

lanche of paper continues to rise. As response rates decline, the direct mailer gets trapped in a vicious circle. Plummeting response rates cause him to spend more in production gimmicks to trigger a contribution. Increased production costs, in turn, force him to ask the donor for a higher average gift. And the request for larger gifts causes the overall response rate to drop even farther.

The direct mailer probably could survive this Catch-22 situation if it weren't for one factor over which he has no control and that is capable of throwing the delicate mathematics of his business completely awry: postage. Direct-mail organizations work with razor-thin profit margins even in the best of times, and a postal increase can be enough to put many of the organizations out of business overnight. Since the Postal Rate Commission is constantly studying the possibility of doing away with the subsidized rate enjoyed by all nonprofit organizations—or taking it away from political organizations—political direct mail, as we know it today, could disappear as quickly and finally from the American political landscape as the dinosaurs once did from the face of the earth.

In 1972, when George McGovern set the standard for the use of political direct mail, not only did a first-class stamp cost six cents, but also political direct mail itself was new and exciting. Receiving what appeared to be a personal letter from a national presidential candidate was something of a novelty, and so were the premiums, buttons, opinion polls, and vinyl records that McGovern pioneered.

"I used to open every piece of political direct mail I got," says political scientist Larry Sabato, "but now I just toss it into the can.

"Nowadays, when you watch television, you can always tell whether a commercial is using an actor or a real person. We've become 'videowise.' And I think we've become 'direct-mail-wise,' too. What would have fooled us, or intrigued us, or delighted us five years ago doesn't do so at all anymore. So we toss it. It's not just oversolicitation [that direct mailers have to overcome]. It's boredom."

But before you can be bored by a direct-mail piece, you first have to be able to read it. And every day, fewer and fewer Americans are capable of doing so. Approximately twenty-three million adults in America today are functionally illiterate. Another thirty-five million Americans are classified as "semiliterate." Among Americans of all ages alive today, it is estimated that as many as seventy million are functionally illiterate and will remain so for the rest of their lives. This figure, equal to approximately three times the population of Canada, is growing fast.

These are not the direct-mail donors of tomorrow.

Everything about Roger Craver is different from Richard Viguerie. Viguerie's hair is thinning on top. Roger's head is a jungle of curls. Viguerie is thin and wiry. Craver is chubby and round. Viguerie dresses in conservative three-piece suits. But on the day I met with Craver, he was wearing a flashy blue blazer with a fire-engine red tie and matching hanky dangling flamboyantly out of the breast pocket. While Viguerie is the archconservative, and Craver the flaming liberal, it is Viguerie who keeps his company in a sleek modern office building, and Craver who runs his agency, like a small-town law firm, from a large Victorian house that has been cleverly converted into a rabbit warren of tiny offices.

Remarkably, Richard Viguerie and Roger Craver are close friends.

"Richard is an extraordinary person," says Craver. "He's willing to risk everything for what he believes in. And it has cost him dearly in recent months. He's lost a lot of money. But I keep telling him, 'Richard, you're not as bankrupt as your ideas.'"

Ideas, however, are one commodity on which Roger Craver will never go bankrupt. Unlike most of the direct mailers I spoke with, here was a man who had clearly thought about virtually all the serious issues raised by his profession. And if he *hadn't* thought about them before, he was more than willing to sit there and think about them while I listened, with his mouth tagging along after his nimble brain like an eager puppy.

"We're not going to get the next generation of political donors with direct mail," he said flatly. "Because they are not print-oriented.

"I'm not worried about the next few years. I'm worried about when today's twenty-eight-year-old gets to be thirty-five. Because today's twenty-eight-year-old doesn't get his political information from *The New Republic*. He watches the evening news. He watches CNN. He watches C-SPAN. We have to be alert to that."

"What are you going to do about it?" I asked him.

Use the new technologies, he said.

Two

The New Technologies

6

Telemarketing:
Reach Out
and Put
the Touch
on Someone

Much has been made of the "front porch" campaign
William McKinley waged against William Jennings Bryan in 1896.
While Bryan was out doing what he did best—making a record
number of stump speeches—McKinley stayed home and let the
campaign come to him. Few people noticed, however, that sitting next to McKinley on that historic front porch in Canton,
Ohio, was a telephone. With it, McKinley directed his campaign
by remote control.

Ironically, history has credited Bryan with running the first
"modern" presidential campaign because it was a campaign based
on image-making, sloganeering, and direct contact with the electorate. But while Bryan was getting all the attention, McKinley
was running history's first "technological" campaign via telephone. Indeed, McKinley's campaign was so intricately tied to
the telephone and telegraph networks that one contemporary
observer described his house in Canton as "looped like a Christ-

mas package with important coils of wire." Not surprisingly, during McKinley's administration the first small telephone switchboard was installed at the White House.

McKinley was using the telephone strictly as an organizational tool; there simply weren't enough telephones among the general public in 1896 to use it as a tool for advertising. But only twelve years later, the situation had changed. The first known use of a campaign "phone bank" took place in Atlanta in 1908. A mayoral candidate installed forty-five telephones in the back of a store and had volunteers place get-out-the-vote calls to his known supporters. By 1906, use of the telephone in politics had become widespread enough for a writer in the trade journal *Telephony* to lament that no one had yet made a serious study of the subject:

> It is time for someone to write a book, or at least an article, on "The Telephone in Politics." The telephone has made it possible for one man to wage a campaign over an entire city. It has curtailed the functions and responsibilities of a district manager as the cable has those of an ambassador. It enables a canvass to be made, or a list of distinguished signatures secured for some "call" or manifesto, without the expenditure of several days' time or the employment of a large corps of workers.[1]

More than eighty years later, those words are still true. Indeed, this chapter—entirely by default—may be the most comprehensive analysis of the telephone in politics ever attempted. Just as we tend to take the phone for granted in our daily lives, we seem to have taken its political impact for granted, too—although if you got a call from Jesse Jackson, like the one many black residents of New Orleans received in 1983, it would be hard to remain completely blasé about it:

TELEPHONE: *Ring . . . ring . . .*
VOTER: Hello?
TELEPHONE: Hello, I'm Jesse Jackson, talking to you via a recording made while in your city. By the way, can you hear me?
VOTER: Er . . . yes, Jesse, I can hear you just fine, I guess.

TELEPHONE: Throughout the United States, we are registering black people to vote for our concern. A special effort is being made in New Orleans. Have you done your part? Are you a registered voter? That's important. Are all the members in your family registered? If you need registration assistance, please wait for the tone. Give us your name and telephone number. [The computer plays a tone and activates the inbound recording tape.]

VOTER: Well, Jesse, let's see. I'm registered, but my wife isn't. Neither is my son, Billy, who just turned eighteen. My name is Robert Thomas and you can reach me at 555-7890.

TELEPHONE: [The computer waits until the voter is finished talking, stops the inbound tape, and reactivates the outbound tape.] We will contact you soon. If you are registered, please help us make sure all your friends and relatives are registered. Please call us at 555-1938 or 555-1983 and give us a hand. Remember, you are somebody and your vote counts. There's a freedom train coming. When you register, you can ride. (Click)[2]

The telephone used in the "conversation" above is essentially the same machine conceived by Alexander Graham Bell and crudely fashioned by Thomas Watson more than a century ago. Remarkably little has changed about the instrument itself during the intervening years. But clearly, much has changed in the way it is being used.

An interesting analogy can be drawn between our use of the telephone for politics and our use of the sun for energy. Like the sun, the telephone has been around for as long as anyone cares to remember, and because of that, we forget how powerful it is. Just as we've always made *some* use of solar power (windmills, for example), we've always made *some* political use of the telephone. In recent years, new ideas and new technologies have been developed to harness the sun's electrical power and the telephone's *electoral* power. But most of these technologies are expensive, experimental, and, quite often, inefficient. As a result we tend to use both solar power and telephone power in a *supplemental* way. Yet almost everyone agrees the potential is enormous. When the right combination of technology and methodology is perfected, the thermal power released by the sun and the political power released by the telephone will boggle the mind.

Although the telephone itself has changed little in the century since it was invented, the American telephone *system* has grown to become the largest and most complex machine ever fashioned by the hand of man. Originally conceived by Bell as a point-to-point intercom linking two customers on a fixed wire, the invention of the switchboard in 1877 transformed the telephone into a point-to-switchboard-to-point system, theoretically capable of linking any telephone user with any other. Miles of copper wire have been replaced over the years with coaxial cable, fiber optic cable, microwave relays, and even satellites to link more and more people at less and less cost. Using this system, it is possible, within seconds, to send a personal message to virtually any individual in the United States and receive an instantaneous, live response.

It doesn't take a genius to realize that this is probably the most powerful political tool ever invented. Yet amazingly, it wasn't until recently that politicians and political organizations began to make anything but the most crude and obvious uses of it. Beginning in the early 1960s, however, three developments changed the telephone's role in both business and politics: (1) the advent of an assembly-line approach to phone banks; (2) the marriage of the telephone to the computer; and (3) the systematic application of direct-marketing principles to telephone selling.

As we've already seen, the use of banks of telephone lines for sales, fundraising, or political advertising dates all the way back to the turn of the century. But the invention of modern telemarketing, as we know it today, can be traced to a single advertising campaign in 1962. The client was the Ford Motor Company. The goal was to develop sales leads for Ford dealers. The Ford executive in charge was none other than a young and ambitious Lee Iacocca. And the consultant Iacocca hired to run the campaign was the father of modern telemarketing, Murray Roman.

Together, Iacocca and Roman came up with a simple but revolutionary approach to telephone sales. Rather than put their faith in the skills of individual salesmen, they created a system-

atic program in which thousands of trained communicators made
millions of calls by slavishly adhering to a brief and standardized script. Like the automobile assembly line pioneered by Henry
Ford himself, the emphasis was taken off individual craftman-
ship—or, in this case, salesmanship—and placed instead on sheer
volume. Make enough phone calls, Iacocca and Roman reasoned, and you would eventually generate a significant number
of leads. It was sort of like the "infinite number of monkeys"
theory applied to the telephone.

As it turned out, the theory worked. Using fifteen thousand
housewives with no previous telephone selling experience and
only a modicum of training, Ford contacted more than twenty
million homes across the country and generated nearly 340,000
leads. On the first day of returns, Ford dealers sold 444 cars as
a direct result of the promotion. Nine days later, they had sold
seven thousand. Harvard business professor Theodore Leavitt
wrote, "[Murray Roman] has pioneered the conversion of the
telephone from an instrument for personal communication to a
machine for production. He has converted a spade into a steam
shovel, a tabulating machine into a computer."[3] By standardiz-
ing the procedure and measuring the results, Roman had transformed telephone sales from a one-to-one, hit-or-miss affair into
a process as predictable, manageable, and productive as a car
factory.

As in any manufacturing business, productivity is enhanced
by technology that saves time or eliminates drudgery. Here, too,
the growth of telemarketing as a commercial and political medium has benefited by significant developments in telecommunications technology. Most of these advances are the result of
marrying an ordinary telephone to a simple computer. In today's
modern telemarketing center, for example, a computer dials the
call, cues the communicator with a script that appears on a CRT
screen, electronically generates a personalized follow-up letter,
and keeps a running tab of results. In some cases a tape re-
corder is added to the mix of machinery, allowing telemarketing
calls to be made with scarcely any human involvement at all.

But the most important factor in the transformation of "phone
banks" into "telemarketing" was the gradual realization in both
politics and business that the telephone was a legitimate direct-
response medium, just like direct mail. As such it could be made
to adhere to all the principles and techniques of direct market-

ing. After all, the very first telephone call was a direct-response campaign. Bell said, "Come here, Watson, I want you," and Watson came—a 100 percent response rate. But it took almost a hundred years before the accumulated wisdom of fundraising and selling by mail was systematically applied to the phone.

To understand how the telephone is used in politics today, one must first appreciate how telemarketing is similar to direct mail . . . and then realize how it is different.

Like direct mail, telemarketing is a *measurable* advertising medium in which the cost of a campaign can be plotted against results. As such it obeys all the rules of mail-order mathematics. Like direct mail, telemarketing has the unusual characteristic of being both a mass medium and a one-to-one medium at the same time. In one expert's memorable phrase, telemarketing is a medium capable of delivering "a volume of messages—one at a time."[4] Most important, like direct mail, telemarketing is a *targeted* advertising medium capable of delivering a message directly to the person deemed most likely to respond—whether the desired response is a contribution, or a vote.

So much for the similarities. The differences are largely matters of degree. You might say telemarketing is just like direct mail . . . only more so.

Much is made of the highly personal nature of direct mail, and direct mailers go to great lengths to make their letters seem as personal as possible. The idea is to achieve the kind of intimate environment in which both trust and persuasion can thrive. But what could be more intimate than entering the donor's home and speaking directly into his ear?

A completely "interactive," or two-way electronic advertising medium is a long-standing dream in the direct-marketing community for obvious reasons. But while many direct marketers pinned their hopes on experimental forms of bidirectional cable TV or interactive videodiscs, few seemed to notice that just such an advertising medium has been around for more than a century: the telephone. "Unlike any other mass medium," writes direct-mail consultant Stephen Winchell, ". . . the telephone provides an opportunity to 'talk back.' "[5] And that, in turn, gives the telemarketer a chance to evaluate his customer's mood, attitude, and reaction to the message while there still is time to change it.

Telemarketing is more aggressive than direct mail. Perhaps because it is an involuntary advertising medium (no one ever *asked* to receive a telemarketing call) and a highly intrusive one, telemarketing has a knack for taking advantage of the customer and putting him on the defensive, making it possible to force an ultimatum on an unsuspecting and usually somewhat passive respondent.

"It's a hot medium," says David Andelman, president of Public Interest Communications, the telemarketing agency founded by Roger Craver. "You're catching the person off-base a little bit. You're not trying to browbeat him, but you have the advantage of knowing what you're going to say."

The sense of immediacy and urgency engendered by an unexpected phone call is an enormously useful tool in politics. We've already seen how direct mailers sometime disguise their appeals as overnight letters and telegrams. But urgent news rarely arrives by telegram anymore. The telephone is today's delivery boy for all important messages, good or bad. Thus, when a campaign worker calls to say the candidate is only 1 percent down in the polls with less than a week to go, it carries more urgency—and more credibility, for that matter—than a fake telegram bearing the same message.

At its best, telemarketing generates a shared sense of excitement between the caller and the donor. Like the hard-core direct-mail donor who willingly plows through a ten-page letter from his favorite candidate, some telemarketing respondents are genuinely thrilled to receive a call from an organization they believe in. And the donor's off-the-cuff comments constitute a kind of electronic "white mail" that is useful not only for modifying the telemarketing campaign but also in refining the goals of the organization itself.

All these factors contribute to the single most obvious and significant difference between telemarketing and direct mail: Telemarketing generates a higher rate of response. Estimates vary, but most experts agree that telemarketing campaigns achieve response rates roughly ten times higher than similar campaigns conducted by mail. Get a 2 percent response to a given list by direct mail, for example, and you're likely to get a 20 percent response if you contact the same list by phone. But telemarketing also *costs more* than direct mail. Lots more. Again, the difference generally is believed to be a factor of ten. It costs between twenty and fifty cents to send a single direct-mail letter; it costs between two and five dollars to make a single telemarketing call. Although the net returns are proportionally higher, the high upfront costs scare away many potential users of telemarketing for political fundraising.

The costs of running a telemarketing operation are more stable than those of managing a direct-mail program. Direct mailers live in fear of postal increases, for example, but telephone rates, especially long-distance rates, historically have only gone down. The price of unskilled labor also is comparatively stable. More significantly, the cost of "testing the waters" in a telemarketing campaign is considerably less than it is in direct mail because telemarketing is the most testable, the most "fine-tunable" advertising medium ever invented.

"If you sit down and listen to an hour's worth of calls," says Charlie Cadigan, president of TransAmerica Telemarketing, a Republican-oriented telemarketing firm, "you can get a good feel for how the script is working."

This high level of "testability" gives telemarketing a significant advantage over direct mail, where even the most modest test requires a substantial investment of time and money. At the first sign that a telemarketing campaign is not returning a profit, the sponsor will terminate the program and cut his losses. Or he may choose to tinker with various elements—the script, the list, the callers—until he gets it right. Telemarketing is the only advertising medium in which the message can be changed while the results still are coming in, making it rather like those anti-tank weapons in which the mortar round can be guided to the target *after* the gun has been fired.

What makes all this fine-tuning possible is the peculiar fact—even the experts are at a loss to explain it—that telemarketing can be adequately tested on a very small sample of calls. The usual direct-mail test, for example, is based on a *minimum* sample of five thousand letters. But most telemarketers feel they can get a reliable sample from just 250 calls. Thus it is possible to test a telemarketing campaign in the morning and roll it out in the afternoon.

The testing revolves around two main factors: the script and the list. A third factor, the person making the calls—or "communicator," as he is known in the trade—is a wild card capable of affecting the results dramatically, but not easily tested or controlled.

The Script

It will come as no surprise that the typical telemarketing script has a lot in common with a political direct-mail letter. Although there is nothing in the world of telemarketing comparable to direct mail's AIDA formula, most scripts are written on a pattern that varies little from one consultant to the next.

The first step is for the caller to identify himself and the organization he is working for. Next, the caller makes sure he has reached the right party, or, if not, that he has reached someone capable of making a decision about whether to give. The donor's wife, for example, may be fair game. But the donor's twelve-year-old kid is off-limits. Having cleared the way for the conversation to take place, the script usually begins by thanking the donor for his past support, or—if this is a first contact—by gathering his involvement through careful questioning.

"We might ask him, 'Are you familiar with the situation in Nicaragua, Mr. Jones?' " says Tom Palma, president of the telemarketing agency founded by Bruce Eberle. If the answer is yes, the communicator will turn immediately to the pressing need for funds. If it's "no," the communicator has the opportunity to launch into an emotional and loaded presentation of the problem similar to the first few lines of a direct-mail letter. As with direct mail, emotionalism is important.

"But you have to walk a fine line," says Charlie Cadigan. "You have more free rein in direct mail" than you do on the phone.

It helps, of course, if you have a devil you can point to. And it helps even more if you have a genuine crisis to talk about. When I asked various telemarketing consultants to tell me about their favorite campaign, I invariably heard about situations in which the client was faced with a bona fide emergency. Andelman's favorite project was typical: an urgent fundraising drive for the Southern Poverty Law Center after the KKK had burned down its headquarters.

Having presented the problem in the most emotional terms possible, the script turns next to the need for the money and makes an urgent request for a contribution. As in a direct-mail letter, the more specific the request, the better.

"We had a program called 'Operation Rescue,'" Tom Palma recalls, "which sponsored a ship in the Gulf of Thailand that rescued boat people. It also managed to get important information of live sightings of American POW's who were still in Vietnam. Well, we figured out that it cost about nineteen dollars a minute to run this ship, if you included fuel, salaries, food, and everthing else. And every time we got on the phone with that it was a success, because we gave them a specific need and a specific dollar amount. We had some people say, 'Put me down for *two* minutes!'"

Although it is permissible to dramatize the need for a contribution in such a simplistic fashion, there are fewer gimmicks in telemarketing scripts than in the typical direct-mail letter. "The prospect," writes Murray Roman, "is in a 'responsive' position at the other end of the line, reserving the right to break in and interrupt with what might prove to be an embarrassing question. . . . Innuendos, tricky offers, half truths, concealed facts, and the old-fashioned 'hard sell' pressure approach have no place in today's telephone-marketing operations."[6]

A notable exception to that rule, however, is what Charlie Cadigan calls "the grand illusion," a technique used by virtually every political telemarketer. Creating the grand illusion is nothing more than fostering a belief in the donor's mind that he is talking to someone at the top echelons of the campaign. In reality he usually is talking to a housewife or a college student, often in a part of the country far distant from the campaign itself.

"We'll have the communicator say something like, 'I'll surely let the congressman know about your concern,' or 'I'll be sure to pass that comment on to the senator,'" says Cadigan. "The key is to make it apparent to the donor that he or she is talking to someone from the organization."

Perhaps the elimination of gimmicks makes telemarketing scripts so much shorter than direct-mail letters. Take all the gimmicks out of a political direct-mail letter and there isn't much left. What remains, in fact, would make a pretty good telemarketing script. A script is similar to a direct-mail letter, Cadigan says, in that it must hit all the chords necessary to make the audience react. "But you don't have two or three pages of copy to do it. You've got about two paragraphs, roughly thirty seconds, to make your point, establish credibility, and ask them for help."

Aside from the donor's short attention span and impatience with an unsolicited telephone call, however, there is also a strictly economic reason for the brevity of telemarketing scripts. As Iacocca and Roman proved in 1962, telemarketing is a numbers game. The more you dial, the more you sell. The point is to spend as little time as possible with someone who is *not* going to give to your cause, so you can move on to someone who will.

Not all telemarketing calls are short, however. Some are quite long, especially if the donor is being asked for a large sum of money and the communicator is under strict orders to negotiate the dollar amount firmly. Negotiations usually proceed from high to low, with the communicator kicking off the process by asking for an amount considerably larger than the donor has ever given before. If he balks, the communicator will drop down and ask for lower and lower amounts.

Even when requesting a small contribution, the communicator must be prepared for some give-and-take. Once the donor feels the fishhook in his mouth, his first inclination is to shake, and squirm, and jump out of the water: "I don't have any extra money right now," "I have to check with my wife (and she's in Sri Lanka this week)," "I just gave to the Republican Party a week ago, for Chrissakes."

In the telemarketing business these verbal convulsions are called "objections," and a skilled communicator is good at overcoming them. Typically, nothing is left to chance. The communicator's response to common objections is scripted as carefully as the fundraising message itself.

By monitoring the telephone calls during the test phase of a campaign, the telemarketer will identify any special objections or questions that frequently recur. These will be added to the standard objections ("I can't afford it," "Who did you say you were again?"), and the answers will be written out and placed on a little plastic flip chart the communicator keeps handy at all times. The flip chart is flagged with key phrases ("CAN'T AF-

FORD IT," "JUST GAVE," etc.) and tabbed so the communicator can turn to them quickly. As soon as he flips to the appropriate page, he sees a short script written especially to overcome the objection at hand. ("Well, Mr. Jones, I understand a lot of our Republican wives go to Sri Lanka at this time of year. But that doesn't mean the party isn't still working hard to protect your interests here in Washington. . . .")

Some fully automated telemarketing centers have eliminated the flip chart by putting objection scripts directly onto the computer. As the communicator reads from his CRT screen, suddenly the donor interrupts and says, "I can't afford it."

No problem.

The communicator looks at the list of objections on the bottom of the screen and sees No. 6—"CAN'T AFFORD IT." He presses "6" on his keypad, and a new script appears on the screen: "Well, Mr. Smith, I know the economy has been bad recently, but that's why we especially need your help. . . ."

Yet no matter how much technology is brought to bear on the problem, some objections just can't be overcome. "When you work for pro-life organizations," says Cadigan, "you encounter a lot of religious donors who say, 'Well, I can't contribute, but I'm going to pray on it.'

"And, of course, you've got to be a humanist at some point," Cadigan adds. "If someone says, 'My wife is dying of cancer and I don't have any money left to my name,' you can't turn around and say, 'Well, I understand, Mr. Smith, but let me tell you why the Republican majority so desperately needs your help this year. . . .'"

But assuming the donor doesn't come up with a zinger like that one, and assuming all his other objections have been satisfactorily answered, he is virtually painted into a corner. Like a dog who has been chased around the room with a rolled-up newspaper, eventually there's nothing left for the donor to do but roll over on his back, stick his legs in the air, and signal defeat.

"Okay," says the donor passively.

And the communicator pounces like a wolf on the fold, following up on the donor's muttered acquiescence with a closing dialogue as stylized and conventional as the murder scene in a piece of Kabuki theater.

"We have a mandatory close," says David Andelman, "which

the communicators have to read word-for-word." This is partly for the donor's protection and partly for the telemarketer's. The idea is to make a solid confirmation of the donor's commitment, to verify his name and address, and to let him know that he will soon receive a pledge envelope that he is expected to return with a check. Finally, the script ends in roughly the same way it began, ladling the donor with gratitude.

The List

As important as a good script is to the success of a telemarketing campaign, Tom Palma is one of several experts who believe the most critical factor is the list. A refugee from the very different world of inbound commercial telemarketing, Palma originally was surprised to discover how important it is in political fundraising to segment the list.

"My assistant was really the first one to discover it," says Palma. "She said, 'You know, the key to this business is all in the list. Either the list is going to work or it's not—or a portion of the list will work.' "

"So we started manipulating the list. Now, we take a list and the first thing we do is break it down by time zones. At 9:00 P.M. you stop calling on the East Coast. But if you've got your list in time zones, you can keep calling California until midnight.

"Then you start to break down the Zip codes. If you're doing something for Jesse Helms, you try North Carolina for a while. If you're doing something for D'Amato, try New York. You hit where you think you're going to be most successful. You always go to the cream of the list if you can find it."

As the calling begins, the results are monitored constantly. And if a certain area or a certain type of donor responds at a particularly high rate, the telemarketer concentrates as many callers as he can on that segment of the file. Of course, direct mailers do this, too, so it's nothing revolutionary. But in direct mail it takes months to compile the data, analyze it, and take advantage of it. In a telemarketing center it all happens with the immediacy and the intensity of a busy day on the floor of the Stock Exchange.

Over the course of time, certain hard-and-fast rules—or "glitches," as Palma calls them—begin to emerge.

"Don't call Utah or Idaho on Monday night, for example. Monday night is family night in the Mormon Church, and they don't like to be bothered with phone calls.

"On Sunday afternoon in the fall, take all the female names from your list and call women. The guys are all busy watching football."

"In Florida, don't call after 8:30 P.M. Older people like to go to bed early, and hit the golf course at dawn.

"Forget about California on a Friday evening. They're gone. You can almost see them rip off their ties as they leave the office and take off down the coast. Don't waste your time trying to reach them."

If all this sounds like flying by the seat of the pants when compared to the painstaking, scientific analysis of direct mail, it is. But like direct mail, it's based on the sound principles of direct marketing: Segment the list and target your message to the most productive portions.

Unfortunately, there is no such thing as a "telemarketing list." All the lists used in telemarketing are adapted in one way or another from direct-mail lists, and that gives rise to certain problems of its own. Foremost among these is simply finding the phone numbers. Until recently, "look-ups" were done by dialing Information until every name on a list was matched with a number. But since the divestiture of AT&T (and the new policy of charging a fee for information), that has become prohibitively expensive. Telemarketers now rely on computers to match contributor lists with compiled lists of telephone numbers. Unfortunately, the process is only about 75 percent effective.

"How is the computer going to find Mr. E. Smith in Manhattan?" asks Bruce McBrearty.

It can't, obviously, so the output of a typical run contains about 20 percent of the list that the computer simply can't find and about 5 percent it matches incorrectly, or "bad hits."

Look-ups add considerably to the overall cost of telemarketing. But the biggest cost—and the biggest imponderable—in any telemarketing center is, not surprisingly, labor.

The Communicator

Given the medium's amazing capacity for testing, one might expect that scripts and lists could be fine-tuned to the point where response rates could be predicted down to the penny. And that might very well be the case if it weren't for a third factor, a factor that has been shown repeatedly to have a dramatic effect on results but that is impossible to predict and difficult to control: the communicator.

"It's the worst job in the world," says Tom Palma. And if you can imagine spending up to eight hours a day calling strangers on the telephone, asking them to send money to a distant address without getting anything in return, you can easily see why. "It's a *god-awful* job," Palma says again.

So it should come as no surprise that good communicators, like good Marines, are hard to find. The ideal telemarketing communicator is well-spoken, mature, intelligent, persuasive, capable of thinking on his feet, and—apparently—thoroughly insane. Because in spite of all these bankable qualities, he must also be willing to work for slightly more than minimum wage.

In search of the ideal communicator (at the ideal price), it has become common for political telemarketing firms to move their phone centers to out-of-the-way communities. Both Palma and Cadigan, for example, maintain sales offices in the Washington, D.C., area, but Cadigan's phone center is in Harrisonburg, Virginia, and Palma's is in Jefferson County, West Virginia. Both firms rely heavily on housewives. Since Harrisonburg is a university town, Cadigan enjoys the added advantage of staffing about a fifth of his labor force with college students. In both cases the main reason for locating in these areas was economic, but Cadigan and Palma each believe the advantages of hiring rural people go far beyond low wages.

"They have a nice, friendly, country charm," says Cadigan

about the people he hires in Harrisonburg. "It's a southern voice, kind of slow-talking, and people like to listen to it."

They're disciplined, says Palma, and polite. "I tried to get them to call me 'Tom,' but it's always 'Mr. Palma' or 'sir.' That's the way they are."

Friendliness, politeness, and discipline are important qualities.

The communicator must be friendly because that's what brings telemarketing scripts alive.

He must be polite, because he will be intruding into a stranger's home and violating his privacy. As a result, he may be subjected to abuse. Yet if he, in turn, allows himself to become short-tempered, he may jeopardize the entire campaign by sparking a complaint.

Most important, the communicator must be *disciplined*, because the delicate mathematics of a telemarketing campaign depend on his ability to stick slavishly to the script and to work as tirelessly as an air-traffic controller for the hours he's on duty. To maintain this level of discipline, communicators are monitored constantly by a team of supervisors. From time to time a supervisor will summon the communicator into a private office and play a tape of his work to point out deficiencies. In some highly automated telemarketing centers, supervisors monitor the communicator electronically and give him advice in one ear about how to handle the donor in the other. Special care is taken to make sure the communicator does not deliberately or accidentally falsify his records. It is not uncommon, for example, for a communicator to mark a "maybe" as a "yes"—especially if he is working on commission or if he is in contention for one of the prizes (color TV's, VCR's) often used as motivation in telemarketing centers. The goal of this relentless supervision is to keep the communicator honest, to keep him dialing, and to keep him sticking to the script.

Many can't take the pressure.

Palma, for example, considers his annual attrition rate of 17 percent amazingly low. And most good telemarketing firms will spend an inordinate amount of time and money on benefits, incentives, and even such things as company picnics to keep the troops happy.

Yet one of the easiest ways to remove the pressure from the communicator, maintain a high level of quality control, and ensure strict adherence to the script is to reduce the communicator's role by using a recorded message.

Murray Roman was the first to try cassette tapes in a telemarketing campaign when he used a recording of Norman Cousins to sell subscriptions to *The Saturday Review*. The technique worked. And a few years later, in the election year of 1980, Roman tried it again on a political fundraising campaign for the National Republican Senatorial Committee. The project was an enormous success, proving not only that using a recorded message was a useful tool in political telemarketing but also that telemarketing had a tendency to increase the receipts from direct mail.

When telemarketing and direct mail are combined, they produce a result greater than the sum of their parts. Indeed, most experts believe that the best use of telemarketing in politics is as a *supplement* to direct mail—a way to draw the donor's attention to prospecting letters, to reenlist the donor who has ignored the cycle of renewal appeals, and to recapture the donor who has let his support lapse. Although telemarketing agencies and direct-mail firms bitterly competed with each other in the past, they now see themselves as partners. To the direct-mail consultant in particular, who has watched his medium suffer under the weight of rising costs and dwindling response rates, the telemarketing consultant is a man on a white horse, riding into town at just the right moment.

As telemarketing consultant Bruce McBrearty aptly put it, "In any given direct-mail campaign of a hundred letters, if you got ten contributions back you'd be really happy. But telemarketing addresses itself to the ninety who *don't* respond. And more often than not, we will find another twenty or thirty people to [make a contribution]."

In recent years the process of wedding telemarketing to direct mail has become more complicated than it was during the 1980 NRSC campaign. In that project, the Senatorial Committee simply went ahead with its usual direct-mail program and added telemarketing in the hope that it would pay for itself while having a salutary effect on the mail. Nowadays the donor is subjected to a systematic, multiwave attack in which telephone and mail are carefully orchestrated to capture the donor's attenion, prime his emotions, soften his resistance, and move in for the kill.

The process usually begins with a "precall."

A precall is placed to the donor a few days *before* the direct-mail letter arrives. Its purpose is to alert the donor to the fact that he will be receiving an important letter in the mail and to urge him to read it. In doing so the precall eliminates one of the most serious obstacles faced by any direct-mail letter: competition in the mailbox. Precalls usually make little or no effort to ask for a contribution. Instead they are designed entirely to "sell" the forthcoming direct-mail piece by creating an aura of urgency and mystery. Such calls have been found to increase the net income of a direct-mail campaign by up to 50 percent.

The opposite side of the coin from a precall is the "lead letter." The telemarketer will mail a lead letter when he is relying on the phone call to bear the brunt of the fundraising message. In that case, a short lead letter is mailed a few days prior to when the phoning begins. In it the donor is profusely thanked for his past support, alerted to the current need, and advised that he will be receiving a phone call within several days.

Sometimes the strategy will be to call the donor *after* he has received the usual direct-mail package. This is called "postcall," and its purpose is to enhance direct-mail receipts, both by increasing the rate of response and by encouraging larger gifts. The postcall concentrates on providing additional information, answering objections, and negotiating a larger-than-average gift. Postcalls must be carefully timed to arrive after the direct-mail package but not so much afterward that the donor's memory of it has faded. If the timing is good and the script persuasive, postcalling can have an even more dramatic effect on direct-mail receipts than precalling, especially when it comes to upgrading contributions. David Andelman estimates that up to 10 percent of a group of hundred-dollar donors, for example, can be persuaded in a postcall to give three hundred dollars or more.

No matter whether the strategy is to postcall the donor or precall him, every telemarketing campaign depends to some extent on the success of a special kind of direct-mail piece called a "pledge letter." The pledge letter is the cleanup hitter of telemarketing. Its purpose is to give the donor a means of fulfilling the commitment made over the telephone. Since credit cards are not widely used in political fundraising, the telemarketer depends heavily on his pledge letter to remind the donor of his commitment and provide him with a convenient way to send his check.

Pledge letters always mention the specific dollar amount agreed to on the phone and usually refer to the communicator's name, as in: "Thank you for taking the time to talk with my assistant, Jim Smith, on the phone the other day." In a non-automated telemarketing center where the communicator himself will be filling out pledge cards by hand, he will be encouraged to include a short personal note relating to something that came up in the conversation, like: "Thanks for your contribution of one hundred dollars; hope you enjoy your trip to Europe next week!"

These and other tricks are designed to make sure the donor remembers the call. But the best way to do that is simply to get the pledge letter out *fast*. Speed, in fact, is the single most important consideration in producing a pledge letter, because the lag time between the call and the letter has been shown to have a dramatic effect on results. Some experts estimate that every day lost between the telephone call and the arrival of a pledge letter will cost the telemarketer a 10 percent loss in contributions.

Does all this phoning and mailing really work?

In most cases, yes.

Generally speaking, a list that yields a 2 percent return on direct mail alone—or 15 percent on telemarketing alone—is likely to produce up to 30 percent when the telephone and direct mail are combined. This means the direct mailer can penetrate deeper into his house list than ever before, skimming the easy contributions with direct mail and dropping a line for the bigger and more difficult fish with telemarketing.

Moreover, an occasional dose of telemarketing seems to make Jack a better direct-mail donor. According to direct-mail consultant Stephen Winchell, donors who receive an occasional phone call become more responsive to their direct mail over a period of time. "Perhaps they feel they have a more personal relationship with the organization as a result of having spoken directly with a representative,"[7] speculates Winchell. As proof of that, Bruce McBrearty cites the experience of Jimmy Swaggart Ministries, which found that a file massaged by telemarketing responded four hundred times better to direct mail than a similar file that had never been called.

From a strictly practical point of view, every time tele-marketing finds or renews another donor, it means there will be one more warm body out there to receive future direct-mail letters. Telemarketing also is an effective tool for recapturing lapsed donors, or "inactives." Since keeping an old donor always costs less than finding a new one, most organizations will go to great lengths to renew their inactives. Quite often a phone call is all that's needed to do the trick. According to Public Interest Communications, even after a group of lapsed donors has ignored seven direct-mail renewal notices, up to 20 percent of them can be brought back into the fold with telemarketing.

Indeed, telemarketing's greatest strength is its ability to cement the emotional bond that exists between an organization and its donors. Properly designed, a telemarketing campaign seems more like a service to the donor than an intrusion.

"Anytime you're touching a contributor in a meaningful way," says Rod Smith, "you are helping to draw him a little closer to your operation."[8] So the wise telemarketer occasionally will use the phone to do more than just pitch for contributions. Cadigan, for example, has a policy of sending "Get well" cards to any donor who says he can't give because he is sick or in the hospital. And Palma has enjoyed success by calling donors just to say thank you. Such use of technology to maintain an ongoing relationship with a donor or customer is direct marketing at its best. And Bruce McBrearty probably is right when he says that political fundraisers are "light-years" ahead of their commercial counterparts in capitalizing on it.

Modern telemarketing is, in fact, a fulfillment of the *Megatrends* concept of "high-tech/high-touch." The more technology brought to bear on a telemarketing campaign, the more personal it becomes.

Automation

In a fully automated telemarketing center, the communicator barely needs to do anything other than stare at his CRT screen and talk with the donor. The computer dials all the numbers on the list and instantly decides how to handle each call. If it reaches a busy signal, for example, the computer will save the number and try it again a few minutes later. If it reaches a "no answer," it automatically reschedules the call for later in the day. When the computer identifies a human voice, the call is instantaneously routed to an available communicator. Should the communicator then discover that it is not a convenient time for the donor to talk, he will reschedule the call for, let's say, 6:10 P.M., and at 6:10 P.M. the number will be dialed again . . . automatically. What's more, each time the computer needs to dial a long-distance number, it pauses to figure out which long-distance carrier has the cheapest rate for that particular call.

Paperwork is virtually eliminated. The complete donor history and often the script itself appear on the CRT screen. When the donor responds to questions, his answers are recorded in the computer's databanks. And if the donor agrees to make a pledge, a single keystroke will generate a fully personalized pledge letter, mailed only minutes after the call. At any given moment the telemarketer can tell exactly how well his campaign is going, with up-to-the-second printouts on such key statistics as cost per call and cost per contribution. He also can monitor the productivity of his communicators, both as a group and individually. Cheating is especially difficult in a computerized telemarketing center, since as Charlie Cadigan puts it, the communicator "leaves his fingerprints" on every call.

Using this kind of machinery, the telemarketer can reach more deeply into a list than ever before, and do so at a lower cost. Not long after Bruce McBrearty automated his telemarketing agency, he conducted a campaign for the National Republican Senatorial Committee that contacted forty thousand people in four weeks, a whopping 85 percent of the total file. "Before computerization," wrote McBrearty, "many campaigns had to be closed down after decisions were secured from only 50 percent or 55 percent of the file. This penetration level was unthinkable only a few years ago."[9]

Indeed, automation has been so successful in telemarketing centers that sometimes it seems as if the manifest destiny of telemarketing is to eliminate human beings altogether. The invention of Automatically Dialed Recorded Message Players (ADRMPs) and interactive systems like The Conversational Computer have given telemarketers the option of running a campaign with scarcely any human involvement.

A candidate might use an ADRMP system like Aristotle Industries' "Watson," for example, to send out a brief get-out-the-vote message to everyone in a telephone exchange. Working with an ordinary PC and a single telephone line, the candidate would enter the telephone exchange—let's say "581"—and a range of suffixes, from "581-0000" to "581-9999." Then he would flick a switch and leave the room as the computer proceeded to call everyone in the exchange with a brief recorded message:

> Hi, this is Bob Smith, candidate for City Council. I just wanted to remind you that Tuesday is election day, and I'm counting on your vote. Please call us if you need any help getting to the polls. And thanks again for your support.

A Texas company called TBS International has taken ADRMP technology a step farther with the invention of The Conversational Computer. Using this machine, it's possible for the candidate to carry on some semblance of a conversation with the voter:

> CANDIDATE: Hello, this is Bob Smith, candidate for City Council. I'm conducting an informal poll of opinion leaders in our community and I'll be transcribing your comments electronically. What, in your opinion, is the most serious issue facing the City Council this year?
>
> VOTER: [Taken aback, the voter hesitates a moment.]
>
> CANDIDATE: [The computer recognizes the hesitation and responds accordingly.] Don't worry, your opinion will be kept confidential. Let me rephrase the question. What do you think is the most serious problem we face here in Middletown?
>
> VOTER: Well, Bob, I guess I'd have to say potholes are probably the biggest problem.
>
> CANDIDATE: Thank you. Now, just to make sure I heard you properly. Let me play that back for you: "Well, Bob, I guess I'd have to say potholes are probably the biggest problem." Is there anything you'd like to add to that?

VOTER: Well, trash collection has been a little slow, too. But I guess that's it.

CANDIDATE: Thanks for your help. And please remember to vote on November second. Good-bye.

A day or so later, the voter will receive a letter outlining Bob Smith's courageous stand on potholes, and a few days after that he'll get another one describing Smith's new ideas about trash collection. Although The Conversational Computer is a relatively new technology, Ted Kennedy and Jesse Helms are just two of the politicians who have already made some use of it.

Fully automated telemarketing systems like Watson and The Conversational Computer are particularly useful for such ancillary political uses of the telephone as canvassing, get-out-the-vote, and voter registration drives. In projects like these the idea is to reach as many voters as possible with a brief message or a simple question. When it comes to such high-volume yet relatively uncomplicated tasks, fully automated telemarketing systems have been quite successful. But so far, every attempt to use them for persuasion or fundraising has been a bust.

Even John Phillips, whose Aristotle Industries developed Watson, admits that the attempt to use Watson to promote his company's products among candidates and campaign managers was a failure. "I guess politicians don't like getting calls from machines any more than their constituents do," he concludes ruefully.

Indeed, nobody really *likes* telemarketing, and many people find it quite obnoxious. For some, the indignity of talking to a machine is heightened by the fact that even when the voter hangs up, an ADRMP will continue to hold the line, happily chatting with itself for several minutes. What's more, since ADRMPs dial random telephone numbers in numerical sequence, they reach many unlisted numbers—people who have paid for the privilege of avoiding unwanted phone calls and are justifiably angry about receiving one.

Most of the complaints about telemarketing, both the automatic and the manual kind, however, revolve around the question of invasion of privacy. Telemarketers themselves admit that theirs is an intrusive medium. After all, the donor can read direct mail at his convenience. But the insistent ring of a telephone demands an answer *now*, whether it's a convenient time or not.

And telemarketing has an even darker side to it. "Boiler-room operations" rip off gullible consumers of nearly one billion dollars a year by selling worthless stocks and fake investments. The tactics employed in boiler-room scams differ from those used by political fundraisers only in degree. Communicators read from carefully written scripts, and if they get an objection, they refer to their flip charts for the proper response. Of course, the pressure on the customer is turned up considerably in a boiler-room operation, but the approach is essentially the same. As a result, boiler-room scams give legitimate telemarketers a bad name, and the government has a tendency to paint them both with the same brush.

In an effort to protect the telephone user's privacy and defend him against con men, both federal and state governments are now considering a wide variety of measures that may cripple outbound telemarketing. In some states telemarketers must submit their scripts to government authorities for prior approval. Other states strictly limit the days of the week and the hours of the day when people can be called at home. But the regulations that telemarketers fear the most are financial-disclosure laws and "asterisk laws."

The proposed financial-disclosure laws may require telemarketers to tell the donor exactly how his contribution will be spent. This will put communicators in the rather embarrassing position of having to announce at the outset of each call that virtually none of the donor's contribution will be used for the stated purpose since most of it is needed for overhead. Several states have financial-disclosure laws in place, although in at least one state the courts have overturned them.

Much worse, from the telemarketer's point of view, is the increasingly popular proposal for asterisk laws. Already under serious consideration in eleven states, asterisk laws are designed to prevent telemarketers from calling any telephone subscriber who has expressed a desire not to be bothered by unsolicited calls. The phone numbers of such people would, in effect, be flagged with an asterisk, and telemarketers would be constrained from dialing those numbers for any reason. Most telemarketers agree that widespread adoption of asterisk laws would virtually put an end to outbound telemarketing. And some telemarketers, like Tom Palma, don't plan to stick around and wait for it to happen.

"The regulations are coming, and they're coming very fast," says Palma, "almost to the point where it would behoove outbound telemarketers to get out of business. My company is about fifty-fifty inbound and outbound right now, and we're looking for more inbound business. You can't fight [government regulation] when it becomes overpowering."

But can political candidates and organizations use inbound telemarketing?

"They better look into it," warns Palma.

So far, though, that's all they've done—look into it.

The ever-alert National Republican Senatorial Committee, for example, has a toll-free "800" number for its members to call whenever they want the inside poop on what's happening in Washington. Jimmy Carter used the "800" number effectively for his talk-radio shows. But when Campaign Management Group, a hugely successful political telemarketing agency, expanded into the inbound marketplace, the firm spent so much money on equipment and found so few political clients willing to try it that the entire agency went out of business.

AT&T's new "900" number, in which the customer pays a small fee to place a call that connects him to a variety of interactive recording devices, shows some potential for political use. Ironically, the very first use of the "900" number was made in connection with a political event. More than five hundred thousand Americans used it to register their opinion on who had won the 1980 presidential debate between Jimmy Carter and Ronald Reagan. In the near future, national candidates may use the "900" number as a kind of electronic position paper: "Call 900-410-2000 to get the candidate's views on gun control; 900-410-3000 for his views on abortion," and so on. In the slightly more distant future, it may eventually be possible to dial a "900" number and use the Touch-Tone buttons on your phone to register the amount of your contribution to a political candidate and have that amount automatically added to your monthly phone bill.

Once the call has been placed and the contact made, inbound telemarketing isn't very different from outbound. The mathematics are much the same, and so are the tactics. If the donor dials an "800" number, he gets a live communicator very similar to the one who places outbound calls, a communicator who sits in front of a CRT, reads from a standardized script, uses a flip chart to overcome objections, and presses hard for a contribution. If the donor dials a "900" number, he gets a recorded message very much like an ADRMP or The Conversational Computer, with all the strengths and weaknesses of those technologies.

Inbound and outbound telemarketing are two sides of the same coin. But inbound telemarketing faces a special problem: How do you get the donor to place the call?

Commercial telemarketers depend on television to generate incoming phone calls, since it has the capacity of reaching a large number of people with a strong message. But conventional broadcast TV is far too expensive for most political candidates or organizations. To make inbound telemarketing work for them, politicians need to find a medium with the impact of television at a fraction of the cost . . . with the reach of broadcasting and the targetability of direct mail.

In other words, they need cable TV.

7

Cable Television: The Trojan Horse of Fall River, Massachusetts

"**I** wasn't very aware of the possibilities of cable television until a consultant by the name of John Florescu came to me in 1982. But at that point, if someone told me *matchbook covers* were an underutilized campaign resource, I would have been on every matchbook cover in town—kitchen matches, of course."[1]

Even in jest, Barney Frank is the kind of simon-pure liberal who wouldn't want to be accused of advocating anything as naughty as smoking cigarettes. But Barney Frank is no run-of-the-mill Democrat. After one term in Congress, his colleagues voted him "Most Outstanding Freshman," the congressional equivalent of "Rookie of the Year." In Washington he quickly became known as a tough, intelligent, effective spokesman for the liberal wing of his party. He also became known as something of a wit.

But Barney Frank wasn't laughing when he came home to Massachusetts after his first term in Congress. A popular Democrat in the most liberal district of the nation's most liberal state, he should have had the easiest reelection campaign of any congressman in the country. Instead he had a nightmare. Barney Frank woke up one morning to find that the state legislature had taken his seat away from him.

The culprit, of course, was the 1980 Census. It revealed that Massachusetts, like several other northeastern states, had suffered a significant loss of population in the sunbelt migration of the 1970s—so much so, in fact, that Massachusetts was forced to reduce the number of congressmen it sent to Washington by one. Thus began the tortuous and highly politicized process of redistricting, or "gerrymandering." Ordinarily a rising star like Barney Frank would be protected from redistricting by a legislature controlled by his own party. But Democrats in Massachusetts suffer from an embarrassment of riches, and in consolidating two congressional districts in that state, at least one Democratic incumbent would have to suffer. Barney Frank was chosen as the sacrificial lamb. Perhaps it was a question of seniority. Perhaps it was just bad luck. But in the case of the *other* congressman affected by the 1982 redistricting, it wasn't a matter of luck at all. It was good, old-fashioned politics. Margaret Heckler lost her seat in Congress because she was a Republican.

And so, in 1982, the Fourth Congressional District of Massachusetts, which Barney Frank had served in Congress for two years, and the Tenth Congressional District, which Margaret Heckler had served for sixteen years, became one. And the race between Heckler and Frank became one of six races around the country that year in which two popular incumbents were forced to battle each other for a single seat.

As it happens, the word "gerrymander" was coined in Massachusetts. In 1812, Governor Elbridge Gerry presided over a legislature that designed a congressional district whose boundaries were so twisted and serpentine that some observers thought it looked like a salamander. But the new Fourth Congressional District, as drawn by the Massachussets state legislature in 1982, didn't resemble a reptile so much as it did a witch's hat, one that had been sat on so the edges were crinkled and irregular, but with the basic shape intact. Imagine this witch's hat standing on the map with its top aiming north and its bottom facing south. Picture the point of the hat sticking straight into the heart of Boston and the wide brim extending from the Rhode Island border on the west to Narragansett Bay on the east. The hat could be divided into three very distinct parts:

The point of the witch's hat, the part that used to belong to Barney Frank, was very much like Barney Frank himself—liberal, Jewish, highly educated, and professional. These were the towns of Brookline and Newton, a traditionally middle-class Jewish suburb, very close to the Boston city line, that in recent years had also become home to many of Boston's college students and university faculty.

The middle of the hat, the part that used to belong to Margaret Heckler, was very much like Margaret Heckler herself. Prim, proper, wealthy, and white, the towns of Wellesley and Dover are the kinds of communities where anyone who cannot trace their ancestry back to the *Mayflower* is bound to feel out of place. The people here wear Bass Weejuns, drive wood-paneled station wagons, and name their kids "Bunny" and "Biff." Not surprisingly, Wellesley and Dover are nearly all that remains of a Republican stronghold in Massachussetts.

The brim of the witch's hat was part of Heckler's original district, too. But the brim was nothing like Margaret Heckler and nothing like Barney Frank. The largest city in the southernmost portion of the Fourth Congressional District is called Fall River. There was a time when plentiful jobs in the mills attracted Yankee farmgirls from around the countryside and energetic immigrants from Ireland to this now decaying textile center. But as the factories died, these groups either left to follow the jobs, or hung around to wait for Social Security checks to start replacing their unemployment checks.

Not everyone moved away from Fall River, though. There was one kind of immigrant who flocked there in droves and continues to do so. In fact, this town and the nearby city of New Bedford, Massachusetts, comprise what is probably the single largest concentration of this particular ethnic group in America. They have come here to take the jobs in the one traditional Fall River industry that has not died or moved away: commercial fishing. And they came here from a nation where commercial fishing is a way of life.

Portugal.

Carrying Fall River was never an easy matter for Margaret Heckler. Her support of Ronald Reagan's tough economic program, which in 1982 seemed to be having no effect other than high unemployment, did not go over well in this working-class, aging, ethnic city. But for sixteen years, Heckler worked at it. She made her name known in the community. She helped the elderly iron out their problems with Social Security. She helped veterans get their pension checks. In short, she did all the things that incumbent congressmen can do to get reelected. And for sixteen years, that was enough. At the start of the 1982 campaign, she was a clear favorite to win the battle against Barney Frank. And in the town of Fall River, where Frank was a total unknown, the polls showed her ahead by a factor of two to one.

For Barney Frank, who now faced the grim possibility of being named Rookie of the Year in his first term in Congress and being sent back to the minors for the next, there was only one winning strategy: Carry his own part of the district by a landslide; stay close in Heckler's part, keeping her margin of victory as thin as possible; and *steal* Fall River. The first two parts of the strategy were relatively easy; the third part was a bitch.

Barney Frank knew even less about Fall River than Fall River knew about him. He ran some polls and learned that while Margaret Heckler herself was well regarded in Fall River, most people in the community were philosophically opposed to her. The elderly, in particular, were worried that the Republican Party might do away with Social Security. The many veterans in Fall River, while sympathetic to Reagan's flag-waving patriotism, had their own entitlements and benefits to worry about. The unemployed were concerned about CETA cuts and cutbacks in other federal job programs. And the Portuguese . . . well, the Portuguese felt that *nobody* was paying enough attention to them.

Perhaps, to a degree, it was their own fault. Perhaps it was the fault of their strange language and peculiar traditions. But the Portuguese in both Fall River and New Bedford had formed a very insular community, one that felt quite isolated, alienated, and ignored by mainstream Americans. These feelings boiled to the surface during the celebrated trial in New Bedford of several Portuguese fishermen who were accused of gang-raping a

woman on a pool table in a local saloon while their fellow fishermen stood at the bar and cheered them on. The city of New
Bedford, amazingly, rallied to the support of the accused, largely
because the Portuguese community felt the publicity surrounding the trial was anti-Portuguese.

Although Heckler had certainly made *pro forma* nods to the
Portuguese community in Fall River, she hadn't really given them
the respect they felt they deserved, certainly nothing on the scale
of what neighboring Congressman Gerry Studds did to ingra-
tiate himself with the citizens of New Bedford. Studds actually
sat down to learn Portuguese from scratch, and it made him so
popular that he won reelection despite the fact he was caught
having homosexual sex with a congressional page.

Clearly, Barney Frank felt he had an opportunity in Fall River
to drive an ideological wedge into Heckler's soft support among
the elderly and unemployed and to form a real bond with the
Portuguese, just as Gerry Studds had done.

But how?

Buying television in Boston (or even in nearby Providence)
to address the insular concerns of Fall River would have been
an appalling waste of money, to say nothing of how TV commercials designed to appeal to Portuguese fishermen would go
over in Wellesley. Radio was a possibility, of course, and certainly the whole gamut of print and outdoor advertising would
have to be used. But Frank needed something more. Billboards
and leaflets alone weren't going to defeat an eight-term incumbent with a two-to-one lead. Frank needed something with the
power of television but the targetability of direct mail. He needed
something that was strong enough to make an impact, but cheap
enough so it wouldn't draw money away from the Boston-based
media campaign central to the first two objectives of his strategy. Finally, he needed something truly *local*, something that
would make the citizens of Fall River—especially the Portuguese—say to themselves, "this guy's one of us."

Barney Frank found what he was looking for when he met
John Florescu.

Despite his foreign-sounding name, Florescu was not a Portuguese fisherman. He was not even from Fall River. He was a
political media consultant who had cut his teeth in Boston politics working for the Kennedys. And he didn't know much more

about Fall River than Barney Frank did. But he knew one thing Barney Frank didn't know: He knew that Fall River had a cable television system.

It was called Whaling City Cable Television, and as cable television systems go, it was an extraordinarily good one. At the time of Barney Frank's campaign, it had more than thirty-six thousand subscribers in Fall River and New Bedford, or nearly 56 percent of all the homes in the franchise area. It carried a full range of satellite-delivered national programming, and it also carried a lively schedule of interesting and informative *local* shows. What's more, Whaling City Cable TV was one of only a relative handful of cable systems around the country with a thriving advertising business.

One of the program services on which Whaling City Cable TV sold local advertising was "The Portuguese Channel." Produced in the system's own studios, The Portuguese Channel featured a variety of programming designed to appeal to the large Portuguese community in both New Bedford and Fall River—from Portuguese-language soap operas to hometown soccer matches.

The Portuguese Channel was unique, but the idea of creating cable program services for narrowly targeted audiences was quite common. In fact, Whaling City Cable TV itself carried such satellite-delivered national channels as Black Entertainment Television, the Christian Broadcasting Network, and MTV. It also carried a range of program services with extremely specific demographic profiles, such as ARTS (which appealed to highly educated culture buffs), CNN (upscale "newsfreaks"), and ESPN (predominantly male sports fans). Working with a well-developed cable system like Whaling City, a clever media buyer could target his message with the precision of direct mail.

John Florescu was certainly clever. He also was a great believer in the political power of cable TV. Earlier in 1982, Florescu had managed to convince both Senator Ted Kennedy and Governor Michael Dukakis to use cable as part of their media strategies, an almost unheard-of idea at the time. Florescu had enough success to convince himself, if no one else, that cable was the wave of the future in political advertising. And he spent a fair amount of time in the summer of 1982 on the phone to local Democratic candidates, urging them to try cable in the fall.

So it was that John Florescu placed a call about cable television to Barney Frank, who, by his own admission, would have been receptive at that moment to a call about anything up to and including matchbook covers. Although Frank was running scared, the one thing he wasn't worried about was money. Together, Heckler and Frank spent more on their race than was spent on any other congressional campaign in the country that year. In part because the race was receiving national attention as a referendum on "Reaganomics," both campaigns were closely attended by outside interests. While Frank certainly couldn't afford to buy Boston TV for the sole purpose of reaching Fall River, he did have enough money to experiment with something new, especially something that wasn't too expensive to start with. "As John described the economics of it," Frank later recalled, "it was a no-lose situation. The cost of reaching people through cable was such that it was worth an effort even if it wasn't likely to be successful."[2]

The strategy John Florescu mapped out for Barney Frank was based around three thirty-minute programs, or "Town Meetings," in which the candidate answered questions from a panel of local citizens. Included among the panel were a World War II veteran, an unemployed worker, a senior citizen, and a Portuguese commercial fisherman. To build an audience for the three shows, Florescu shot thirteen thirty-second commercials featuring each of the panelists standing in front of a recognizable local landmark and urging TV viewers to tune in to the panel discussion. The ads ran on The Portuguese Channel, the local cable news, Cable News Network, and ESPN.

With scarcely more equipment and effort than one would expend on videotaping a family picnic, Florescu filmed each panelist making a personal appeal to the constituency he or she represented. Then, at a cost of sometimes no more than twenty dollars a spot, he saturated the ads on every bit of advertising time Whaling City Cable TV would sell him. "No matter what you were watching in Fall River," said Florescu, "if you were watching cable, you were seeing these spots drawing your attention to these shows."[3] And the "pitchmen," so to speak, were not slick Madison Avenue announcers but the friends, relatives, and neighbors of the people watching at home.

"We used a Mrs. Rita Gibney," said Florescu, "whose children permeated every civic institution in town. When she got on the tube, all of a sudden half of Fall River knows who they're dealing with."[4] And by extension, half of Fall River suddenly knows Barney Frank.

From a production standpoint, the panel discussions were as humble and inexpensive as the tune-in ads. Producing and buying time for a thirty-minute panel discussion on broadcast television is an enormously expensive and difficult proposition. But Whaling City Cable TV provided the production facilities for a song and sold Florescu a half hour on The Portuguese Channel for the whopping price of $150.

"Of all the paid media I did," said Frank, "these half-hour shows were the ones that most closely conformed to what a democratic campaign ought to be. Thirty seconds on TV isn't the best way to describe Social Security or nuclear arms reduction. But here we were able to talk in greater detail about the nuances of the issues."

Especially the *local* nuances.

"We were always dealing in specifics," said Florescu. "We didn't talk in 'Washingtonese' about millions of dollars in budget cuts. We spoke about how we wouldn't be able to put wheelchair ramps in the post office. When you can translate some of these national issues to the local level, cable becomes the perfect medium because you can speak about specific streets, or post offices, or bus lines.

"Another important issue was fishing rights."[5]

Not that there are many people interested in fishing rights, but in the town of Fall River, it's a pretty good draw. It's not "the broadest audience in the world," says Frank, but "it's a self-selected audience of people who are reasonably sophisticated and interested in politics."[6]

Or in Florescu's memorable phrase, "It's not how many are watching that counts, it's *who*."

Margaret Heckler probably wasn't among those watching the ads for Barney Frank on Whaling City Cable TV. Unless she happened to turn on the television when she was campaigning in Fall River to shore up her two-to-one lead, she may never have realized that Frank was saturating every television screen in town. Like Helen of Troy, Margaret Heckler probably thought her insulated, walled fortress of Fall River was safe from all enemies. She knew that this fishing town, with its elderly and foreign-speaking population, wasn't the kind of place to welcome newcomers easily. It had taken her sixteen years of hard work to be accepted there. To wage a frontal attack on such a stronghold would have been political suicide.

But Barney Frank did not wage a frontal attack on Fall River. He slipped into the city in the middle of the night, bearing gifts. Three soft-spoken programs featuring local issues; thirteen homespun ads starring the guy next door. As night fell on Fall River, three thousand years after the legendary fall of Troy, out of the horse, one by one, they came: the Portuguese fisherman, the World War II veteran, the unemployed worker, the senior citizen, and Mrs. Rita Gibney and all her children. And as Margaret Heckler sat in her home in Wellesley, wondering if her own hard-hitting television ads would have any effect on Frank's liberal strongholds of Newton and Brookline, Mrs. Rita Gibney and the others quietly went to work.

When the votes were counted, Barney Frank had gone from being a two-to-one underdog in Fall River to being a two-to-one winner. His strategy worked as planned. He won big in Newton and Brookline. He ran close enough in Wellesley and Dover. And he stole Fall River. His overall percentage of the vote was 60 percent—a landslide.

It would go down in history as the first, and still the best, use of cable television in a political campaign.

To appreciate fully the political implications of cable TV, one must first fly into outer space for a bird's-eye view of the growth pattern of cable TV as it spreads its tentacles across the United States . . . and then burrow down into the ground for a worm's-eye view of the coaxial cable itself.

If you could look at the growth of cable television in America over the past forty years from the vantage point of a time-lapse film shot from outer space, you'd notice that cable's growth has been rather like that of a bed of clinging ivy—not quite planned, but not exactly random, either. Just as the ivy follows the sun and the moisture, so the growth pattern of cable TV is strongly influenced by a variety of external factors. Generally speaking, cable will grow in areas that offer a combination of one or more of the following conditions: (1) weak television reception; (2) weak local government; (3) high income; and (4) high population density.

Thus the small-town and suburban areas across the country were the first to be wired. With poor reception and no strong government to stand in the way, small towns and suburbs have the density of homes and the middle-class incomes necessary to provide highly fertile ground for the growth of a cable TV system. Big cities, on the other hand, have been the last to be wired. Urban areas generally have excellent TV reception; they have large pockets of low-income residents; and they have greedy municipal governments that demand high franchise fees and expensive additional services from anyone who applies for the right to build a cable system. Finally—with a few exceptions—truly rural areas never will be wired for cable TV. The extremely low density of homes makes it almost impossible for a cable operator to recover the initial investment of laying cable. And that is why a drive through the countryside in America today reveals a most startling and peculiar sight: the enormous number of homes equipped with their own satellite dishes.

From this high vantage point, let's now dive down into the ground for a close look at a piece of coaxial cable. In fact, let's worm our way into the cable itself, where we will discover it is different from any kind of wire we've ever seen before. As its name implies, coaxial cable consists of a variety of different materials centered around an inner axis, or copper core. Surrounding this highly conductive core is a layer of plastic foam, and surrounding *that* is another layer of conductive metal, usually aluminum. The foam keeps the two metals apart and creates an electrical field between them. Meanwhile, all of this is surrounded by a protective plastic jacket, which keeps the electrical signals in and the moisture out. Arranged in such a way, a wire like this is capable of carrying electrical frequencies from forty million cycles per second to three hundred million cycles per second. And since a television signal requires a band width of six million cycles per second, a piece of coaxial cable can carry about forty different television channels.

Forty channels!

That may not seem too exciting until you realize that because of the limitations of electromagnetic radiation (and the many demands placed on a limited radio spectrum), broadcast television must operate within a range of only seventy-six million cycles per second, or just *twelve* channels. And since channels close to each other on the spectrum tend to interfere with one another, the practical limit is only six. Millions of Americans are served by even fewer channels.

As a result, broadcast television has developed a programming philosophy based on a *scarcity* of channels, while cable had developed a philosophy based on an *abundance* of them. Television programmers refer to the difference between these two philosophies as the difference between "horizontal" and "vertical" programming.

Just like the program schedule that appears in your daily guide to TV, broadcast programming is scheduled horizontally across the hours of the day. Since the broadcaster must take one channel and make it appeal to as many different people as possible, he puts one kind of programming on at a certain hour and a different kind of programming on at a different hour. Thus if the broadcast viewer wants to watch news, he must turn on his set at 7:00 P.M., and if he wants to watch a movie, he must turn it on at 9:00 P.M.

The cablecaster, on the other hand, has an abundance of channels to work with, so his philosophy is quite different. He can take one channel and completely dedicate it to a certain kind of programming or a certain kind of audience. Because the programming is scheduled vertically throughout a twenty-four-hour period, the cable viewer never has to wait for what he wants. If he wants to watch news, for example, he turns to CNN. If he wants to watch movies, he turns to HBO. If he wants to find out about the weather, he turns to The Weather Channel.

As a practical matter, if a broadcaster knows his town has an enormous Portuguese community, he might decide to put an hour of Portuguese news and discussion on on Sunday morning after *Meet the Press.* But the cable operator can take one channel among the forty available to him, call it "The Portuguese Channel," and put it on twenty-four hours a day, every day, until the end of time.

Given cable's unique characteristics and its distinct differences from broadcast TV, cable offers political candidates a number of useful advantages.

Foremost among these is cable's ability to target specific audiences. Just like direct mail, cable television can zero in on particular voters based on where they live, how much they earn, and what interests them. An advertiser would say that cable was geographically, demographically, and psychographically targeted.

Geographical Targeting

To many political candidates, the *geographical* targeting of cable television is its strongest appeal.

"Right now," says John Florescu, "a candidate from New Jersey is sending his message to Westport, Connecticut. It doesn't make sense."

What does make sense in that situation is cable.

Cable franchises usually are awarded on a county or municipal basis, so the boundaries of a cable system often are precisely matched to the boundaries of a political district. Since the signal is carried through wires, there is no accidental spill. The advertiser knows exactly where his message is being delivered, and he rarely has to pay for homes he doesn't need.

Demographic Targeting

But it's not just a question of where the cable viewer is, it's also a matter of *who* he is. Because of the economic and geographic factors influencing the growth pattern of cable television throughout the United States, the population of Americans served by cable TV has a readily definable political character. The typical cable viewer is, for example, 19 percent more likely than the average American to have written a public official about an issue of concern to him, and he's 13 percent more likely to have visited that official. He is 14 percent more likely to have volunteered time to a political candidate; 21 percent more likely to have contributed money; 10 percent more likely to vote. On the other hand, the person who does not subscribe to cable is considerably *less* likely than the average American to have done these things: 8 percent less likely to have voted; 13 percent less likely to have contributed to a campaign; 12 percent less likely to have written a public official. So when it comes to political activity, the gap between the person watching cable and the one watching conventional television is significant.

Most of that gap can be attributed to the difference in income between cable and noncable homes. The mere fact that subscribing to cable costs money skews the cable audience toward a higher-income, more highly educated, active, and involved demographic profile. By paying his cable bill once a month, the cable subscriber demonstrates a level of responsibility and stability that makes him an attractive audience to anyone who has something to say in the public interest.

Psychographic Targeting

The vertical programming schedule on cable television— a channel for "newsfreaks," a channel for rock 'n' roll fanatics, a channel for Hispanics, for Christians, for Jews, for blacks— creates a kind of video direct mail in which targeted political messages may be aimed directly at the people deemed most likely to respond.

"Cable is the MIRV missile of politics," says Ed Dooley, former spokesman of the National Cable Television Association, as he spreads his fingers on both hands widely and lets them fall into his lap like missiles from outer space. "You've got 'multiple independent reentry vehicles' for targeting your message to different areas and different audiences."

Most of the national satellite-delivered program services offer two or three minutes each hour of "local avails," advertising time that may be sold by the cable operator on a strictly local basis. Thus a mayoral candidate seeking to reach the predominantly black audience in the southeastern quadrant of his city might choose to buy thirty seconds of local time on the national program service Black Entertainment Television (BET). He also may wish to create a synergy between his commercial and the programming that surrounds it, perhaps having a black leader endorse his candidacy. This kind of programming environment tends to include all the people you're trying to reach with a particular message and exclude all those you don't want to reach.

Although no politician in his right mind would attempt such a thing, it's theoretically possible to use cable television to take an anti-abortion stand on the Christian channel CBN, and a pro-choice stand on the women's channel LIFETIME. But even if the politician doesn't speak with a forked tongue, he can use cable to sink his fangs directly into the audience he considers most likely to listen . . . and most likely to vote. "If you have five thousand people watching a program called *Inside City Hall*," says Florescu, "that's a better hit from a campaign manager's point of view than ten thousand watching the Harvard-Yale football game."

But campaign managers would be inclined to like cable even if it didn't give them a better hit, because cable offers one advantage over broadcast TV that is music to any campaign manager's ear: It's cheap.

Low Cost

"The cost of cable overcomes a lot of the questions I have about how effective it is," says one well-known Republican media consultant. And most other consultants agree. Cable gets a certain amount of play in political media plans nowadays just because it's there and because it doesn't cost much to try.

To anyone familiar with the cost of advertising time on broadcast television, the cost of cable time seems almost absurd. Florescu paid twenty dollars each for the thirty-second ads he ran on Whaling City Cable Television. His thirty-minute panel discussions cost $150. In cable systems with less established advertising departments, the prices run even lower. It's possible in some areas to buy a thirty-second ad on cable for five dollars, and this is in markets where a comparable amount of time on the local broadcast station might cost as much as five thousand dollars. Although the audiences are smaller on cable than they are in broadcast television, the low cost of a single ad allows the candidate to build what advertisers call a "cumulative audience" through frequent repetition.

Production costs are lower, too. Eager to build their fledgling local advertising departments, many cable operators willingly give studio equipment and technical assistance to anyone who is making a substantial purchase of airtime. And since local cable channels offer an informal programming environment, the cheaply produced ad does not appear as out of place as it would if it were dropped into *Dynasty*. This was certainly the case in Fall River, where the total cost of Barney Frank's pivotal use of cable television—including media, production, and even Florescu's consulting fee—came to less than ten thousand dollars. Although it probably was the most crucial expenditure of Frank's campaign, the price tag came to less than 1 percent of his total budget.

The low cost of cable also has a democratizing effect on the use of television in politics, making its power accessible to candidates who never would have had the opportunity before. It used to be that only statewide and national candidates could afford to use television. But nowadays even the town dogcatcher has the chance to show the public how he works in action . . . and do it cost-effectively.

A pleasant by-product of this low cost and high accessibility is that cable commercials tend to have a hometown look to them, which, in a political sense, translates into greater credibility. "The medium is less other-worldly than broadcast television," says Florescu. "There are no slick ad men, no fancy Madison Avenue accents. You're using people from the community whom the audience may know personally. And if you use a woman who has lived on Main Street for the past twenty-five years, her credibility is conferred on the candidate himself."

Freedom of Expression

She might also be able to speak her mind more freely on cable than she would on broadcast TV. "Cable operators," writes Tom Belford, former president of Vanguard Communications,* "are far more 'culturally inclined' than broadcasters to accept controversial material."[7]

As proof of that, Belford cites his own experience with a series of ads that Vanguard produced for Planned Parenthood. In one, an emergency-room doctor talks about his experiences with women who were victims of crude illegal abortions and desperate attempts to perform abortions on themselves. Broadcast stations refused to air the ads, but Belford had no such problem with cable. The commercials ran, and they worked.

Sometimes the question of freedom of speech centers around not *what* can be said but *when* it can be said. Broadcasters, for example, usually ban political ads from appearing on or near news programming. Apparently they're afraid the audience will have trouble separating fact from fiction. News programs, however, offer the ideal audience for political advertising, and media consultants always are a little angry that they can't buy it. Yet no such problem exists on cable.

In theory, cable operators follow the same rules on fairness and equal time that the FCC imposes on broadcasters. But in practice these rules are hard to enforce in the realm of cable TV, and the current administration of the FCC doesn't really like to enforce them anyway.†

Although they are almost always mentioned in the same breath, "equal time" and "the fairness doctrine" actually are two very different laws. "Equal time" applies only to candidates for

*Vanguard Communications was formed by Roger Craver to explore the political applications of Cable TV and the new electronic media.
†The FCC officially revoked the fairness doctrine in August 1987. However, there is now a movement in Congress to codify the doctrine by making it law.

political office, and it states that a broadcaster must: (a) make time available to all qualified candidates; (b) make that time available at the lowest unit rate currently being offered by the station to any advertiser; and (c) make sure there is no discrimination among candidates when it comes to the price and availability of time. Cable operators generally obey this rule as dutifully as broadcasters do (although neither one is particularly fond of the part about "lowest unit rate").

The fairness doctrine, on the other hand, has to do with the presentation of political *issues*, and here there is a substantial difference between the broadcaster's attitude toward the law and the cable operator's. The fairness doctrine states that broadcasters must provide a reasonable opportunity for the presentation of conflicting views on important issues of a controversial nature. In other words, if a broadcaster airs a documentary in support of the Sandinistas in Nicaragua, he must provide a similar amount of time for a program in support of the Contras.

Unfortunately, the greatest effect of the fairness doctrine over the years has not been to encourage broadcasters to handle controversy fairly but to cause them to avoid controversy altogether. Because of the fairness doctrine, broadcasters just don't *like* controversy. They don't want to touch it. And the doctrine has become a handy excuse not to do so.

Fortunately, the cable operator feels very differently about the question of fairness. And the reason he feels differently goes back again to the sheer abundance of channels on cable. The cable operator's attitude toward a controversial program is, "Why not?" After all, he knows that if an opposing group comes to him and demands time, he has plenty of it to give. So, in many communities, cable TV has become a kind of video soapbox open to all comers. In Pocatello, Idaho, for example, a neo-Nazi group called "The Aryan Nations" uses the public access channel on the local cable system to air a weekly talk show on what's new in the world of white supremacy. In San Francisco, the local poopah of the Ku Klux Klan produces a cable program called "Race & Reason." And in Manhattan, the publisher of *Screw* magazine, Al Goldstein, uses the local cable system to air a hard-core sex program called *Midnight Blue*.

This extraordinary level of freedom on cable television applies not only to the content of programming but to its length as well.

Expandable Time

"We are the world's leading producers of the forty-two-second spot," says media consultant Bob Squier with the rueful air of a man who has spent many hours hunched over a film editing machine. "But unfortunately nobody will sell it to us."[8]

Squier probably couldn't buy a forty-two-second spot on cable, either. But he could buy a sixty, a ninety, a two-minute, a five-minute, a thirty-minute, maybe even a two-hour-long advertisement if he so desired.

In fact, you can buy just about anything you want on cable. And for politicians, many of whom candidly agree with the common charge that thirty-second commercials can't adequately address the issues of a campaign, the flexibility of cable time represents an important opportunity. By their very nature, thirty-second broadcast ads produced for a mass audience must emphasize style over substance. Issues are drastically oversimplified. And the differences between the candidate and his opponent are likely to be expressed in the puerile tone we are accustomed to hearing when Burger King talks about McDonald's.

"You hear people decrying the fact that we're selling candidates like soap or soft drinks in fifteen or thirty seconds," says Bob Alter of the Cabletelevision Advertising Bureau (CAB). "But with cable you really have an opportunity to communicate."

When you combine the flexibility of time on cable TV with the flexibility of content, it's possible to create some interesting new video formats. And that's exactly what many politicians—especially incumbents—have done. Perhaps the most successful new format has been the "video newsletter" in which senators and congressmen—most notably Senator Bill Bradley of New Jersey—produce and host a weekly program featuring the legislator answering constituent mail, interviewing guest experts, and even grilling witnesses at committee hearings.

While Bill Bradley runs what Tom Belford calls "the Mercedes

of video newsletters," he is by no means alone. Dooley estimates that hundreds of congressmen and senators now produce
similar monthly programs for the cable systems in their states.
Thrilled with the idea of having the folks at home see them in
action, some congressmen have taken the video newsletter a
step farther and produced "A Day in the Life of Me" documentaries that they thoughtfully distribute to cable systems back
home and, sometimes, to local high schools as an object lesson
in civics.

To sum up, then, cable is geographically, demographically,
and psychographically targeted. It's dirt cheap and highly credi-
ble. It offers more freedom and longer formats than broadcasting.

So how come cable hasn't lived up to its promise?

After Barney Frank's highly publicized campaign in 1982,
both the cable industry and the community of political consultants were ready for cable television to make a huge impact on
the elections of 1984 and 1986.

"I've always viewed cable as the future of this whole business,"[9] said the top Democratic media consultant, Bob Squier,
at a seminar on the political use of cable hosted by the CAB in
1984.

"I don't know if it is there yet," famed political TV producer
David Garth told a reporter in 1982, "but in the next couple of
years cable is going to become one of the leading political vehicles."[10]

"In 1984 we'll see increased usage of cable TV, and then as
we move ahead to 1986 and 1988, it will play a greater and greater
role," John Florescu said to me in the fall of 1983.

But when I called Florescu in the summer of 1986 for an
update, he was out of politics entirely and producing televised
debates for PBS. Presumably he'd grown tired of waiting for
cable to arrive.

What happened?

As it turns out, cable television has a number of significant
weaknesses to go along with its celebrated strengths.

Foremost among those weaknesses is the fact that the cable
audience is almost impossible to measure. It's "like trying to
grab hold of fog,"[11] said one frustrated media consultant. Since
the cable audience is much smaller and more fragmented than

the broadcast audience, none of the techniques that have evolved over the years to measure TV viewers applies to it. Only the most popular cable services like ESPN and CNN will register at all on the Nielsen scale, where they appear as a tiny blip on the radar screen. Statistics on people watching the more narrowly targeted program services, like Black Entertainment Television or The Jewish Television Network, simply don't exist.

Even if someone could come up with a precise system for audience measurement (and, in fairness, the cable industry has made strides on this in recent years), on the local level the numbers are so small that politicians must wonder if it's worth the effort.

"Look," says Tom Belford as he grabs a pocket calculator from the top drawer of his desk, "CNN has a daily average rating of about 0.8 nationwide. Suppose you're running for office in a town where there's a cable system with 40,000 subscribers. When you buy a local avail on CNN in that town, you've got to multiply 40,000 times .008."

He taps out the numbers on his calculator.

"You come up with an audience of 320 people. Now, how much time do you want to devote reaching 320 people?"

When it comes to measuring the audience of satellite-delivered program services on the local level, Belford says the ratings are an "asterisk to an asterisk."

"You can take the time and stand in a shopping center and shout and reach as many folks.[12]

"Who wants to screw around with it?" he wonders.

Indeed, many cable operators around the country don't want to screw around with advertising in the first place. Because people pay to receive cable TV, most cable systems can make a nice profit without any advertising at all, and relatively few systems have made the investment necessary to get into the business. The automatic insertion equipment used to put local ads into national programming is expensive, and the cost of assembling an advertising sales force is even greater. Of the roughly eight thousand cable systems around the country, only about twelve hundred, or 15 percent, sell local advertising. The cable industry is fond of pointing out that the systems that *do* offer advertising reach 65 percent of the total cable audience, but that fancy statistic won't do a politician any good if he happens to live in an area that doesn't have it.

Another reason cable TV hasn't developed more quickly is that political media consultants have a built-in disincentive for using it. Most TV consultants nowadays charge a flat fee to the candidate plus a 15 percent commission on the media buy. The amount realized from the commission often far exceeds the fee. Victor Video, for example, might charge a U.S. Senate candidate a sixty-thousand-dollar fee plus 15 percent of the two million dollars the candidate will spend on television, or another three hundred thousand dollars. Tell Mr. Video you've found a way to spend five dollars for a thirty-second commercial instead of five thousand dollars and he might have mixed emotions about it.

Of course, a strong candidate who truly believed in the power of cable ought to be able to override the financial interests of his own consultant. But candidates have a disincentive for using cable, too. You might call it "the inevitability of election day." Unlike the grand opening of a store, election day can't be postponed. Unlike a clearance sale, it can't be held again the next month. The political candidate has only one chance to succeed or fail, and then his opportunity is lost forever. Faced with limited time, limited manpower, and limited resources, the candidate rarely wants to hear about something "new" or "different" or "something that's never been tried before."

Yet in spite of all these problems, cable television has the potential to become an effective political weapon. Barney Frank's campaign is proof of that. And it probably has been proven hundreds of times over in local races around the country that haven't come to the attention of the national media. Indeed, since cable is most effective on a local level, it's quite possible cable TV will have an impact on American politics without anyone every realizing it. The evolution of cable TV in politics will take place on a micro, not a macro sale, and we might start to notice the symptoms of its widespread use before we notice any evidence of it.

Like everything in the cable industry, the political use of the medium has been overpromised. There's a tendency in the cable business to put everything on a hypothetical timetable—e.g., cable will be in X million homes by 1990, penetration rates will exceed X percent by 1995, and so on. When the reality doesn't match the projections, critics and naysayers come out of hiding to say there must be something wrong with cable TV. They never consider the possibility that something was wrong with the timetable. Clearly, the same thing has happened with projections about the *political* use of cable. It was expected to have a big impact in 1984, and it didn't. It was expected to be important in 1986, and it wasn't. But to conclude from this that cable won't play an important role in American politics in the future would be a big mistake.

The key to using cable in politics—and the key to understanding its *effect* on politics—is to realize that it always will be a supplemental and tactical medium. Cable never will replace broadcasting as the medium of choice for swaying the mass of voters. But it can be very effective in reaching the small percentage of voters who might make the difference in an election.

Most political media consultants—despite the financial disincentive—have started to use cable as a supplemental part of their overall media strategy. They have to. Thanks to the increasing penetration of cable television in America, the percentage of people watching broadcast television has steadily declined in recent years. Several years ago, more than 90 percent of the people with television sets had them tuned to one of the three networks during prime time. That figure now is down to about 73 percent. And in cable homes it approaches 50 percent. As a result, even media consultants who are skeptical about the value of cable television in politics have been forced to buy *some* cable just to fill in the gaps in their media plan. As long as cable TV continues to grow in America, it will remain important in politics as a supplement to broadcasting.

But the key to using cable effectively is to deploy it not just supplementally but also *tactically*. It must be used as a field weapon rather than as a strategic one. Or, to carry the analogy farther, broadcasting is a wave of B-52's overhead saturating an area with fire bombs; cable is a tank commando knocking out specific bridges and supply depots. Florescu recommends a five-step plan for using cable effectively: (1) Examine your polling data to find out where the candidate is especially weak (whether that happens to be in a particular geographical area or with a particular bloc of voters); (2) determine which issues your candidate can emphasize to gain strength among those voters; (3) make sure you have at least a 45 percent cable penetration rate in the area; (4) determine who is watching the programming (not how many, but *who*); and (5) develop a style and message consistent with the issue you want to emphasize and targeted to the audience you want to reach. "We're only targeting 2 or 3 percent of the vote," says Florescu. "Let broadcasting take care of the rest, and we'll look for that little edge that might make the difference."

Will cable have an impact on American politics?

In subtle ways, I think the answer is yes.

Most of the speculation about cable TV in politics so far has centered around the question of which political party, or which political ideology, is ahead . . . or which side has an advantage. But the question is moot. While the Democrats clearly have the advantage in using satellite-delivered programming to build ethnic coalitions, Republicans seem to have a built-in knack for new technology.

The difference in the attitude toward technology between the two parties is dramatic. Democrats have lots of registered voters and no money. Republicans have lots of money and comparatively few registered voters. As a result, the GOP has both the means and the motivation for trying new technology. The Democrats have neither the justification nor the wherewithal for doing the same.

"I used to get calls from the Republicans all the time asking me how they could use cable TV to get their message across," says former NCTA president Tom Wheeler. "And I was happy to tell them. But in fairness, I would also call my friends in the Democratic Party and suggest they get involved, too. They always used to say, 'Well, we're studying it.' "

The Democrats aren't entirely ignorant, though. Democrats are fond of both the targeting ability and the low cost of cable, and on an individual basis some of them have used it quite well. It's at the national committee level where the Democrats seem to lag behind. "It's not what they're doing that puts the Republicans light-years ahead," says Florescu, "it's the skill with which they're doing it."

Republicans also may be slightly favored by the upscale skew of the cable audience and cable's small-town, suburban growth pattern. But the *future* growth of cable television will take place in densely populated urban areas, and this may favor the Democrats. The question is: Will the lower-income, ethnic, Democratic households in America's inner cities be able to *afford* cable TV?

Some say yes. Some say that at twelve dollars a month cable television will be a comparatively cheap form of entertainment for families who are hard-pressed to take the kids skiing in Aspen. The urban poor are known to be avid fans of television anyway, and they're likely to jump at the chance to get more of it.

But others disagree. They say that by putting more and more political information on cable we will be disenfranchising the nation's poor, creating an even greater political boundary between the "haves" and the "have-nots." One critic of politics on cable speaks in terms of creating an "information underclass." And even Florescu is concerned about the "discrimination of political information" that may result from relying too heavily on cable TV for political messages.

"Take any big urban area," says Florescu, "and you'll find that the black neighborhoods may not have cable TV because the operator doesn't have the economic incentive to wire that part of town. If you can afford to own a certain kind of equipment, then you can afford access to political information. What if we create a situation in which the presidential candidates can talk only to the people who can afford to hear them? That's a dangerous thing."

But Tom Belford is unconcerned. "If I don't get a C-SPAN, I don't feel like I've been cut off from the U.S. Congress. I can always find out what's going on."

As already noted, cable's longer formats and its ability to target messages to special-interest groups will have a tendency to make it, like direct mail, an intensively issue-based advertising medium. Cable gives the candidate more time to concentrate on the issues and less need to rely on image-making and sloganeering. On the face of it, that sounds like a good thing. And it probably is. But just as we found in direct mail, issue-based advertising can be a double-edged sword. Commercials based on issues are certainly more substantive than those based on image, but they also can be more emotional, more divisive, and more polarizing. When we consider the fact that cable, like direct mail, can "narrowcast" its message only to those most likely to agree . . . *and* the fact that cable, like direct mail, has almost no restraints on what can be said, we shouldn't be surprised to see some cable commercials that are as wild and woolly as political direct mail. Imagine how much fun it will be to turn on the TV and see someone call a U.S. senator a "baby-killer" or accuse the Democratic Party of promoting "cannibalism" and "wife-swapping."

Like direct mail, cable television may be seen as one more force encouraging the splinterization and factionalization of American politics. For all its faults, broadcasting tends to cast a unifying blanket across the land. Wherever one travels in America today, it's fascinating to realize the extent to which regional differences have eroded over the years and to discover how much we are all alike, mostly thanks to the impact of television. In a political sense, broadcasting is capable of focusing national attention on an issue and forging a broad-based consensus. Network television was able, for example, to change the national will on the war in Vietnam, force a resignation from a president, and help create a tidal shift in the nation's attitude toward civil rights. For better or worse, broadcast television brings people together. Cable, on the other hand, may drive them apart. By its very nature, cable accentuates the differences between people: geographical differences, economic differences, differences in interests and in religions and ethnic backgrounds. And as the technology of cable grows, there may be ways of addressing those differences literally from house to house.

With his eyes ablaze and his mouth almost watering, Robert Squier told attendees at a CAB seminar on politics and cable of a recent lecture he had given at Princeton University on the future of political media:

"I described the ultimate Buck Rogers scenario," said Squier.

"A person would sit in front of their TV set on a given evening, and they would get a quiz. It would be a combination of questions about themselves and questions about politics—kind of a *People* magazine quiz. If you were willing to play along, maybe you'd get a free movie later in the week. Then after you've played the game, you'd go back to watching your regular programs. But that night you'd find that the commercials for a certain political candidate would be very interesting to you, more interesting than usual. It was as if they were aimed at your own head. The reason is that the computer had analyzed the data from the quiz, and it could read your particular form of 'undecidedness.' Then it could reach out and pull a particular commercial off the shelf, put it on the machine just for you and people like you. Then, of course, at the end of the evening, we would ask, 'How are you feeling *now* about our candidate?' And if you were feeling better, we knew we wouldn't have to work on you the following night.

"I described this scenario to these Princeton students, and I had them sitting there with expressions of horror on their faces. But they were even more horrified when I then told them that every piece of technology needed to pull off this kind of thing now exists."[13]

And indeed it does.

Just because something is possible, however, doesn't mean it's profitable. And there's a great deal of doubt in the cable industry as to whether bidirectional, interactive, addressable, computer-enhanced cable systems will ever be built on a large scale. As it stands now, there probably are only two or three systems in America where anything remotely like Squier's Buck Rogers scenario could take place. And when you're working on a single, local system, you're dealing with numbers so small that they're scarcely worth the effort. In terms of conventional TV ratings, the number of people Squier is talking about is equivalent to taking Belford's "asterisk to an asterisk" and adding another asterisk to it. It would be less expensive and time-consuming to have the candidate take each family out to dinner at the local Pizza Hut.

No matter what new technologies are added to the basic capabilities of coaxial cable, the political effect is apt to be primarily local, and the resulting changes in American politics will occur on a micro, not a macro, scale. One might be tempted to argue that cable systems will have a decentralizing effect on politics in America, forcing us to pay less attention to national issues and to put more emphasis on issues of local concern. Indeed, that certainly would be the case if it weren't for another force pulling in the opposite direction. It is a technology that is already in place and already having some effect on cable TV and politics, a technology that takes the essentially local character of cable television and gives it a national scope.

Imagine each cable system in the United States as a separate island in a communications archipelago.

Now imagine a force that is capable of bringing all those cable systems together and making them act as one cohesive unit.

A force from outer space.

8

Satellites: Gutter Politics in the Global Village

There's a place in outer space called the Clarke Belt. Located exactly 22,300 miles above the equator, it was named after science-fiction writer Arthur C. Clarke—not because he was the first person to visit the place, but because he was the first person to believe that such a place might exist.

Back in 1945, more than a decade before the first communications satellite was launched, Clarke proposed the use of manned space stations for relaying radio signals between distant cities on earth. Working with a sharp pencil and a better-than-average knowledge of astrophysics, he calculated that a satellite placed in orbit at 22,300 miles above the equator would have a period of rotation around the earth exactly the same as the earth's *own* rotation around its axis. Although the satellite would be zooming through space at nearly seven thousand miles per hour, it would appear to people on the ground to be standing perfectly still. It would always be located in the same spot in the sky. And since it was so high up, it could be "seen" from almost a third of the earth at the same time.

Imagine a flashlight standing, lens down, on the floor in front of you. You lean over, flick the switch, and gradually begin to lift it up. As you do, the circle of light on the floor grows wider and wider. When you first lift it off the ground, the circle is only about two inches in diameter. By the time you have the flashlight as high as your head, however, it has grown to several feet. Theoretically, if you could lift it all the way into space, its beam would cover the entire continent. And if you flashed out a little message in Morse code, people all over the United States would be able to read it.

But a communications satellite is less like a flashlight than it is a kind of electronic mirror. It does not transmit messages of its own; it simply receives radio signals from the earth, gives them an electronic boost, and sends them flying back down to anyone equipped to receive them.

Most communications satellites have several different "transponders," or channels. Each is tuned to a particular frequency on the radio spectrum. For example, transponder No. 23 on the satellite known as *Galaxy I* will respond only to signals transmitted at 6,385 megahertz, ignoring any other signal. In this way a single satellite can handle many different transmissions at the same time, including long-distance telephone calls, cable television programs, network TV programs, banking transactions, and weather information.

Back on the ground, anyone who owns a parabolic microwave antenna (sometimes called a "dish" or an "earth station")—and knows where to point it—can receive any of the many signals bouncing back from outer space. For example, if a dish owner aims his antenna at *Galaxy I* hovering above the Pacific Ocean and tunes his receiver to 6,385 megahertz, he will receive a cable television service called HBO.

There was a time when only large, successful cable television systems could afford to own a satellite dish. But as Home Box Office began to revolutionize the cable industry—and as the technology for manufacturing dishes improved—eventually *every* cable system in America bought a dish.

In time, broadcast TV stations followed suit. The network television system began by distributing its signals on long-distance telephone lines. Nowadays most network affiliates take their company's feed from a satellite. Even independent television stations have found that owning a satellite dish is a useful way to receive programming from remote sources.

As the price of a dish began to approach about five thousand dollars (ready-made) or two thousand dollars (some assembly required), many private citizens began to buy dishes of their own. Satellite dishes became especially popular in rural areas that were too remote to get good broadcast reception and too sparsely populated to attract the interest of cable operators.

The growth of privately owned satellite dishes in the United States is a phenomenon some experts believe has only begun. Using the latest technology, it's now possible to build a dish only two feet in diameter, a dish you could practically put on top of your television set and point out the window. A different kind of television is developing to allow the mass production of a *flat* satellite antenna that would fit onto the roof. We are quickly reaching the point where Americans will have a chicken in every pot and an earth station on every roof.

As the cost of receiving a satellite transmission has declined, so has the cost of sending one. Again, there was a time when only large corporations could afford to use this means of communication. But now the technology is available to anyone.

Suppose, for example, you live in Connecticut and own a small videotape camera to go along with your VCR. You use the camera primarily to take pictures of your newborn infant. The child's grandparents live in South Dakota and own their own satellite dish. They would love to see their new grandson, but they are old and unable to travel. So you make a ten-minute tape of your baby playing in the bathtub, and you take it to the nearest broker of satellite time. You buy the time and arrange for an "uplink" facility to transmit your tape. You call your parents and tell them where to aim their dish, what frequency to tune it to, and when to turn on their TV. When the appointed hour arrives, Grandma and Grandpa sit in front of their TV and watch their grandson blow suds at them over a distance of some forty-four thousand miles.

The whole thing would only cost you about three hundred dollars.

Of course, if the only people interested in seeing your baby romp in the tub were your parents in South Dakota, it would be much cheaper to send the tape through the mail. That would only cost about three dollars. But what if there were *millions* of people interested in seeing such an unusual form of television programming? What if your baby were so newsworthy that there were cable systems and independent television stations around the country eager to take the feed and put it on the eleven-o'clock news? Or what if there were a cult of some three hundred thousand people in various parts of the country to whom bathing babies was a sacred rite?

What if, in fact, your baby was running for president?

Then you might be on to something.

Many years ago, when I was in high school, on a day when the weather was too bad for us to go outside and the gymnasium was occupied by the wrestling team, our physical-education instructor decided to show us a filmstrip on "the fundamentals of basketball." We learned that the proper way to shoot a layup is with the right hand when approaching the basket from the right and with the left hand when approaching from the left. We learned how to plant the left foot and pivot with the right. And we learned all about the "bounce pass."

The bounce pass, as its name implies, is a way of conveying the ball from one player to another by means of a pass that bounces once upon the floor and up into the hands of a teammate. The great advantage of a bounce pass is that it's very hard to intercept. Even if the defensive player has positioned himself directly in the line of sight between the two offensive players, a properly executed bounce pass may come within inches of the defender without being stolen.

To understand how satellites are used in politics, it's useful to hold this image of a bounce pass in your mind.

But the image requires some modification.

Imagine that our hypothetical basketball game is on a court where the ceiling is very low—let's say only fifteen feet off the ground. Thus it becomes possible to execute a bounce pass off the ceiling as well as the floor. Such a pass would be virtually impossible to intercept.

Now imagine that the ceiling had a kind of magical quality, so that any ball hitting it would be transformed into several balls, and each of these new balls would bounce back into the hands of your teammates all over the court. With one pass you would not only avoid interception, you also could reach all your teammates at once, no matter where they happened to be standing. It would be as if the ball could be in more than one place at the same time. And if your opponent was unaware of the ceiling bounce pass, your team would have an enormous advantage.

Such is the advantage enjoyed by the relatively few politicians and political organizations who understand and use satellites.

When satellites are discussed in Washington today, the word heard most often in the cloakrooms of Congress and in the offices of political consultants is "bypassing." It is not a word heard very often in the media, because the media are the ones being bypassed. Yet whenever political people gather nowadays to talk about campaign communication, they talk not about how to get the press to cover their campaign but how to cover it themselves.

Public-relations consultant Ed Dooley describes a hypothetical use of satellite bypassing in a national campaign:

"Look at what happens when a presidential candidate gives a speech nowadays," says Dooley.

"Let's say the speech gets one minute on network news. Well, first you see him get off the plane and shake hands with the crowd. Then there's the motorcade into town. Now, maybe a voice-over tells you what the speech was about. Finally, if you're lucky, you get to hear about ten seconds of the candidate actually talking. Don't you suppose there was more than ten seconds of important stuff in that speech?

"Well, in the future, the candidate will tape the speech himself, and he'll uplink it to a satellite. Local news stations will pick out things of local interest, and cable stations will probably play the whole thing. In the future, a candidate will cover his own campaign."

No question about it. When it comes to bypassing, the communications satellite is the most valuable tool ever invented. And that goes for bypassing the press, bypassing a political opponent, or—in the case of international politics—bypassing foreign governments.

The Use of Satellites in Politics

Before the off-year elections of 1986, few people had ever heard of a political media consultant by the name of Frank Greer. On November 5, 1986, the morning after election day, his name was on everyone's lips.

A Teddy-bearish man with a friendly, open face, Greer doesn't look like anyone's idea of a political mastermind. But in 1986 he scored the media consultant's equivalent of a grand slam, winning all but two of the thirteen campaigns he took on. The national media hailed Greer as the newest political genius. But few reporters noticed what really distinguished Greer from all the geniuses who preceded him. Although it would be hard to say it was the sole reason for his success in 1986, it's not entirely coincidental that Frank Greer is the first major political consultant in America to specialize in the use of satellites.

"We try to keep it simple and not mysterious," Greer says about using satellites in politics. "A lot of people in this business make it sound incredibly complicated and avant-garde. But it's not. It's just a tool, just another way of communicating your message."

"There are really only four ways to use satellites in politics," says Greer. "You can use them for remote press conferences. You can use them to feed new stories [to local media around the country]. You can use them for fundraising. And you can use them for organizing."

It's that simple. But more than enough to have an impact on the outcome of a political campaign.

Remote Press Conferences

John Glenn, of all people, should have known better. How ironic that the first American to go into orbit would be out-smarted by a mere earthling like Walter Mondale! But that's what happened when the former vice president hired Frank Greer to consult on his 1984 presidential campaign.

In the presidential primaries, each week brings a new election and a new battleground. Occasionally there are as many as seven different elections in seven different states on a single day. During the heat of a primary campaign it's not unusual for the candidate or his aides to lament, "If only there were a way for us to be in two places at once."

It sounds impossible. But if you know how to use satellites, you can do it.

During one such impossible week in 1984, when both Florida and Georgia were preparing for their primaries, Walter Mondale took an hour out of his campaign schedule in Georgia to go to an Atlanta television studio. Greer had arranged for an "uplink" to a satellite and had made appointments with the news anchormen of Miami's three biggest television stations. As Mondale stared into the camera, each Florida newsman took turns asking him questions over long-distance phone lines. Mondale's replies were shot in Atlanta, relayed by microwave to an uplink dish outside the city, beamed 22,300 miles in space to a satellite over the equator, reflected back to the downlink dishes in three Miami television stations, and recorded for use on the evening news later that day.

Meanwhile, John Glenn was doing it the old-fashioned way. He took a precious day out of his own campaign schedule in Georgia (a state of crucial importance to him) and traveled to Miami, where he held a rally. As it happened, Glenn's rally and Mondale's satellite news conference took place on the very same day.

When the six-o'clock news came on in Miami that evening, the interview with Walter Mondale was the lead story on all three network-affiliated television stations. In each case Mondale appeared on the "chroma-key" blackboard behind the news desk as the anchorman swung around in his chair and repeated the questions he had asked on the phone earlier. To the viewers it appeared to be a live interview in the studio, a real coup for the local news team. But as virtually everyone in southern Florida watched Mondale "live" on local TV, Mondale himself was busy meeting his commitments in Georgia.

John Glenn's rally was covered by only one TV station in Miami. "It was the fifth or sixth story," says Frank Greer with a smile.

The Satellite News Feed, or Video Press Release

What we're running here, says Robert Vastine of the Senate Republican Conference, "is a miniature news bureau for the Republican Senate."

Like any newsroom, Vastine's is a beehive of activity. Telephones ring. Typewriters clatter. Technicians and cameramen swarm around a small TV studio. Two mobile crews await word from a harried assignment editor, who sends them scurrying out the door to cover this event or that.

But Vastine's newsroom is very different from all the others in Washington, D.C. For one thing, it's on the grounds of the U.S. Capitol. For another, it's completely financed by the federal government. And for a third, it has only one "beat": the U.S. Senate. In fact, Vastine's newsroom is even more narrowly focused than that: It covers the statements and activities of only *Republican* senators.

Whenever a Republican senator as much as burps on Capitol Hill these days, the Senate Republican Conference is on hand with its cameras to record the event and prepare it for transmission to a satellite later that afternoon. When the Senate is in session, the Conference has a thirty-minute block of time reserved on either *Westar IV* or *Galaxy I* every day at 3:45 P.M. On a busy day they might contact their satellite broker and expand that to as much as two hours of transponder time.

They don't have to worry about renting an uplink dish, though. They have their own. It's on the roof of the Hart Senate Office Building.

Although the Conference has a state-of-the-art television studio, with a set large enough for one moderator and two guests, most of the videotape is shot by two mobile crews, who roam the Hill looking for Republican senators in the act of making news.

"We might shoot them making comments as they leave a committee room, holding a press conference, emerging from the Senate chamber . . . anything a senator does that's newsworthy," says Vastine.

These two crews and the TV studio are tightly scheduled by two assignment editors, who use a variety of sources to find out what's happening on any given day. Once they assign a crew to cover an event, they check with each senator's press secretary to make sure it's okay.

The raw videotape is brought back and prepared by two editing crews for the afternoon feed to the satellite. According to Vastine, the type of material being fed varies widely. But most of it consists of what people in the electronic news-gathering business refer to as "actualities": video newsclips of Republican senators presenting bills, interrogating witnesses, answering questions from reporters, or giving speeches.

Although the programming never smacks of campaign politics—the Republican Senate Conference and its Democratic counterpart, after all, receive six hundred thousand dollars of annual funding from the federal government—it obviously has some cumulative political effect. To put it bluntly, more and more Republican faces are appearing on more and more television screens more and more often. What isn't appearing there as often as it used to is the filtering—some might say, the cynical—effect of the national political reporter. "The boys on the bus" and "the boys in the press gallery" are standing alone in center court while Republican senators send a bounce pass sailing over their heads to local TV reporters back home.

Are local reporters less skeptical? Less sophisticated? Easier to manipulate? More likely to accept things at face value? More respectful?

Who knows?

But whether they are or not, Republican senators have clearly made the judgment that—just like the "telephone game" they played as children—the message is more likely to come out intact when you eliminate the middlemen.

Former National Cable Television Association spokesman Ed Dooley is very impressed with what the Senate Republican Conference has accomplished. In fact, said Dooley in a letter dated October 1986, "[The Conference has] done a really first-rate job. Their equipment—from uplink to studios—is one of the Hill's better kept secrets. The odds a year ago seemed against the Republicans retaining control [of the Senate]. But if they do, I'd be brash enough to give substantial credit to satelcasting."[1]

As it turned out, of course, the Republicans *didn't* retain control. But that doesn't mean Dooley was wrong in his assessment, because if the activity of the Senate Republican Conference is one of Washington's better-kept secrets, then Washington's *best*-kept secret is this:

The Democrats are doing it, too!

The Democrats call their committee the Senate Democratic Policy Committee, and its communications director is a woman, Linda Peek. But aside from those superficial differences, and aside from the fact that the Republicans have enjoyed a substantial head start, Democrats are busy promoting their own senators in much the same way the Republicans are.

Since the Senate Democratic Policy Committee continues to use its six-hundred-thousand-dollar annual budget to provide a variety of services other than electronic publicity, Ms. Peek does not have the wide range of equipment and resources enjoyed by Mr. Vastine. Her biggest problem, however, is not getting more hardware; it's getting more support from her senators. Although some are better at it than others, Republican senators have, for the most part, taken to the cameras like fish to water. The Democrats, on the other hand, have been camera-shy. Perennial underdogs when it comes to using new technology, some Democratic senators may not even realize that the cameras they see could be their own.

"They've seen us developing [this technology] so fast," says Vastine, "some of them don't realize their own party is doing it, too."

In fact, when I spoke with Mr. Vastine shortly after the November elections of 1986, he expressed some concern about how the new Democratic majority in the Senate would respond to his cameras now that they would be in power.

"I think January will be a miserable month for me," he said ruefully.

And indeed it was.

January was scarcely more than a week old when Senator Wendell H. Ford, Democrat of Kentucky, sent a stern letter to the architect of the Capitol. Under the new Democratic regime, Ford would become head of the Senate Rules Committee. In that capacity, he told the architect to remove all microwave antennas—except those of the national television networks—from the roof of the Hart Senate Office Building. Aside from the network antennas, however, there happens to be only one other dish up there, the one belonging to the Senate Republican Conference.

How odd that one of the first things Senator Ford would want to do after becoming Chairman of the Rules Committee would be to sweep off the roof of the Hart Building. What a tidy man! In politics, this is what's known as "cleaning house" . . . or, er, Senate.

The Republicans were, of course, incensed. And they threatened to fight back. But it didn't really matter. If the Democrats wanted a clean roof, Vastine could always get his uplink from another source. And in time the Democrats would want their own dish on the roof, anyway. After all, you can't stand in the way of progress.

One group that would very much like to stand in the way of this kind of progress, however—that would, in fact, like to throw their limp bodies in front of it—is the national press. If Democratic senators are uncomfortable with the new technology, members of the Washington press corps are downright appalled by it. And although it is the electronic media who presumably are being "controlled" and "manipulated" by the use of video actualities, ironically it's the print reporters who seem to get the most exercised about it.

"The print media find these [satellite] feeds extremely offensive," says Vastine. "They get on their high horse and inveigh against the scandalous practice of [a] television station's using someone else's footage. But ask them how many press releases their reporters just rewrite . . . or how many they don't even bother to rewrite.

"The analogy to a press release is exact," says Vastine. "What we're doing is helping nonnetwork affiliate and nonmetropolitan television, radio, and cable stations build their own programming base. They don't have to scrape to hire their own Washington Bureau."

As with any public-relations tool, however, the point of a satellite is not just to help the press tell your story but also to help the press tell your story in the way you want it told. And while the material is not packaged or slanted in any way, it also is not what one would characterize as a warts-and-all view of the Republican Senate.

"You're certainly not going to feed them both sides of the story," says Greer bluntly.

More worrisome from the press's point of view is that the "beat reporter"—the guy who sits in the press gallery every day and who is in a position to know when Senator Jones is telling the truth and when he's not—is being bypassed. In the past he could report the senator's comments and add his own analysis. But now he watches helplessly as the senator's remarks fly over his outstretched arms to a local television reporter, who—as one wag once characterized all local TV anchormen—is scarcely more than a thirty-dollar haircut on a three-dollar head.

Vastine is right when he says that the video actuality and the paper press release are exactly analogous. But in the world of public relations, getting your press release published intact without comment or analysis is the publicist's equivalent of hitting a grand-slam home run. In the world of video actualities, it seems to happen all the time. While network-affiliated and large independent stations look disdainfully at actualities, small broadcast and cable stations gobble them up.

If anything, admits Vastine, "[these stations] would really like for us to do more of the story for them. If [there's a committee hearing] on hazardous dump sites, they'd really like us to put in a picture of a hazardous dump site.

"But that does get to where you're canning the feed," Vastine adds primly.

The Satellite As a Fundraising Tool

Why go a few miles to attend a fundraising dinner when you can go forty-four thousand miles?

That must have been what some Democratic fat cats asked themselves when Walter Mondale held a fundraising dinner in Washington that was beamed by satellite to thirty other locations around the country.

One of those locations was in Alexandria, Virginia—only a few miles from where the event was actually taking place. Although the price of a ticket was the same in both locations, approximately three hundred Democrats decided they'd rather watch Mondale on the satellite than cross the bridge to see him in person.

"It was the craziest thing," says Greer, who organized the technical aspects of the event, "but some people are just fascinated by the technology."

Evidently a lot of people were fascinated by it, because the dinner raised more than a million dollars. And the money came at a time when Mondale desperately needed it. You could say Mondale owed his nomination to *Satcom III-R.* But when he finally made it into the general election, Mondale had to face a man who had been raising money by satellite for some time.

Ronald Reagan's experience with satellite fundraising dated all the way back to 1982, when the president conducted what must have been the shortest, least expensive, and most lucrative whistlestop fundraising tour in history.

On October 14, 1982, Reagan left the Oval Office and drove two blocks to the U.S. Chamber of Commerce building just across Lafayette Park from the White House. He stepped into a two-million-dollar television studio the Chamber had built to broadcast their own satellite-delivered cable program service, BIZ-NET. When the cameras came on, Reagan's face and voice could be seen at fundraising events in dozens of different locations around the country. He "visited" ten states, spoke on behalf of fourteen GOP congressional candidates, answered questions from dozens of local GOP donors, raised untold thousands of dollars, and did it all without spending more than an hour away from the Oval Office. The satellite campaign swing was so successful that four days later he did it again.

But you don't have to be a president of the United States with commitments all over the country to take advantage of the satellite's unique ability to put you in two places at one time. In 1986, Representative Bill Richardson, Democrat of New Mexico, demonstrated that even a congressional candidate can use the satellite as a fundraising tool. Richardson held a fundraiser in Santa Fe that was televised live and beamed up to *Westar IV*. At various locations throughout his district, campaign volunteers invited their friends and neighbors to watch the show on cable or on their own private satellite dishes. When everyone was gathered around the set, the hosts passed peanuts, passed the hors d'oeuvres, and passed the hat.

The Satellite As an Organizational Tool

In one sense, the use of satellites as a tool for political organization is still in its infancy. In another, it is more highly developed and more pervasive than many people realize.

As an instrument for the nuts-and-bolts work of campaign organization, some labor unions have enjoyed success using satellites. The American Federation of State, County, and Municipal Employees (AFSCME), in particular, has made a substantial investment in satellite technology. So has the AFL-CIO. Both organizations used their facilities to help organize the involvement of their rank-and-file members in the 1984 Mondale campaign. By using satellite teleconferences, the unions could afford to have top-notch political consultants conduct private seminars for their field operatives all over the country. As the technology becomes cheaper and more available, it's likely that more and more political organizations will be using satellites for internal communications. As noted in Chapter One, satellites are also being used by media consultants to transmit television commercials from the studio to the field instantaneously, thus contributing to the punch/counterpunch style of today's media campaigns.

But the satellite's greatest impact on politics so far has been as a tool for *external* communications, as a way of reaching out to the uninitiated and bringing them into the fold. No communications medium casts a wider net than a satellite. It literally drops its message like a blanket over an entire continent. It can bring together millions of like-minded individuals, no matter how far apart they may live or how different their lives may be on a superficial level. When it comes to reaching out to a broad constituency, inculcating them with a system of values and beliefs, encouraging them to give their time and money, building a corps of activists and volunteers, creating a sense of shared interests and culture, satellite technology is without peer. And if you need proof of that, consider this:

Pat Robertson is a child of the satellite.

Or is the satellite the child of Pat Robertson? It's hard to tell. Although Ted Turner usually gets the credit for inventing the "superstation," it was actually Pat Robertson who first came up with the idea of taking an ordinary UHF TV station in Virginia and beaming its programming up to a satellite. Turner's ambitions were to make himself a zillionaire and create a fourth national television network. But Robertson had bigger things in mind. Much more than Turner, Robertson understood the new communications technologies. He understood database marketing, computers, cable TV, direct mail, and telemarketing. He understood that putting your programming on the satellite and signing up cable affiliates across the country were just the first steps. What Pat Robertson has is a kind of power that Ted Turner can only dream about. Robertson owns the hearts and souls of every person who watches his television network. More important, he owns their names and addresses.

The gateway to the byzantine empire of the Christian Broadcasting Network passes through what appears to be some very innocuous television programming. If you came across CBN while flipping around the channels on your cable converter, you would be hard-pressed to tell that it was a religious television network, or even that it was noticeably different from any other independent television station. The programming fare consists primarily of old network reruns like *Daktari, Gunsmoke, Dobie Gillis,* and *Flipper.* Only the most observant viewers would notice over a period of time that the shows seem to be chosen for their wholesomeness, especially for their adherence to traditional family values. Reruns of *Dynasty* certainly are not here, and neither are any of the Norman Lear comedies.

The religious component of CBN is no more evident to potential advertisers than it is to viewers. In recent years the word "Christian" has dropped out of CBN's corporate vocabulary. The network now refers to itself only by its initials. When I requested a press kit from CBN, I pored through dozens of documents without finding a single reference to God, religion, or Christianity. Clearly, CBN does not want to put off any potential viewer—or advertiser—by pigeonholing itself as a religious television network. The door to salvation, in other words, is unmarked and open to anyone. But once you become hooked on *Flipper* or *Groucho* or *Gunsmoke*, once you find yourself sitting in front of the television set on a rainy night, feeling alone and depressed and yearning for some of those good old-time family values, eventually you will come face-to-face with the radioactive core of CBN: *The 700 Club.*

It appears on CBN only three times a day and lasts for only an hour, but *The 700 Club* is the engine that makes everything else at CBN go. At first glance *The 700 Club* looks like nothing more than a kind of Christian version of *Good Morning America*, complete with a congenial host, an attractive blond sidekick, and even a token black man. The basic format of the show consists of Robertson, Ben Krinchlow (the black man), or Danuta Soderman (the blonde) interviewing a variety of people who have achieved success or have had extraordinary experiences in life as a result of their faith in Jesus Christ. They range from the famous (like ex-Watergate burglar Chuck Colson) to the ordinary (my own great-aunt was once interviewed on the show because she does missionary work in Texas prisons). But what they all have in common is their belief in God. It's sort of what you'd imagine Johnny Carson's show might look like if it were broadcast out of the Bible Belt instead of Hollywood.

At least twice during each show, however, an effort is made to reach out directly to the television audience. At some point during the program, Robertson will put himself into a kind of a trance in which he seems to be seeing the faces of people who are suffering from various illnesses. As he speaks and repeatedly invokes the Lord's name, the diseases are miraculously cured. It sounds something like this:

> I'm expecting Jesus to do something tremendous on this program. . . . Somebody has got this really serious phlegm in their lungs and they have been coughing and coughing. The Lord is healing those lungs, right now, in Jesus' name, amen. . . . God is taking that bone spur away and you are healed in Jesus' name.[2]

This goes on for several minutes, and as it does, viewers are encouraged to phone the program and speak with "prayer counselors" about their special needs. Approximately three to four million people avail themselves of this service every year. When a viewer calls, he hears a soothing voice who leads him in prayer and takes his name and address.

At another point in the program, Pat will come out to center stage, sit on a stool, ask for the houselights to be turned on, and take questions from the studio audience. No matter what the question is—whether it's theological (Aren't John 2:16 and Matthew 4:12 contradictory, Pat?), political (Should freedom of speech apply to child pornography, Pat?), or philosophical (Why is there air?), Pat's response always is basically the same. He gives a quick, sketchy, and, one suspects, deliberately unsatisfactory reply, and then he says the *real* answer is in his book, which he holds up to the camera. It's called *Answers to Life's 200 Most Probing Problems*, and it's free. Well, not quite free. It's more of a barter deal. You give us your name and address; we give you the book.

One way or another, CBN is going to get your name and address. And when it does, you will become part of a labyrinthine network of multimedia database marketing that is probably the most sophisticated moneymaking operation in the world today. When it comes to the use of communication technology to raise money and exercise power, nothing in private industry or government comes close to it. Forget the fact that CBN admits to having a half-million donors, making it one of the largest nonprofit organizations in the country. Consider instead that these donors give an *average* of $214 a year! When you ask Pat for a free copy of his book or have one of Pat's counselors lead you in prayer, you are reaching up to the satellite and pulling a lever that, unbeknownst to you, will cause an avalanche of direct-mail letters and telephone calls to fall down on your head. You may not choose to contribute, but many others will.

Where does the money go?

Well, most of it is plowed back into running the communications empire. To be fair, a decent amount goes to charity and missionary work, including a CBN university. But in one way or another, all of it contributes to the greater glory and power of Pat Robertson.

Two of the things you will inevitably be asked to support after you have earned a place on CBN's mailing list are Robertson's own private political action committee, the Committee for Freedom, and his political *education* committee, the Freedom Council. These groups enjoy a base of at least two hundred thousand donors and employ more than forty full-time staff members. Prior to his official announcement, they were the primary vehicles of Robertson's campaign for president of the United States.

It's easy to pooh-pooh Pat Robertson's political ambitions by saying he'll never be elected president. Of course he'll never be elected president! Not unless the nation's water supply is tampered with. But the presidency isn't really what he wants, any more than Gene McCarthy wanted it, or George Wallace, or, more recently, Jesse Jackson. What Robertson wants is to place his own ideological agenda on the national menu. He wants the return of public-school prayer. He wants an end to abortion. He wants "creationism" taught in public schools. At the very least, he wants these issues to be taken up, debated, and voted on. And if he can use his satellite-based political organization to become a kingmaker at the Republican National Convention, he will get what he wants.

Nor does Robertson have to confine himself to working in presidential politics. Like his friendly rival Jerry Falwell, Robertson has encouraged his supporters to be active politically on the local level. And although it's hard to tell exactly where his hand is at work, the recent success of born-again fundamentalists in state and local politics has been remarkable. Senator Robert Packwood, Republican of Oregon, almost lost his reelection campaign to one in the 1986 GOP primary. Two evangelical ministers won congressional primaries in Indiana in 1986. And in many cities around the country, the local Republican Party organization is literally swarming with them—even though, like termites, you don't always know they're there.

"Hide your strength," advised a Christian political primer entitled *How to Participate in a Political Party* that was found at a recent Iowa state GOP convention. "It is important not to clean house of all non-Christians. . . . Try not to let on that a close group of friends are becoming active in the party together. . . . Come across as being interested in economic issues."[3]

What Pat Robertson has created in CBN is what Jesse Helms was dreaming about when he planned his quixotic raids on CBS— a national television network that indoctrinates its viewers with a particular ideology and uses them to exercise deliberate political power. Everyone agrees that television is the most powerful communications medium ever invented. But in the United States, only its power to sell products is used fully; its political power sits underutilized and unheeded, like a dormant volcano.

Through his mystical incantations in front of the camera and his sly manipulations behind it, Robertson has brought the volcano to life. Like a primitive witch doctor, he's concocted a potent brew that's different from any network programming we've ever tasted before. It tastes like a holiday punch, with the same sneaky effect. You put in a quart of old TV reruns, add a pint of news and weather, toss in a cup of comedy, a dash of old-time religion, and you'll never notice the shot of pure grain alcohol— the hardball politics—until you drive to the polls and run smack into a bridge abutment by the name of Pat Robertson.

All of this wouldn't be so bad if it weren't for the fact that Robertson, alas, is not the only power-drunken speedster racing around the Clarke Belt. Indeed, Pat Robertson's success with satellite programming has spawned a variety of imitators outside the realm of electronic evangelism. So far most of these political program services have crashed off the side of the road, either because they couldn't find money or because they couldn't find an audience. But it's probably only a matter of time before one of them succeeds.

Tom Belford almost succeeded with something he called the Vanguard Network. Belford's idea was to form a consortium of five or six of the most active liberal public-interest organizations. The National Audubon Society, the National Organization for Women (NOW), Common Cause, People for the American Way, SANE, and the ACLU all expressed interest in the idea.

Although none of these organizations were in a position to do much with satellites on their own, Belford felt that as a group they could afford to lease a permanent and regular block of time on the satellite for documentaries, public-affairs programming, and even entertainment.

The Vanguard Network was to begin with four one-hour specials to be aired on consecutive weeks over the Satellite Programming Network (SPN). Each special would cover one topic. Nuclear disarmament, civil rights, ecology, and women's rights were the first four programs on tap. Although the Vanguard Network's initial budget was just $350,000—with only $125,000 earmarked for programming—there's little doubt that Belford had bigger things in mind. With CBN as a model, it's likely that Belford's eventual goal was to create a twenty-four-hour network featuring a variety of nonpolitical programming. Unfortunately, the Vanguard Network never got off the ground.

"It's more complicated than we expected,"[4] Belford said to a reporter from *CableVision* magazine as negotiations among the competing public-interest groups began to break down.

For Belford, the demise of the Vanguard Network was the end of a dream. But his idea attained a kind of rebirth a few years later when Belford met Ted Turner, and together they formed The Better World Society, a nonprofit organization designed to produce television programs on global issues.

Meanwhile, Larry Kirkman of the AFL-CIO was trying to create a satellite-delivered program service that would do for the labor movement what CBN did for fundamentalism. After a successful three-market test of labor-oriented programming on cable TV in 1983, Kirkman began finalizing plans for a satellite-delivered program service that would include comedy and variety shows in addition to public-affairs programming. Among other things, the channel would feature a syndicated program called *America Works*, which had been well received in the initial test. The goal, said Kirkman to *CableVision*, is to provide labor-oriented programming that "viewers want, but cannot find on the dial,"[5] and to "make the public interest interesting."[6]

The U.S. Chamber of Commerce also is trying to make the public interest more interesting with their satellite-delivered program service BIZNET. When it isn't being rented by Ronald Reagan, the two-million-dollar television studio at the U.S. Chamber of Commerce is used to broadcast a complete menu of legislative and economic programs to business subscribers around the country. They include local chambers of commerce, trade associations, and large corporations. The programs themselves go by such names as *Washington Watch*, *Economic Update*, and *Small Business Report*.

"[BIZNET is] a very powerful force," says a former communications staffer from the Democratic National Committee, "because it's keeping constituents around the country informed. A grass-roots lobbying effort could be put together in a matter of seconds."

All of this raises the possibility that the national political parties themselves will eventually want to create their own satellite-delivered program services. The Senate Republican Conference's now-defunct *Conference Roundtable* program certainly was a stab in that direction.

Conference Roundtable was produced every two weeks at the Senate Recording Studio, beamed up to a satellite, and offered free of charge to some three hundred cable systems and sixty PBS affiliates around the country. What was remarkable about the *Conference Roundtable*, while it lasted, was how much it resembled the usual fare of Sunday-morning public-affairs shows and how little it looked like partisan propaganda. The show always began with a pop version of one of the Brandenburg concertos, while the camera panned portraits of great Republicans from the past. "*This* is the *Conference Roundtable*," said the voice of a professional announcer in a grave and momentous tone. From there the show proceeded very much like *The McLaughlin Group*, with two senators, two national political reporters, and one moderator sitting in a semicircle and informally discussing the week's hottest issues. The viewer would have to be fairly well acquainted with the names and faces in the U.S. Senate to notice that no one but Republicans were ever invited to appear on the show. When the credits rolled at the end of each episode, the program was identified as a production of the "Senate Conference of the Majority." It did not use the word "Republican." Just as CBN subtly avoids the word "Christian," so the *Conference Roundtable* clearly wanted to attract new people into the fold without running the risk of dredging up old prejudices about the GOP.

"I don't think it's unrealistic at all to think that the major parties will have their own network," said one former director of campaign planning with the Republican National Committee.

"When I buy cable today, I get ESPN. Someday I might get RNC."

By their very nature, satellites are deeply involved in international politics. That's true for no other reason than that the signal reflected off any communications satellite almost always falls down on more than one country. And every nation in the world wants to reserve its little piece of the Clarke Belt.

The Clarke Belt, in fact, is the most crowded place in space. It's a man-made replica of the Asteroid Belt, with scores of communications satellites whirling around the earth at seven thousand miles per hour, all within a relatively confined area. After many nations had launched their own communications satellites, it became obvious that some form of international regulation was needed. Eventually it was agreed that satellites could not be placed less than two degrees apart, and each nation on earth was assigned its own slot. Some of the world's smaller nations now lease their slots to larger countries in the same hemisphere.

Aside from such territorial matters, however, the law north of the stratosphere is very similar to the law west of the Pecos—there just ain't much law up there. "Space law" is the hottest topic on law school campuses today because every new deal sets a precedent. As in the days of the Wild West, the law in outer space is pretty much whatever you think you can get away with. Similarly, there seems to be no shortage of people willing to take advantage of it.

On April 27, 1986, a man calling himself "Captain Midnight" became the first space outlaw by aiming a powerful uplink dish at *Galaxy I*, Transponder 23, and jamming the transmission of Home Box Office. Millions of Americans were sitting at home watching *The Falcon and the Snowman* when suddenly the movie faded from the screen and was replaced by a test pattern with digital lettering. "Good evening, HBO," the message said, "from Captain Midnight. Twelve-ninety-five per month? No way! Showtime, Movie Channel beware!"

Three months earlier, HBO had begun to scramble its signal to prevent private dish owners from enjoying the service without paying for it. The cable systems authorized to carry HBO were provided with descrambling equipment, and HBO was offering the same equipment to dish owners for $12.95 per month. But dish owners are an ornery lot, and they were used to getting the service free. They didn't want to pay HBO's monthly fee, and they certainly didn't want the other pay-cable services to start scrambling their signals, too.

Eventually the FCC caught up with Captain Midnight. He turned out to be a relatively harmless fellow who, as near as anyone could tell, was motivated only by a sense of mischief and a love for free movies. But in playing his little trick on HBO, Captain Midnight exposed one of the great untold secrets of modern communications technology: Satellites are incredibly vulnerable to attack. They can be jammed, overriden, used without authorization, and even pointed in different directions by satellite hackers on the ground with amazing ease and surprisingly little expense. With the proper equipment you can use satellites to eavesdrop on private telephone calls, to intercept unsecured messages from *Air Force One*, or to listen in on the fleet commands in U.S. naval exercises. Drug traffickers in South America have been known to use unoccupied transponders to relay information about the time and location of a forthcoming drop.

"Those of us in the business have known for a long time that something like this was possible," confided one experienced user of international communications satellites. "People weren't talking about it much, because we didn't want to give anybody ideas. But with Captain Midnight, it's out of the bag."

Not long after Captain Midnight was caught, *Mother Jones* magazine published a harrowing account of the incident that clearly showed how a person with something more serious on his mind than free movies could use the same technology to wreak havoc with American military satellites.

"If he were feeling particularly venturesome," wrote Donald Goldberg, "Captain Midnight might have aimed at a spot a hundred degrees west longitude, above the Galapagos Islands, situated off the coast of Ecuador, and set his frequency at 293.975 megahertz. In that case he would have jammed a channel on the U.S. Navy satellite *Fleetsatcom I*, which is used to send emergency wartime messages from the president to U.S. submarines, silos, and bombers, telling them to launch their nuclear weapons."[7]

Communications satellites could not only start the next world war, but they could also be used to fight it. We already have spy satellites, some of which are capable of reading the headline on a newspaper sitting on a park bench. The Russians have deployed an antisatellite weapon that cozies up next to an enemy satellite and explodes, taking the enemy along with it. And if President Reagan gets his way, we soon will have a satellite-controlled antiballistic-missile system.

The immediate effect of satellites in international politics, however, will not be to help us fight World War III but to help us fight the Cold War. The communications satellite is, after all, the most potent propaganda tool ever invented. It throws a bounce pass to the citizens of other nations that foreign governments are almost powerless to intercept.

Under the administration of the Great Communicator, the U.S. Information Agency (USIA), the primary vehicle of American propaganda in the world, has enjoyed a resurgence of power. And much of it is due to the advent of new technology. While the Voice of America continues to be its most visible project, the real excitement at USIA these days is being generated by a satellite program service called WORLDNET.

WORLDNET began simply as a satellite link between Washington and American embassies in five European cities. Private dish owners, cable systems, and broadcast stations were invited to take the signal as well. In time, many of them did. In Western Europe, for example, WORLDNET is now carried by fifty-seven cable systems and 107 hotels. All told, the service now reaches a hundred cities in eighty different countries, and if you look at its cumulative ratings you could say that WORLDNET is viewed by nearly half the people on this planet.

According to USIA director Charles Wick, the purpose of WORLDNET is the same as that of Voice of America: "to present American society, in its diversity, energy, and spirit, to audiences around the world."[8]

A typical week on WORLDNET might include a live telecast of an American rodeo on the sports-anthology program *Sports Machine*, an interview with singer John Denver on the talk show *Almanac*, an award-winning documentary film on *Cine Showcase*, and a live report direct from the location of a breaking news story on the morning news program *America Today*.

In addition to this kind of entertainment programming, WORLDNET also provides a public-relations service to members of the Reagan administration similar to what Robert Vastine offers to Republican members of the Senate. A large block of time is reserved on WORLDNET satellites each day for interactive press conferences in which foreign journalists can ask questions directly of American political leaders. Edwin Meese, George Shultz, Caspar Weinberger, and Jeane Kirkpatrick are just a few of the administration officials who have used WORLDNET to meet the foreign press.

Meanwhile, WORLDNET seems to be forging a kind of "Satellite Free Europe" with growing numbers of private dish owners around the world, even in Eastern bloc nations. The USIA has received many letters from Eastern Europeans asking for information about how to get WORLDNET, including one letter from a viewer in Poland who wrote: "I very beg leave of information in the construction of the aerial to take away the program."[9]

A satellite dish isn't the easiest thing in the world to build from scratch, but at least one expert I spoke with said he had seen it done. At a science fair in Sri Lanka held to honor one of the island's most celebrated residents, Arthur C. Clarke, one young student demonstrated a downlink dish he had fashioned out of a fifty-five-gallon metal drum. "He sort of moved it around and aimed it at *Gorbizon* [the Soviet satellite *Horizon*], which happens to be directly overhead. And he could get this fuzzy image of Soviet TV in Sri Lanka. On zero technology!"

Of course, Sri Lanka is just north of the equator, where satellite signals are so strong you can practically pick them up on your hearing aid. But if a twelve-year-old Sri Lankan student can do this, it's not unreasonable to suggest that a forty-five-year-old Russian engineer might be able to pull off the same feat.

The dynamic of WORLDNET isn't very different from that of the Christian Broadcasting Network: Attract an audience with glitzy entertainment, soften them up by exposing them to a particular system of values, and then nail them with a stiff dose of politics.

As a patriotic American, I can't find anything wrong with WORLDNET; I rather like the idea. But I can't help but wonder how I'd feel if the Russians were doing the same thing.

But, of course, the Russians *are* doing it. Every time one of their spokesmen appears on *Nightline* via satellite, or whenever *The Phil Donahue Show* does a "space bridge" between

New York and Moscow, the U.S.S.R. is using satellite technology to get their point across. Nor are the Americans and the Soviets alone in this. Nowadays the entire planet is tied together by an intricate web of satellite technology, a fulfillment of Marshall McLuhan's prophetic image of the "global village."

If you look closely, you can already see a new kind of politics taking shape in the village. Public opinion is playing an increasingly significant role in the actions of foreign governments, and satellite technology is helping to mobilize world opinion more quickly and effectively than ever before. The sudden fall of Ferdinand Marcos in the Philippines, the demise of "Baby Doc" Duvalier in Haiti, the rise of Solidarity in Poland, and the gradual dissolution of apartheid in South Africa are internal political developments that have largely been fomented by outside forces—not *military* forces, but merely the forces of information and public opinion. It's getting harder and harder to be a despot these days, and that, of course, is a good thing. But how long will it be before some despot tries to seize the high ground by commandeering a spot on the Clarke Belt?

What satellites offer the budding tyrant is the ability to cast a wide net over an enormous geographical area, and—through the use of packaged news or packaged entertainment—inculcate millions of people with a particular set of values and beliefs. What you have as a result is a large mass of people who are broadly sympathetic to your political goals. But this is just the raw material of politics, a formless, shapeless blob of undirected power. To turn it into real political power, it must be organized. You must gather names and addresses, compile information about your constituency, uncover their innermost motivations, and learn how to manipulate them. It's been said that a million mosquitoes have more combined energy than an elephant. But an elephant is much easier to harness. The satellite gives you a million human mosquitoes buzzing around the vast territory blanketed by your transponder. But to harness those mosquitoes into votes, you need a different kind of technology.

If I could have the ear of Charles Wick for five minutes, I would tell him this: "Figure out a way to get the names and addresses of everyone who watches WORLDNET and you will become the most powerful man in the world."

And I'd have one other piece of advice for him:

"Buy a computer."

9

Computers: Mayor Daley on a Disk

"I wish you'd quit calling me," said the elderly woman's voice as it crackled out of the telephone receiver into Matt Reese's ear.

Matt Reese was exasperated. He was tired and tense. It was late in the afternoon on election day, and he'd been making calls like this since early in the morning. He reached for a handkerchief to wipe the sweat off his brow.

"Lady," he said, "if you get out and vote, I *will* quit calling you. I'm not asking you to go to a motel with me. Just go vote!"

Matt Reese had a right to be a little testy.

But so did the lady on the phone. All told, this was the *tenth* time someone working for Matt Reese had telephoned her, written her, or knocked on her door in the past month to ask her if she was planning to vote against the right-to-work referendum. In fact, it was the *third* time that day! At 11:00 A.M., someone called to ask her if she'd kept her promise to vote by ten o'clock. No, she said, something came up and she wasn't able to. Would she promise to vote by two? Yes, she said. And at two o'clock, someone else called. Did you keep your promise? No, I haven't been able to get to it yet. Will you promise to vote by four? Yes, she said. But now it was three-thirty in the afternoon and Matt Reese was calling. Reese was holding a little card with the woman's name on it. All day long, he and his assistants had been tearing up cards like this as voters arrived at the polls. The fact that this woman's card was still intact meant she still hadn't voted. And there were now only three hours left. So Matt Reese called again. This time he offered her a ride. You can hardly blame her for losing her temper on the phone.

Who *was* this woman, and why was her vote so important? Why was Matt Reese willing to go to such great lengths to get this one woman to the polls?

In fact, she was no one important, or unusual. She was a typical citizen of Missouri, barely distinguishable from her neighbors. She wasn't even particularly interested in politics. On most off-election years like 1978, she probably wouldn't even bother to vote. But this year, by God, she would definitely vote. Because this year, her name had been selected by computer.

The story of the 1978 Missouri "right-to-work" ballot initiative is, on its surface, not very different from dozens of similar referenda that were held in many other states throughout the 1970s. According to federal law, when a new employee is hired by a unionized company, he or she is required to join the union. Each individual state, however, is permitted to modify the law according to the wishes of its own citizens. If a vehemently antilabor state like New Hampshire, for example, wants to outlaw the union shop requirement, they may pass something called a "right-to-work" law.

In the 1970s, right-to-work became one of the major issues fueling the New Right direct-mail machine. The various organizations of the New Right succeeded in placing right-to-work initiatives on the ballots of many states. By 1978, twenty states had modified the federal labor laws by passing their own right-to-work amendments, and according to the opinion polls in the summer of 1978, the state of Missouri was about to become the twenty-first.

Perhaps confusing "right-to-work" with the literal *right to work*—a confusion that the law's sponsors did everything in their power to promote—nearly two thirds of all voters in Missouri supported their initiative. Labor leaders knew they had to do something to stem the tide. What they decided to do was hire Matt Reese.

Matt Reese is a mountain of a man. Tall, heavy, with a thick mane of white hair, he looks a lot like a polar bear. Reese got his start in politics by helping John F. Kennedy pull off a surprising victory in the 1960 presidential primary in West Virginia, Reese's home state. He came to Washington with Kennedy and stayed, working first as the deputy director of the Democratic National Committee and later in his own consulting firm. In a world dominated by "media consultants" who specialize in the glamorous business of producing radio and television ads, Reese is a throwback to an earlier time. He is an "organizational" consultant, an expert in the painstaking task of doing what Abraham Lincoln once called "finding 'em and voting 'em."

In hiring Reese, the United Labor Committee* knew that staging a massive media campaign against "right-to-work" would be the worst mistake they could make. Waging war on television would serve only to increase the overall voter turnout, which, according to their polls, would bring two supporters of "right-to-work" to the voting booth for every one opponent. Clearly, the United Labor Committee would have to wage a silent campaign, using the "quiet" media of direct mail, telephone, and personal visitation. But that decision raised a problem of its own.

How do you find your supporters? Who are they? What are their names and telephone numbers?

The range of opinions on the question of "right-to-work" is surprisingly heterogeneous, cutting across the usual demographic lines with no apparent pattern. Democrats are as likely to be for it as Republicans. Blacks, Catholics, Jews, businessmen, poor people, wealthy people, the highly educated, and the functionally illiterate might be in favor of "right-to-work" . . . or they might be against it. There's almost no way of telling. Even labor households showed an amazing diversity of opinion on the subject.

The United Labor Committee hired pollster Bill Hamilton to conduct a benchmark opinion survey in the summer of 1978, and what he discovered was frightening. Even in households where the breadwinner was a union member, 57 percent of the people polled were *in favor of* "right-to-work." When union

*The United Labor Committee was a coalition of the AFL-CIO, the UAW, and the Teamsters organized for the sole purpose of fighting "right-to-work."

members themselves were polled, a shocking 42 percent said they planned to vote for "right-to-work," with only 52 percent voting against. Thus, even if the referendum were held only among union members and their families, the election would be close.

Following an age-old principle of political organization, Reese divided the electorate into three main groups: (1) union members and their families, who, he hoped, would eventually vote the labor line; (2) businessmen, conservatives, and others who, if the opinion polls were correct, would almost certainly vote *for* "right-to-work"; and (3) people who, for whatever reason, might be persuaded to vote against the initiative. (Reese liked to call these people "the fairminded.") The strategy was simple. Using his lists of union members, Reese would do everything possible to explain "right-to-work" to the first group and urge them to turn out in force on election day. He would keep his activities as quiet as possible so as not to arouse the interest or the ire of the second group, hoping they would stay at home on election day out of both overconfidence and lack of interest. And he would focus the bulk of his efforts on the third group, the persuadables.

But who the heck were they?

Pondering that question in the summer of 1978—or perhaps I should say *agonizing* over it—Matt Reese suddenly remembered a man he'd met a year earlier. The man's name was Jonathan Robbin. And he was as different a man from Matt Reese as one could imagine.

Matt Reese is a backslapper and a bear hugger, a man with a bawdy sense of humor and with such an innate fondness for pressing the flesh that he probably would work in politics whether anyone paid him to do it or not. Jonathan Robbin, on the other hand, is a numbers man. A scholar and a scientist, he is cool, theoretical, and abstract. Robbin is the perfect exemplar of the old joke "Ask this man what time it is and he'll tell you how to build a watch."

What was occupying Robbin's mind throughout most of the 1970s, however, was not building a watch but building a rather unusual mathematical system for analyzing Census data. As a statistician and a sociologist, Robbin had been dealing with Census figures for most of his adult life. Working under various contracts with the federal government and with commercial marketing firms, he had gained an insight into Census data that eventually led to an important invention, one now known generically as "geodemographics." Robbin named his patented system Prizm, and the company he formed to promote it Claritas.

Prizm is an extraordinarily complex statistical system based on a very simple idea: "Birds of a feather flock together."

It occurred to Robbin that he could pump his computer full of Census data and ask it to sort the information into groups of neighborhoods that were similar along certain demographic lines. The computer came up with forty different neighborhood "types," which together are capable of describing nearly 90 percent of all the communities in the United States. Robbin called these neighborhood types "clusters," and he assigned each of them a number, a description, and a colorful nickname.

Cluster 8, for example, is called "Money & Brains" and is described by Claritas as follows:

Cluster 8 enjoys the nation's second-highest socioeconomic rank. These neighborhoods are typified by swank, shipshape, town houses, apartments, condos, with relatively few children. Many Cluster 8's contain private universities, and a mix of upscale singles. They are sophisticated consumers of adult luxuries—apparel, restaurants, travel, and the like.[1]

Farther down the socioeconomic ladder is Cluster 6, nicknamed "Hard Scrabble":

The term "hard scrabble" is an old phrase meaning to scratch a hard living from hard soil. Cluster 6 represents our poorest rural areas, from Appalachia to the Ozarks, Mexican border country, and Dakota Badlands. With very few blacks, Cluster 6 leads the nation in American Indians (including many Indian reservations) and shows a high index for both Mexican and English ancestries.[2]

As I type the manuscript for this book in my office on the corner of West Fifty-seventh Street and Broadway in Manhattan, I am sitting in an area that Prizm has categorized as a typical Cluster 21, "Urban Gold Coast":

Cluster 21 is altogether unique. It is the most densely populated per square mile, with the highest concentration of one-person households in multi-unit, high-rise buildings, and the lowest in-cidence of auto ownership. Other mosts: most employed, most white collar, most professional, most rented, most childless, and most New York. Cluster 21 is the top in Urbania, a fit address for the 21 Club.[3]

Having identified these forty neighborhood types, Rob-bin returned to his computer, chock full of Census data, and asked it to assign a cluster number to every single neighbor-hood in the United States based on the smallest geographical unit possible—the Census Block Group. In an urban area, a Cen-sus Block Group usually is comprised of four square blocks and contains roughly three hundred households. When broken into small units, neighborhoods display a remarkable homogeneity.

"The average behavior of the community," says Robbin, "will more or less represent the behavior of the individuals in it." For example, Robbin explains, if you determine that the mean edu-cational level of an area is one year of college, you'll probably find some people in that area who have finished college and some who never went beyond high school. But it's unlikely that you'll find many Ph.D.'s or high-school dropouts.

Most neighborhoods also show a remarkable stability. Al-though Americans are extremely mobile, our neighborhoods tend to retain their basic character for a generation or more. People move in and out of a given community every day, depending on what point they've reached in their life cycle, their income, or the size of their family. But the community itself remains in a state of dynamic equilibrium, experiencing very little change from one Census to the next. "People move," says Robbin, "but their houses stay put."[4]

These two factors combine to make the behavior of individ-uals in particular neighborhood amazingly predictable. And pre-dicting behavior, especially *consumer* behavior, is precisely what Claritas and Prizm are all about. Working for a variety of cor-porations, Claritas analyzes a client's current customer base to see which clusters dominate. The client then concentrates his future marketing efforts on people who live in those clusters nationwide. A manufacturer of hair curlers, for example, might want to target his promotions to all the neighborhoods in Amer-ica categorized as Cluster 28, "Norma Raeville."

Although the major use of Prizm has always been for commercial purposes, Jonathan Robbin felt from the beginning that one of the best uses of his system would be politics. "I wrote a monograph on the use of Census data in a political campaign way back in 1971," says Robbin, "but it took seven years before someone applied it in a campaign."

That someone, of course, was Matt Reese.

By 1978, Reese had been eyeing Prizm for at least a year. He was privately convinced of the system's merit and eager to put it to the test. But until the Missouri right-to-work campaign came along, he hadn't been able to find a client who could afford it. Fortunately, money wasn't a problem in Missouri, where labor had decided it was time to draw the line on right-to-work. And since they had also decided not to sink their dollars into television advertising, it meant there was plenty of money left for organization.

For Matt Reese, Prizm was the looking glass through which he could see his persuadables. He rented a list of 1.5 million households in Missouri, complete with addresses and telephone numbers. Using a computer, he matched this list against a list of registered voters, kicking out the people who weren't registered to vote. Each remaining name was assigned a cluster code. If a person lived in downtown St. Louis, for example, he might be in Cluster 23, "New Beginnings." If he lived in the small southwestern town of Ozark, he could be in Cluster 19, "Shotguns & Pickups."

Meanwhile, Bill Hamilton conducted an opinion poll in which each cluster group was represented. The results were tabulated cluster-by-cluster, so it was possible to tell which clusters generally supported right-to-work, which ones were generally against it, and which ones were undecided. Furthermore, the polling data were analyzed to find out *why* people were against right-to-work or why they remained open-minded about it. As it turned out, eighteen clusters showed significant levels of persuadability on the issue. So Reese returned to his master list and pulled out the names, addresses, and phone numbers of every person in Missouri who lived in one of those eighteen clusters. Then he formulated a simple message designed to appeal to each particular group. Some clusters, he felt, could be persuaded by a basic pocketbook argument: namely, that the overall standard of living in the state would go down if union members lost their buying power. Others might respond to an argument based on state pride, especially if it was pointed out to them that most of the other right-to-work states were somewhat impoverished and backward.

At this point Matt Reese began the process that climaxed with that little old lady yelling at him on the phone.

"It is difficult to describe the voter-contact program initiated by the Reese team in Missouri without the word 'harassment' coming to mind,"[5] recalled one of Reese's assistants in an article he wrote about the campaign. Some lucky people were contacted by Reese's workers as many as ten times.

It all began with a telephone call in which voters were asked flatly whether they were for right-to-work or against it. If they said they were for it, they were scratched off the list. If they were undecided, they would remain on the list to receive persuasion mail. But if they were definitely against right-to-work, they were asked to become a block captain. Two more letters followed. A few days later, the people who agreed to become block captains went around the neighborhood distributing literature to the people who didn't. Ten days before the election, another phone call: "It's very important that you vote early on election day," said the volunteer. "Will you promise to vote by 10:00 A.M.?" On the Saturday before the election, a volunteer from organized labor knocked on doors, distributing more literature—all of it written especially to the neighborhood's cluster. On Monday, another letter: "Don't forget to vote tomorrow. Here's the address of your polling place." On the morning of election day, Reese had his computer print out three cards for each targeted voter. A pink card went to the volunteer who originally extracted the voter's promise to vote by 10:00 A.M. A green card went to the block captain. And at the polling place a blue card was held, to be torn up as soon as the voter walked in. At 10:00 A.M. the block captain knocked on the voter's door and said, "rise and shine—it's time to vote." At eleven o'clock the volunteer called and said, "Did you vote at ten o'clock, like you promised?" If not, a new commitment was made for later in the day. In the afternoon, another call. Did you keep your promise? By three-thirty, all the blue cards that hadn't been torn were rounded up and given to volunteers, who went back and knocked on doors. "Hurry up and vote—there are only three hours left!"

"They'll go to the polls just to get us off their backs!"[6] said Reese.

And indeed they did.

Bill Hamilton's initial poll showed that 63 percent of Missouri's voters planned to vote in favor of "right-to-work" and only 30 percent planned to vote against. The election day results were almost exactly the opposite. Sixty percent of the voters rejected the initiative, and only 40 percent voted in favor. It was a massive victory for the labor coalition in Missouri.

Yet if Hamilton had conducted *another* opinion poll on the day after the election, he probably would have found that Missouri's overall opinion about right-to-work had hardly changed at all.

"On election day," said Reese, "there were still more people in the state who wanted the right-to-work proposition to pass than who didn't."[7]

There simply weren't very many people in Missouri who truly agreed with labor on this issue. But Matt Reese had used the computer to find them.

And "vote 'em."

"Finding 'em and voting 'em" was not Abraham Lincoln's only observation on the science of organizing a political campaign. Lincoln also wrote this rather remarkable prescription for winning elections, one that remains as valid in today's high-tech campaigns as it was when Honest Abe shared the stump with Stephen Douglas:

> Organize the whole state, so that every Whig can be brought to the polls . . . divide the county into small districts and appoint each in a subcommittee . . . make a perfect list of voters and ascertain with certainty for whom they will vote . . . and on election day, see that every Whig is brought to the polls.[8]

The key to winning elections in Lincoln's day, and throughout the days of the party bosses and ward heelers who controlled American politics until the advent of television, was *information* and *organization.*

A ward heeler's power rested primarily on the information he possessed about his own district and the voters in it. He knew who the neighborhood leaders were, and he knew who could be bought, who could be sweet-talked, and who could be bargained with. He knew where the Italians lived and where the blacks lived and what was on their minds. He knew what the Poles wanted to hear, and the Jews, and the Germans. After years of practice he learned how to say the exact same thing in fifty different ways. He usually told the truth, but it was a truth made to fit the particular interests of his audience as neatly as a tailored suit.

Yesterday's party boss also possessed the organizational resources to apply this information systematically toward winning elections—to "process" it, if you will. From canvassers to block captains to poll watchers to precinct chairmen, he controlled the organizational structure necessary to make sure *his* vote got to the polls and the other guy's vote did not. Machine politics was a matter of counting heads, making lists, checking them twice, knocking on doors, making phone calls, making more lists, passing out literature, and—most important—getting people to the polls on election day.

Although it exists in vestigial form today, the party machine as we used to know it began to disappear when television gave candidates a direct route of communication to the voter. Even Chicago, the last stronghold of machine politics in America, now has had a two-term black mayor who successfully bucked what was left of Mayor Daley's once-powerful machine. But machine politics is making a comeback in America today—not under the control of the Democrats or the Republicans, but under control of a machine that often sits on top of the candidate's desk. We are entering a new era of machine politics in America. Only this time the "machine" is a computer.

To picture the role of the computer in politics today, imagine the contents of Mayor Daley's brain being electronically transcribed into a floppy disk.

Such a disk would contain many megabytes of stored information about the city of Chicago: its ethnic neighborhoods, its voting history, its opinions, its biases, its hopes for the future, and its memories of the past. The Mayor Daley disk (if it were formated for the Apple MacIntosh, I suppose its trade name would be "MacMayor") would also contain the programming—the knowledge, in other words—of how to organize and apply all this information systematically. Finally, if you put "MacMayor" into a computer that was equipped with a full range of output devices, it would be able to generate lists and reports, write letters, type envelopes, make phone calls, communicate with other computers, control the campaign's budget, comply with federal paperwork, print speeches and press releases, and keep track of the candidate's schedule. In short, the machine could do all the same things that used to be done by "the machine."

Now look at how Abraham Lincoln's famous quote would read in the computer lingo of today's campaign technologists:

> Download historical election data from the registrar's mainframe and voter-ID every Whig . . . target the electorate into geodemographic clusters and other segmented audiences . . . develop a multivariate database and use regression analysis, multidimensional scaling, and statistical modeling to ascertain with certainty for whom they will vote . . . on election day, program the computer to output automatically dialed GOTV calls and lasered slate cards.

As the French are fond of saying, the more things change, the more they remain the same.

It was the French, in fact, who were responsible for inventing the primary use of computers in politics today—although they didn't realize it at the time. They were simply trying to save lives.

During the French Revolution, a system was developed for applying first aid to the wounded that—although it could be cruel at times—was designed to save the maximum number of lives on the battlefield. The system was called "triage," and even today it is one of the fundamental principles of emergency medicine. If you've ever been treated in a hospital emergency room, you've been the subject of some form of triage.

As its name implies, triage works by dividing all the wounded into three groups: (1) the people who are injured so badly that no amount of medical attention could possibly save their lives; (2) the people who are hurt so mildly that they are bound to survive whether they are treated or not; and (3) the people whose injuries are such that if they are given immediate medical attention, they will probably survive . . . and if they are not given that attention, they will probably die.

In a first-aid program operating under the principle of triage, the first group of people will be ignored entirely. They're goners (or in the lingo of today's hep young doctors, "Gomers," an ac-

ronym for Get Out of My Emergency Room). The second group
are kept waiting, sometimes indefinitely. (You've certainly had
this experience if you've ever arrived at an emergency room
with a cut finger or a broken arm.) And the third group receives
all the time, manpower, talent, and money needed to save their
lives.

Like an emergency room, the resources of time, manpower,
talent, and money in a political campaign always are in short
supply. Decisions must be made early in the campaign about
how to allocate those limited resources. And those decisions
almost always involve some form of voter targeting.

In the old days, according to Matt Reese, electoral targeting
consisted of little more than saying, "The South Side's good, the
North Side's bad."[9] But nowadays, targeting is computerized, and
it's considerably more sophisticated. It *has* to be, because there
simply are more people around today than there were in Lincoln's day. With the number of people in a typical congressional
district now exceeding five hundred thousand, it's almost impossible to run a successful political campaign aimed at the entire
electorate. "The obvious solution," writes political scientist Larry
J. Sabato, "is to target voters and geographic areas selectively,
based on where the greatest number of votes can be harvested
with the least amount of effort."[10] And the way to do that is to
triage the electorate.

Most modern political campaigns divide registered voters into
three groups: (1) the voters who are so opposed to the candidate that nothing he does or says will convince them to vote for
him; (2) the voters who are so supportive of the candidate that
all they need is a gentle reminder on election day; and (3) the
voters who are undecided. In this system, the first group is ignored entirely. They are the political Gomers; the campaign se-
cretly wishes they would shrivel up and die. The second group
is made to feel comfortable and appreciated, but they don't receive any real attention until election day approaches. And the
third group, the undecideds, receive all the time, manpower,
money, and talent the campaign can possibly expend.

In many cases, the third group may also receive a further
triage. In other words, they may be divided into thirds again: (1)
the people who are undecided but leaning toward the candidate,
the "soft favorables"; (2) the people who are undecided but
leaning toward the opponent, the "soft unfavorables"; and (3)

the truly undecided. Again, group two is ignored. Group one is lightly massaged until election day. And group three is besieged throughout the campaign.

"You can't grow flowers in the desert with a bucket of water," says Reese, "if you just throw the water every which way at once. But if you use the water intelligently, you can do it."

In politics today, it's the computer that tells you where to pour your water.

The process of targeting voters with a computer can be broken down into three steps: (1) Get ready; (2) aim; and (3) fire.

"Getting ready" consists of acquiring and enhancing a database of voters' names and addresses, with as much useful information under each name as possible.

"Aiming" is a matter of choosing which of those voters to target and what should be said to each of them. It's done with polling, geodemographic analysis, and historical election data.

When it's time to "fire," the computer is hooked up to a variety of peripheral devices such as modems, laser printers, and automatically dialing telephones. Thus equipped, it begins spitting out direct-mail letters, personalized absentee ballots, computer-generated slate cards, individualized palm cards, walking lists, automatic phone calls, and so on.

Get Ready!

"Database" is a sneaky word, one of those annoying examples of high-tech jargon that's really a lot simpler than it sounds . . . and also, unfortunately, a lot more complex. On the surface, a database is not much more than a list, usually a list of names and addresses. In practice, however, a database may contain an almost unlimited amount of information about the people on it. And all this information can be sorted, selected, related, compared, merged, purged, and manipulated in a thousand different ways to predict voter behavior or to influence it. When Lincoln wrote about the "perfect list," he might have had something like one of today's political databases in mind.

The process of developing a campaign's database almost always begins with the purchase of a voter registration tape from the local registrar or secretary of state. Until the computer came along, voter registration lists were considered worse than useless in a political campaign. They were cumbersome, unreliable, and frequently out-of-date. But the computer's ability to process large volumes of data has converted the humble voter registration list into a powerful tool.

The typical voter registration tape, however, requires lots of tinkering before it can be put to work. It must be cleaned of errors, updated, converted into a useful format, and—most important—enhanced with added information. As it arrives from the registrar, the average voter tape contains little more than basic data about each voter and where he lives. The first problem faced by the campaign's computer expert is simply to convert this existing information into a format compatible with the campaign's own hardware and software. But that's just the beginning. From there the data undergo a filtering and treatment process reminiscent of what happens to water at a brewery. First is added a lot of barley and hops—the additional information acquired when the candidate or his volunteers canvass the district.

A "walking list" is created by sorting the voter registration names into households and sorting the household addresses into odd and even numbers. In that way volunteers can stay on one side of the street as they knock on doors collecting information. In a typical canvass conducted early in the campaign, the ostensible purpose is to give the voter preliminary information about the candidate. The real purpose, however, is to give the candidate preliminary information about the voter. Armed with a three-by-five card for each registered household, the candidate (or his volunteers) will engage each voter in conversation and take down as much relevant information as possible: the voter's occupation, his interest-group affiliations, his union memberships, the number of children in the household, whether they attend public or private school, the make and model of car, the presence of any pets in the household, and so on.

Of course, not all information can be acquired by canvassing. Some of the juiciest tidbits of data are among the toughest things to ask people face-to-face, things like: "How old are you? How much money do you make? Are you gay? Are you Jewish?" and so forth. Some of these things can be estimated in a canvass and noted on the three-by-five card. But a more reliable method is provided by turning again to the computer.

At this point the computer filters the existing data by mixing and matching the data with the information contained on other readily available lists. Matching the data with the county assessor's list, for example, will provide information about home value (and, therefore, income). Matching against labor lists will yield union members. The Department of Motor Vehicles tape gives age and race. Census data provide the usually demographic statistics on a given neighborhood. Comparing addresses on the voter registration tape with a computerized version of the phone book will yield correct telephone numbers for about 80 percent of the list. "Ethnic dictionaries" analyze each voter's surname and, with varying degrees of certainty, assign it to one of several different ethnic and religious groups.

A particularly clever computer expert can "merge/purge" two or more lists so the end product is a list containing information that none of the earlier lists possessed. Political computer expert Frank Tobe describes this process for a hypothetical campaign that needs to target gay people:

> Imagine a candidate running for Mayor in a city said to have a 25% gay population (like San Francisco). Obviously, that's an important group which the candidate needs to reach (or exclude). In order to do so, he needs to identify them.

> Here's how we would go about finding gays using our mainframe computer. . . . First, we identify a broad geographical boundary where a large portion of them are supposed to live. Then we start to eliminate households: married couples, unmarried male/female couples living together, and families—multiple male or female households with the same last name. From those that are left, we count the number of two-person households of the same sex but different last names and where the age spread is less than 20 years (to eliminate parent/child combinations). Where the number is high, in comparison to heterosexual households, we encode the results as gays and we also encode the single households as possible gays (in those areas

where the ratio of gays to non-gays is highest). This vastly increases the probability that the couples we identify are gay. Because of the geographical knowledge, moreover, we know that even if those individuals aren't gay, they are likely to be receptive to gay issues.[11]

The ultimate goal is to come up with a database in which each name is coded with as many as 160 bits of useful information in a record format similar to the one used by Frank Tobe (see Table 4).

"Consider [the following] example regarding John and Mary Jackson," writes Tobe. "They live in a hotly-contested district in a nice apartment in a moderate-income area. They're both 28 years old; he's a teacher and her occupation is unknown. They're black and both are Democratic. He's a member of the local school board (an elected job) and they're both members of the local Southern Baptist Church.

"Thus," Tobe concludes, "John and Mary Jackson's computer record could be coded 1, 13, 28, 41, 81, 89, 112, 140, and 158. Simple!"[12]

Simple indeed.

But what *about* the good old 1-13-28-41-81-89-112-140-158 family? What's really on their minds? Can they be persuaded to vote for the candidate? And if so, what kind of a message will it take to convince them?

Aim!

Picture the database just described as a large, colorful dartboard with dozens of concentric circles around the center. Each ring stands for a different voter group: Democrats, Republicans, Jews, Catholics, blacks, senior citizens, Hispanics, and so on. Limited by time, money, and manpower, the campaign cannot afford to spray its darts at the target blindly. It must decide which ring, or combination of rings, will provide the winning score. It must aim carefully. And it must dip each dart in the appropriate type of poison.

Table 4

Sample Assembly District—Voter Database Fields

1. Democrat	45. Social Worker	88. Condo
2. Republican	46. Accountant	89.
3. Libertarian	47. Armed Forces	90. Black code
4.	48. Teacher	91. Gay code
5. Minor Party	49. Student	92. R1
6. Decline to State	50. Other Profession	93. R2
7. American Independent	51. Civil Service	94. RM2
8. Peace and Freedom	52. Misc. Medical	95. RD2
9. Pro-Candidate	53. Show Biz	96. RDM2
10. Moved	54. High Tech	97. DM2
11. Opponent's Supporters	55. Finance	98. D2
12. 18–25 yr. old	56. Aerospace	99. D1
13. 26–30 yr. old	57. Real Estate	100. M1
14. 31–40 yr. old	58. Pro-rent control	101. M2
15. 41–50 yr. old	59. Anti-rent control	102. 2nd Supervisorial
16. 51–64 yr. old	60. Mr.	103.
17. 65+	61. Female	104. West Hollywood
18. No age on file	62. Mrs.	105. Burbank
19.	63. Ms.	106. Old 45th AD
20. Jews	64. Miss	107. Old 24th CD
21. Italian	65. No title	108. New 24th CD
22. Armenian	66. Phone #	109. New 23rd CD
23. Hispanic	67. Education Concern	110. New 26th CD
24. Japanese	68. Crime Concern	111. New 27th CD
25. Greek	69.	112. 20th SD
26. Black	70. Candidate met	113. 22nd SD
27. Chinese	71. Volunteer met	114. 23rd SD
28.	72. Observed gay	115. 28th SD
29. Non-ethnic	73. Liberal	116. Income Group A
30. Other Asian	74. Conservative	117. Income Group B
31.	75. Celebrities	118. Income Group C
32. Philipino	76. Unions	119. Income Group D
33. Foreign Born	77. SEIU	120. Income Group E
34.	78. Supporters of	121.
35. Retired Sr. Citizen	Affinity Legislators	122.
36. Business	79.	123.
37. Blue Collar	80.	124. Miracle Mile/Park
38. 9 to 5	81. Apartment	LaBrea Jews
39. Law Enforcement	82. Mail Address	125.
40. Doctor	83. P.O. Box	126.
41. Dentist	84. Rural Route	127. Miracle Mile mixed
42. Construction Trade	85. No House number	128.
43. Pharmacist	86. No address	129.
44. Lawyer	87. Mobile Home	130. Blax

Table 4

Sample Assembly District—Voter Database Fields (cont.)

131. N. Hollywood Crackers	141.	151. Mixed
132.	142.	152. Flatland Valley
133. Mt. Olympus	143. Wilshire LaBrea Polyglot	153. Hills
134. Laurel Canyon	144. W. Hollywood Polyglot	154. East District
135. Hollywood Hills	145. Hollywood	155. Hollywood
136. Shrecklach Hills	146.	156. Cracker households
137. Lk. Hollywood	147. Schwab's	157.
138. Park LaBrea	148. Atwater	158.
139. Toluca Lake	149.	159.
140. Hancock Park	150. Fairfax	160.

As already noted, most campaigns will choose to concentrate their limited resources on the undecided and soft favorables. But who exactly are they? Where do they live? And how can they be persuaded to vote?

To answer these questions, campaigns rely on three techniques, all of which depend heavily on the computer: (1) analysis of historical election data; (2) public-opinion polls; and (3) geodemographics.

Election Data

Most political professionals would agree that the single best predictor of a voter's future behavior is that voter's past behavior. Given a similar set of circumstances and similar candidates, most precincts will vote in the next election exactly the way they did in the last one. The analysis of historical election data, therefore, probably is the oldest form of electoral targeting. And all things considered, it's probably still the best.

The computer has not revolutionized this particular aspect of campaign strategy, but it certainly has made it a lot easier than it used to be. Historical election data that once were buried in the ward heeler's brain or filed away on dog-eared sheets in the party headquarters can now be entered on a simple spreadsheet program, like "Visicalc." At a glance, the campaign strategist can triage his precincts into the strong favorable, the strong opposed, and the "swing" precincts that will probably make the difference.

The wild-card factor when it comes to analyzing election data is the question of *turnout*. A safe Democratic precinct, for example, can suddenly vote Republican if the overall turnout is low and the Republican candidate does a particularly good job of getting his supporters to the polls. Again, the spreadsheet comes to the rescue. It's a simple matter for a computer-literate campaign strategist to build on the spreadsheet a model that will tell him how various precincts *would have* voted in the last election if the turnout had been higher or lower than it actually was. From that information he can tell where to focus his get-out-the-vote efforts on election day.

Predicting the outcome of elections is a little like predicting the weather. If you simply say tomorrow's weather will be pretty much like today's, you'll be right almost 90 percent of the time. The problem is, you'll miss all the important changes. So to stay on top of the important changes, the campaign strategist uses public-opinion polls.

Public-Opinion Polls

"Polling" is a word that is misunderstood by most Americans, or at least as the word applies to modern political campaigns. Contrary to popular belief, polls are not primarily used to determine "who's ahead" in a given race, except late in the campaign when tracking polls are used to determine where last-minute resources should be spent. This kind of horse-race poll probably is the most worthless and unreliable aspect of opinion sampling, and the frequent mistakes in this area have given the whole business of polling a bad name.

The primary use of polling in politics is to find out what kind of people plan to vote for the candidate, what kind of people plan to vote against him, and what kind haven't made up their minds. Equally important, polling is used to determine *why* people feel the way they do about the candidate. Armed with that information, the campaign strategist formulates messages that will fortify the soft-favorables, persuade the undecided, and convince the soft-opposed.

Computers have utterly revolutionized the world of political polling.

"I'll tell you a simple story about how things have changed since the computer came into this business," says Peter D. Hart, who broke into politics working with Lou Harris, John F. Kennedy's celebrated pollster.

"When I first started working with Lou, he didn't know how to use a slide rule. But he had this little booklet of percentage tables. So he'd say, 'Well, the base is three forty-two, and the amount is sixty-seven,' and he'd go through this little booklet and say, 'Aha, the percentage is nineteen point five percent.'"

By comparison with such a primitive instrument, the wooden slide rule Peter Hart brought with him when he started working for Harris in 1964 was at the cutting edge of advanced technology.

"I'll always keep this slide rule as a reminder of where the business was then and where it is now."

But where the business is now is not just a matter of performing arithmetic calculations faster and more accurately than before—although that's certainly part of it. A more important part is the computer's ability to analyze raw data and explain those data in ways that are more meaningful and revealing than a flat percentage of how many people are in favor of a certain candidate and how many are opposed. In the twenty-five years since Peter Hart brought his wooden slide rule to Lou Harris & Associates, technology in polling has gone from being able to tell *what* people are thinking . . . to *who* is thinking what . . . to *why* they're thinking what they're thinking . . . to *how* their thinking will affect the election. And most of that progress has been driven by the computer.

What they're thinking. This is what most of us have in mind when we hear the word "polling." The pollster writes some questions. He places about fifteen hundred random phone calls. He learns that 75 percent of the people in the district are in favor of gun control, 15 percent opposed, 10 percent undecided. He tells the candidate it might be a good idea if he came out in favor of gun control. Lou Harris's dog-eared booklet of percentage tables was perfectly adequate for this kind of work.

Who is thinking what. When the pollster adds some basic demographic questions to his survey ("How old are you?" "What's your household income?"), he can run some simple cross-tabulations to find out how his overall statistics break down by subgroups. He may learn, for example, that 84 percent of the blacks surveyed were in favor of gun control, but only 45 percent of the whites. Peter Hart's slide rule could do this kind of work reasonably well. An electronic calculator could do it even faster. But a computer, of course, can do it fastest, more efficiently, and in greater volume.

Why they're thinking what they're thinking. By examining the statistical relationships among the answers to various questions on the survey, the pollster begins to understand the underlying reasons why people feel a certain way about an issue. He might pose a statistical question like this: Of the middle-class black people who answered yes to question 5 ("Do you think the availability of guns in our society contributes to high crime rates?") and no to question 2 ("Do you think policemen should carry guns?"), what percentage also answered yes to question 10 ("Do you favor some form of gun control?")? By running a series of such analyses, the pollster may discover that the people in the candidate's district really don't care as much about gun control as they seem to. What they're really worried about is *crime.* Thus if the candidate promises to get tough on crime, his personal stand against gun control may not hurt him at all— even though the district appears on the surface to be very much in favor of gun control.

This kind of statistical computation usually is based on some form of linear algebra or regression analysis. Theoretically the pollster could do it by hand, but it might take him the rest of his life.

"It's sort of like one of those eighteenth-century astronomers," says pollster Charlie Welsh. "The poor guy spends half his life working out the perturbations in the orbit of Mars. But nowadays you pop your figures into the computer and you get a model of the orbit on your screen."

Because the computer makes such calculations so quick and easy, the pollster is much more likely to continue asking questions, running cross-tabs, and examining the data from every conceivable angle. And the presence of microcomputers and minicomputers in the pollster's office simplifies the process even further.

How their thinking will affect the election. The latest and most advanced use of computers in polling involves the statistical modeling of survey data to uncover ways in which the emphasis of the campaign may change the outcome of the election. Most of the pioneering work in this area has been done by President Reagan's pollster Dr. Richard Wirthlin.

Wirthlin's masterpiece is a computer program he calls the Political Information System, or "PINS."

How does PINS work?

"Imagine you have thirty-six switches in front of you," says Wirthlin, "one for each potential issue in the campaign. And you could turn on any one of those switches—or any *combination* of them—and the computer would tell you how it would affect your vote.

"There weren't many moments in the 1984 campaign when we were concerned [about the outcome]," says Wirthlin. But there was at least one time when PINS told Reagan's strategists something they didn't know. "It told us how important it was to remind people that Reagan had brought inflation under control. Our survey research data wasn't telling us that. Our best political instincts weren't telling us that. But PINS identified it as a key theme for us to use in the fall campaign."

To return to the hypothetical example I used earlier, a candidate who didn't have a computer-modeling system like PINS might keep fretting about gun control, trying to formulate a position that would satisfy his constituency. The candidate with PINS, on the other hand, could begin experimenting with different issues and combinations of issues. He pulls the switch marked "Abortion," and nothing happens. He pulls the switch marked "Gun Control," and the data show that he probably will lose the election. But when he pulls the switch marked "Crime," suddenly the whole thing lights up. Bells go off. Smoke comes out of the top. A little clown pops up and hands him a piece of paper saying, "Congratulations, Senator!"

Lou Harris's booklet of percentage tables could not do that.

But no matter how sophisticated the use of computers in polling gets, public-opinion polls have a fundamental weakness that always will limit their usefulness in a political campaign: A poll tells you what the voters are thinking, but it doesn't give you their names, addresses, Zip codes, and telephone numbers. For that you need some form of geodemographics.

Geodemographics

"The best system, of course, would contain data about individuals," says Jonathan Robbin. "You knock on one door, and you know that behind that door there is an individual of a certain type. If you were a politician, that would be the ultimate."

But Robbin's Prizm system comes remarkably close to that. It breaks the United States into approximately 240,000 block groups or enumeration districts, each of which contains only about three hundred people. It's as if the map of the United States had been covered by a giant grid, and each little square in that grid was a place where we knew a great deal about the people who lived there.

"Politicians were among the first people ever to use a system like this," said Robbin. "Because they did it naturally. If the candidate had an Italian last name, campaign managers knew they had to work the Italian wards."

What makes Robbin's system so much more powerful than the primitive geodemography practiced by politicians in the past, however, is that Prizm is a "multivariate" system, not "unidimensional." Back then, if a candidate had an issue he thought might appeal to blacks, he could easily target his mail and telephone contacts into black neighborhoods. But neighborhoods targeted on the basis of only one demographic characteristic ("unidimensional") may not be homogeneous enough in other characteristics to account for the whole range of political attitudes. When it comes to the question of welfare, for example, middle-class blacks and lower-class blacks may have very different opinions. Of course, the candidate can cross-tabulate his demographics to yield more narrow groups (black males earning over twenty-five thousand dollars per year, for example). But too much cross-tabbing creates "statistical noise," making the resulting information not only meaningless but also downright misleading.*

*This is one of the most serious problems with any kind of statistical sampling, and ironically the problem has gotten worse as pollsters have gotten better at using computers to analyze their data. When the pollster keeps cross-tabbing and cross-tabbing his sample, eventually he starts dealing with a uni-

The cluster system, however, is a "multivariate" system. It takes into account hundreds of variables compiled on a nationwide basis and organized into recognizable patterns that can, in turn, be overlaid on any neighborhood in the United States. Jonathan Robbin can walk into a neighborhood for the first time and know as much about the people who live there as he would if he'd spent twenty years studying them. But that's because he has spent twenty years studying the people in neighborhoods exactly like it.

When the latest technology in geodemographics is combined with the latest technology in polling, the result is a remarkably accurate printout of who is thinking what and where they're thinking it. A cluster-by-cluster poll may determine, for example, that Cluster 33's are soft favorables, Cluster 22's are soft opposed, and Cluster 9's are undecided. At that point the candidate will select the names, addresses, and phone numbers of people living in his targeted clusters and start phoning and mailing them into submission.

Fire!

The database has been assembled. The target has been selected. Now it's time to fire. And here is where today's computer technology really shows its stuff. There are really only four ways to get a political message to the voter: mail, telephone, personal visit, and the mass media. Nowadays all four of these channels are driven largely by the computer.

Earlier in this book we looked at the use of direct mail and telemarketing in politics. By now the reader is well acquainted with how computers are used to produce personalized letters and automated phone calls, so there's no need to rehash that

verse that's too small to be statistically meaningful. For example, he may be shocked to discover that 50 percent of middle-class black males above the age of thirty-five support Ronald Reagan. But once he has cross-tabbed his fifteen-hundred-person sample that many times, he may be working with a universe of six guys, three of whom happen to support Reagan because they loved his movies. Key campaign decisions often are made on the basis of such faulty information.

material here. It should be noted, however, that while much evidence exists to suggest that both direct mail and telemarketing are on the wane in fundraising, their use as tools of political persuasion and advertising is clearly on the rise.

The variety of personalized campaign literature produced by Frank Tobe's firm, for example, is indicative of both the growth and the increasing sophistication of computer technology in voter-contact mail. Browsing through a pile of Tobe's "products," one sees such things as:

- A personalized slate card that tells the voter where to vote and whom to vote for.
- A preaddressed absentee ballot application that needs only be signed and dropped in the mail (prepaid postage) for the voter to receive a free absentee ballot.
- A computer-printed persuasion letter that appears to be a personal note from a concerned neighbor of the voter. The outside of the envelope and the entire letter are completely "handwritten" and personalized by a laser printer.
- An imitation overnight express package containing a computerized sample ballot.
- An endorsement letter from a major labor union mailed to its members on a national basis. The computer has automatically filled in the name of the union's chosen candidate in the recipient's own congressional district.
- A grass-roots lobbying letter in which the recipient is asked to sign and mail an enclosed note to his congressman. The note is laser-printed to look as if it were typed on the recipient's own letterhead, and the text has been varied by the computer so each letter the congressman eventually receives will be different.
- A series of last-minute, get-out-the-vote postcards. The endorsed candidates are the same, but each voter sees a slightly different message. On one postcard, for example, the voter is urged to vote for the candidate because of his support for civil rights; on another, because of his work for better schools. One contains a testimonial from a leading black politician; one has an endorsement from a leading Hispanic.

In short, the whole range of gimmicks, tricks, and computer personalization devices developed over the years by direct

242   The New Technologies

mail fundraisers to elicit a contribution are now being applied
in voter-contact mail to elicit a vote.

"In the old days," says Frank Tobe, "we thought it was wonderful to be able to put 'Mr. and Mrs. Armstrong' on the letter.
Then when we were able to say 'Dear Dick,' we were thrilled.

"But nowadays we can say things like 'Dear Dick: As a fellow writer, especially one who lives on the East Coast . . .' We
can insert and reformat the letter to an unlimited extent."

The result is that today's candidate is really running twenty
different campaigns at once. He's got one campaign to senior
citizens, one to blacks, one to Jews, one to Jewish senior citizens, and so on . . . almost *ad infinitum.* One of Tobe's clients
actually will write a special version for every subgroup consist-
ing of more than ten people. And not only does each group get
a different message, but depending on where the group fits into
the campaign's overall strategy, it also may receive vastly different levels of attention. Single black women, for example, might
receive only a single postcard throughout the entire campaign.
Jewish senior citizens, on the other hand, might get two postcards, three slate cards, an overnight express letter, one fake
telegram, five computer-automated phone calls, two live phone
calls, three personal visits, and one ride to the polls.

Juggling all the factors of a single campaign was hard enough.
How does today's candidate manage to keep on top of twenty
different campaigns at the same time?

He has a "PC," of course.

Young John Phillips's science project was a real doozy.

It wasn't at all what you'd expect from a science project—
not even at Princeton. No papier-mâché. No sugar cubes. No
plastic models of a molecule. None of that silly kids' stuff for
John Aristotle Phillips.

No. John built an atom bomb.

Well, he didn't actually build one. He more or less designed
one and drew up the blueprints for it. He did it with no more
information than one could get from published sources, scientific texts, and declassified government documents. John's point,
presumably, was that anyone—including terrorists and renegade
Third World governments—could make an atom bomb.

His point was well taken, but John Aristotle Phillips was not
just anyone.

He was, in fact, quite an extraordinary young man—good-looking, thoughtful, and deeply concerned about nuclear disarmament. When John's physics paper attracted nationwide publicity, he was not the kind of person just to sit back and enjoy his sudden fame. He wanted to *do* something with it. He wrote a book, of course, and there was some talk about making a movie. But eventually John decided that the attention and interest created by his atom bomb project would be put to best use if he ran for public office. So in 1980, at the tender age of twenty-four, John Aristotle Phillips returned to his home in Connecticut and ran for Congress.

Working on John's campaign that summer was his younger brother, Dean, a student in electrical engineering at MIT. Dean Phillips was as handy with computers as John was with nuclear weaponry. Since the campaign was forced to operate on a budget of only $150,000, John decided to rely heavily on computer-generated persuasion mail for the bulk of his advertising. He also relied heavily on the expertise of his brother to keep most of the computer work in-house.

Considering the fact that John Phillips was running in Connecticut's most Republican community (Fairfield County) and that he was running against a popular five-term incumbent, it should come as no surprise that he lost. What *was* surprising is that he did as well as he did. Indeed, John's percentage of the total vote was high enough to encourage him to try again in 1982.

By 1982 Dean had graduated from MIT and was able to devote his efforts to his brother full time as campaign manager. Perhaps more significantly, the two years between 1980 and 1982 were pivotal ones in the history of computer technology. During this relatively short period of time the microcomputer burst on the scene. Suddenly it was possible to put all the power of a 1960s mainframe computer on the candidate's desk. In 1982, the Phillips for Congress campaign produced more in-house direct mail than any other congressional campaign in the country. They pioneered the use of automatically dialed telephone messages. They developed a highly targeted database. And, unhappily, they lost again.

But this time they lost by only twenty-two thousand votes.

As it became apparent late in the campaign of 1982 that they were going to lose, John and Dean Phillips gradually began to think about their future. Shortly after the first election, they had formed a company to manufacture digitalized voice recordings for use in automobile dashboards—the little computers that say things like, "Your seat belt is unfastened." But cracking into that market proved to be harder than they thought, and after the second election the Phillips brothers began casting about for another high-tech field that would take advantage of their unique background.

By 1983, microcomputers were becoming common in small businesses, and since the price of a micro had dropped dramatically, the use of a personal computer in a low-level political campaign suddenly became feasible. John and Dean approached an acquaintance who was running for mayor of Stamford with an interesting proposal: Buy a personal computer, they said, and we'll create an integrated package of software on which you can run your whole campaign. All they asked in return was the right to market whatever software they invented.

During that year, John and Dean worked closely with the candidate's staff to develop a program that would guide and manage every aspect of the campaign. A political database program, of course, was the heart of the software, and word processing was its primary function. But the program they invented also contained modules for budgeting, polling, media buying, generating FEC reports, and even scheduling the candidate's time. They called their invention Campaign Manager, and John and Dean's unique relationship with the Stamford mayoral campaign enabled them to field-test the software even while it was still in development. By the time the campaign was over, John and Dean's friend was the mayor of Stamford (an upset victory) . . . and the Phillips boys were in business—one they called Aristotle Industries.

Aristotle Industries immediately tapped into an enormous if somewhat hidden and elusive market. It's been estimated there are approximately five hundred thousand electoral offices in the United States, with roughly 750,000 candidates vying for them. These candidates spend about 1.25 *billion* dollars a year in cash and, most likely, receive several billion dollars more in donated services in their effort to get elected. Congressional, gubernatorial, and senatorial campaigns make up only a tiny fraction of this market. The bulk of it is comprised of local politicians who spend five, ten, or fifteen thousand dollars to get elected to city councils, state legislatures, school boards, and county commissions. In the past, only big campaigns could afford to use computers. In the future, 90 percent of the use of computers in politics will be in the smaller campaigns.

The effect of this untapped market on young Aristotle Industries was somewhat like striking oil.

"We mailed a promotion to twenty-five hundred hard-core political people," Dean Phillips recalls. "We hadn't even finished working on the software when they started calling, writing, sending checks. We made a killing in the beginning."

Aristotle responded to the demand by diversifying its product line. John and Dean now have a second-generation version of their original program, called Campaign Manager Plus . . . a high-volume database program called Get Out the Vote . . . a telecommunications program named Billboard . . . office software for incumbents dubbed Constituent Service! . . . and an automatically dialed recorded message player named Watson.

Meanwhile, John and Dean Phillips have had to fend off a fair amount of competition. Campaign software has become the hottest-selling item in the world of political technology, with at least half a dozen other companies peddling their own version of it. Some of these firms have carved out a niche in the market for themselves by selling to only one party. A program called Hannibal (hint: It has to do with elephants) is only for Republicans, while The Election Machine is sold only to Democrats.

In truth, all campaign software at this moment is pretty much alike. The differences are largely a matter of degree and capacity, where the age-old rule of consumer quality—"you get what you pay for"—certainly applies. Most brands of campaign software will offer some version of these ten modules: (1) a database program to maintain information about voters and volunteers; (2) a word-processing program for direct mail; (3) a spreadsheet program for precinct targeting; (4) a polling program capable of running simple cross-tabs on tracking polls; (5) a scheduling program for organizing the candidate's time; (6) a simple office budgeting program; (7) a program designed to maintain and produce printouts of periodic financial reports for the Federal Election Commission; (8) a program for media buying; (9) a public-relations program for composing press releases and storing information about reporters; and (10) a program for storing opposition research in a file that can be searched by key words.

Not surprisingly, many of the other purveyors of campaign software are critical of Aristotle Industries, suggesting that Aristotle's software tends to be inflexible and unsophisticated. But John and Dean Phillips are not the kind of young men it pays to underestimate, and I came away from Aristotle Industries with a very different impression. Their office on Capitol Hill is located in a converted town house, with John and Dean sitting across from each other in an attic room reminiscent of a ship's crow's nest. Beneath them are two floors teeming with the kind of clean-cut, brilliant, athletic-looking young people I used to detest in college. Most of them come from both a technical and a political background, and they seem as comfortable with ballots as they do with bytes. If there are going to be any major breakthroughs in the world of campaign software, I wouldn't be at all surprised if they came from here.

What's the political upshot of putting Mayor Daley on a disk?

Some critics worry that we're creating another "haves vs. have-nots" situation between the well-heeled candidates who can afford to use computer technology and the poor candidates who cannot. But the evidence overwhelmingly suggests the exact opposite. The computer has been used most effectively by the underdog, the maverick, the underfinanced and unknown candidate. Assuming such a candidate has enough money to enter the game with an ante of roughly five thousand dollars in hardware and software, he suddenly has a million dollars' worth of political organization sitting on his desk. The computer—especially the microcomputer—will serve not only to make political campaigns more competitive but also to encourage a wider variety of citizens to get involved.

"Our best customer," says John Phillips, "is not the guy with a lot of money, it's the guy with a little bit of money. They are not the entrenched incumbents, they are the challengers. They must use the technology because the only thing you can do when you're being outspent two to one in a political campaign is to spend your own money twice as efficiently."

Some observers argue that computers are diminishing the

role of the volunteer in political campaigns while encouraging the rise of political consultants and political technologists. Again, I disagree. I do see a change in the kind of work volunteers will be doing (and where they will be doing it), but that change is clearly one for the better. No longer confined to doing assembly-line work in the campaign's headquarters, tomorrow's political volunteer may be part of a network of computer users who access the campaign's mainframe from their home computer via modem and do everything from routine keypunching to taking part in on-line strategy meetings. Far from encouraging the "professionalization" of political campaigns, so far the computer has been a mighty force for the "amateurization" of them. More and more political campaigns are recruiting bright kids from local high schools and colleges to help develop customized computer programming. Meanwhile, some candidates are finding that a strong computer and good campaign software can replace hiring an outside consultant.

The consultants themselves scoff at this.

"If they think that software package can substitute for me," sniffs GOP consultant Eddie Mahe, "then I'm not even remotely interested in working for them. Because they so thoroughly fail to understand what it is we're all about that it would be painful to work for them."

Of course, Eddie Mahe is in no danger of being replaced by a floppy disk. Neither is Matt Reese. They are at the top of their profession. But what about the several thousand other people around the country who call themselves political consultants? I'm not sure they can afford to be so cavalier about it. Even coming from the mouth of Eddie Mahe, this kind of comment has that faintly familiar ring of "famous last words" uttered by many craftsmen over the years whose irreplaceable skills are now almost fully automated.

Perhaps the most serious problem posed by the increasing use of computers in American politics is the matter of voter turnout. We live in a country where the percentage of voting-age citizens who are registered to vote is low, and the percentage of those who actually show up at the polls—especially in nonpresidential elections—is amazingly low. Ordinarily this is not something that bothers me very much, since I'd rather have our elections decided by a few people who are involved and informed than by a lot of people who are ignorant and unconcerned. But what I see happening with the continued use of the computer goes beyond "low turnout" to the point where it looks more like "minority rule." And that's a little scary.

It's a fact known to just about everybody inside of politics and amazingly few outside of it that political campaigns really don't have very much effect on the electorate at all. They don't do a particularly good job of changing anybody's mind, and they are rarely capable of turning the entire electorate around to vote in a way it hadn't been planning to vote all along. Presidential campaigns, for example, are traditionally supposed to begin on Labor Day. But by the month of September, the vast majority of voters have already decided whom to vote for, and they have no intention of changing their minds. Only a relatively few voters remain truly undecided, and assuming the race is close, they are the ones who decide the election. In the old days, both campaigns had to bombard the entire electorate with mass media to make sure they reached this small group of undecided voters. In doing so they created an air of excitement about the election that, in turn, would bring comparatively large numbers of voters to the polls. Although it was still a far cry from bringing *every* registered voter to the polls, the turnout was enough to provide a snapshot of what the entire electorate was really thinking.

But the computer is changing all that. Using the techniques described in this chapter, it's now possible to find out exactly who those undecided voters are. Candidates can now focus *all* of their attention on the undecideds and soft favorables, letting the rest of the electorate lie like sleeping dogs. As candidates learn to use the computer more effectively, we are likely to see many more "silent campaigns" in American politics—especially when it comes to ballot initiatives and off-year congressional elections. Matt Reese's campaign against the right-to-work initiative in Missouri was so quiet that people actually called their labor unions to complain that nothing was being done. Suffering a slight failure of nerve toward the end of the campaign, Reese authorized the production of some last-minute TV commercials because he was afraid if he didn't use at least *some* TV, his undecideds and soft favorables wouldn't take the campaign seriously. "It's like balloons and funny hats," says Reese. "They don't do any good, but you've got to have them or people don't think you're running a real campaign." In the future, however, political strategists will have more faith in their computers. They won't worry about the five million people who don't vote; they'll worry only about the five thousand who do. As a result, even *fewer* people in this country will vote until eventually, I suppose, elections will be decided only by those people who have either slept with the candidate or received expensive gifts from him.

I'm also a little concerned about the computer's role in something that has come to be known as "grass-roots lobbying," a phenomenon that deserves much more attention than it has yet received in the press. As I conducted the interviews for this book—and particularly for this chapter—the single most common thing I heard from the people I spoke with was this:

"We don't do much political campaign work anymore."

Now, mind you, these were America's top political consultants who were saying this. If these people aren't doing much political campaign work anymore, what *are* they doing?

The answer, it seems, is grass-roots lobbying.

Grass-roots lobbying is the business of affecting the outcome of legislation by communicating with the voter so that he, in turn, will communicate with his representatives in government. This bizarre trade has become big business in Washington these days among smart political consultants who are devoting more and more time to it. It's more lucrative than campaign work, not as seasonal, and considerably less taxing. As a result, some of our best political minds are spending less time trying to elect good people to Congress and more time trying to influence incumbents with messages sponsored by special-interest groups and the *Fortune* 500. This book has concerned itself almost entirely with how technology is being used to elect political candidates. But there's another story to be told someday, and that's the story of how technology is being used to manipulate politicians *after* they've been elected.

Finally, most observers who have looked at the use of computers in politics and government have expressed some concern about privacy, and I share those concerns. After unveiling his elaborate algorithm for finding gay people with a computer, Frank Tobe brushes off the ethical ramifications of what he has done by saying that all the information he used was readily available. "I think we can dispense with the privacy issue," he writes. ". . . The information used is forthrightly acquired, in the public domain, and only used for campaign purposes."[13]

But I don't find that particularly comforting. To the contrary, Tobe is using a lot of readily available information about me (my age, my driver's license information, my address, etc.) and manipulating it to find out something about my life that is extremely private (namely, my sexual orientation). I find that somewhat more disturbing than if I caught some political consultant rummaging around in a secret file about me, or even peeking through my window. I could always have him arrested for that, after all. But I can't stop him from using the phone book.

Of course, I am not impugning any bad motives to Frank Tobe himself. He is a liberal Democrat, and he seems to have more than the usual amount of caution about the clientele he accepts. What's more, he wrote his article back in 1984, when the only possible use one could imagine for acquiring information about gay people would be to help them. But nowadays, when some very responsible people are talking about quarantining gays, the idea of using a computer to identify gay people is nightmarish. Many states have laws against using voter registration data for any purpose other than political campaigning, and I'd have to say that's a very good law.

After staring at the ceiling for a few moments and clucking their tongues in serious contemplation, most political consultants eventually wind up dismissing the question of privacy when it comes to using computers by saying:

"It's only a tool."

The computer, in other words, is only as good or as bad as the human beings using it.

As long as human beings remain in control, I guess that's true.

It's when computers start talking to computers that the real fun begins.

10

Telecommunications and the New Electronic Media: The Political Cocoon

My computer—the one I'm typing on right now—is nothing to brag about. "Low-tech," you might call it. It's roughly the size and shape of a small suitcase or overnight bag. The computer is encased in plain gray metal. It has two built-in floppy-disk drives and a very small built-in TV screen. From a distance it looks like I have a tin crate sitting on my desk. It's as sturdy as hell. When the dealer first showed it to me, he banged on the top with his fist while I winced and muttered, "Please stop, please stop."

I don't know much about my computer's innards, but from reading the owner's manual it's clear that the physicists at Cal Tech won't be asking to borrow my machine. It's got sixty-four bytes of Random Access Memory. The two disk drives give it another 380 or so bytes. Sounds like a lot, but they'll be putting that much memory into electric can openers before long. This machine cost me about fifteen hundred dollars new. That was four years ago. I understand that now you can get a similar model (similar, but better) for less than a thousand. I read somewhere that if commercial air travel had progressed at the same rate as computer technology, the Concorde would be carrying half a million passengers at twenty million miles per hour for less than a penny apiece. Twenty-five years ago, in fact, a machine that had as much computing power as mine would cost more than a million dollars and occupy several large rooms in a high-security research facility. When my desk gets crowded with papers, I've been known to eat lunch off the top of my computer.

All things considered, my computer is about as plain and simple as they come. But I'm rather fond of the old crate. Nowadays, in fact, I often bang my fist on it myself—not to demonstrate its sturdiness, but just out of affection.

When I do bang it, however, I'm careful not to strike a little instrument that sits on top of the computer in the near-right-hand corner. This instrument, which is about the size of a small cigar box, cost me nearly half as much as the entire computer. But I've never regretted spending the money. Unlike my computer, it looks very "high-tech"—almost like something from the bridge of the *Enterprise* on *Star Trek.* When I turn it on, a whole panel of little red lights flashes on. And when I put it in use, the lights flicker and oscillate, just like Lieutenant Uhura's control board always did before she said, "I'm having trouble reaching the Federation, Captain."

It's a modulator/demodulator, a "modem" for short. For all its fancy appearance, what it does is very simple. It allows my computer to "talk" to other computers over the telephone line by translating written numbers and characters into audible tones. When the other computer answers back, it "demodulates" those tones so they appear as letters and words on my computer screen. If, for example, I tell my modem to dial my friend Jimmy in California, I might begin by typing on my keyboard:

"Jimmy, are you there?"

The little red lights would flash, and a moment later I'd see the following message on my screen:

"Where do you think I am, stupid?"

Same old Jimmy.

Sounds simple. So simple, in fact, that upon first seeing a

modem demonstrated, the usual reaction is, "So why don't you just pick up the phone and say hello?"

Indeed, if casual conversation were the only use of the modem, it would have a hard time supplanting the telephone. But you can't just pick up the phone and read an eighty-page document to your friend, hoping his stenography is good enough to get it all down. You can't share software programs over the phone, or use the phone to run your friend's computer by remote control. All this and more, however, can be done with the modem.

The effect that a modem has on a personal computer and its owner is electrifying. It's the same effect Disneyland has on children or cocaine has on professional baseball players. It's an eye-popping, mind-expanding, occasionally addictive experience. No longer is your computer confined to mundane local tasks like word processing and spreadsheets. Suddenly it is part of a worldwide network of technology, capable of visiting great libraries of information, conveying important messages across the globe by electronic mail, participating in computer conferences with people from all over the planet, playing games with giant mainframe computers, tapping into the latest news or stock quotations, sharing computer software, transmitting lengthy documents, or simply—as it's come to be known—"chatting."

Add a modem to your personal computer, especially a plain-Jane computer like mine, and after a few minutes you'll turn to it and say:

"Toto, I don't think we're in Kansas anymore."

Many of the newest communication technologies used in politics today are the result of connecting one computer to another, usually by modem. Or by connecting a computer to another machine, usually a television set. In the first category are such technologies as local area networks, bulletin board systems, information utilities, electronic mail, and electronic funds transfer. In the second category are bidirectional cable, addressable cable, videotex, teletext, and laser optical videodiscs. One last technology, videocassettes, belongs to neither category. But it brings this book full circle, tying one of the newest political campaign technologies to one of the oldest. Herewith, then, is a survey of some of the most significant of the "new electronic media" and how each is being used in politics.

Local Area Networks (LAN)

A LAN is the simplest form of computer communications and the one that has enjoyed the widest use in political campaigns to date. As its name implies, a LAN consists, in the same office, of two or more computers that have been "hard-wired" into one system. What distinguishes a LAN from the more common "multiple-user" system is that each LAN terminal retains its own independent computing power. Not merely a "dumb" terminal accessing a central database, each computer in a LAN is capable of doing its own calculations and word processing . . . or sharing central data and central output devices whenever necessary.

A LAN makes it possible for several personal computers in one campaign office to share a single printer. It also makes it easy for users to share files. Using a LAN, for example, the press secretary might electronically distribute a copy of the latest press release with a note saying, "Make any changes on your own word processor and send this back to me by 3:00 P.M."

LAN users can send messages to each other using an informal system of electronic mail. Such messages will range from passing along the latest political joke . . . to placing one's order for a chicken salad sandwich . . . to, occasionally, matters of substance. LANs also allow computer conferencing, both real-time and ongoing.

Two months before a major address at local farmers' cooperative, the campaign manager might want to start an *ongoing* computer conference titled, "WHAT SHOULD WE SAY TO THE FARMERS?" Over the course of the next eight weeks, everyone in the campaign will have the chance to put in their two cents' worth. Some ideas will be criticized and rejected. Others will receive subtle refinements. By the time the speechwriter sits down to write the speech, he will have the benefit of a written outline reflecting the ideas, opinions, and concerns of everyone on staff.

After the first draft of the farm speech has been written, the campaign manager may distribute a copy electronically to everyone on the LAN and hold a *real-time* computer conference to discuss it. The advantage of holding such a meeting is not only that people can remain at their desks but also that everyone has a transcript of exactly what was said. Instead of walking out of the conference with a sick feeling in the stomach and no idea of what he should do, the speechwriter walks away with a blueprint for a final draft that will please everyone.

Despite their usefulness and apparent simplicity, local area networks can be very tricky to set up. Putting together a workable LAN usually requires the advice of a computer consultant who specializes in designing them. As a result, when it comes to sharing data many campaign computer managers prefer using something called the Nike Network, after the running shoe of the same name. It consists of taking a floppy disk out of one computer and running it down the hall to the other one.

Data Transmission

The vast majority of political campaigns can get along fine with a Nike Network. Larger campaigns may need a LAN. But statewide and national campaigns—particularly campaigns with offices in more than one media market—ought to invest in a modem.

With a modem, a campaign can share data between the computers at headquarters and the computers in the field. A U.S. Senate campaign in Ohio, for example, may have headquarters in Columbus with field offices in both Cincinnati and Cleveland. Managing the flow of paperwork among three such offices is no easy task, especially if it has to be done through conventional mail. The problem becomes particularly intense during those occasions when the candidate himself must spend time working in the field.

But with a modem, he is never out of touch. The headquarters in Columbus can send him a last-minute revision of the speech he will deliver in Cleveland that evening. It can transmit a list of Cleveland VIP's and fat cats to call in the morning. Up-to-the-minute results of direct mailings and voter-contact programs can be flashed from city to city daily. And with the help of specialized telecommunications software, it's even possible for a staffer in Cleveland to operate the computer in Columbus.

Once having invested in several modems to carry out such tasks, some campaigns might find it useful to set up a Bulletin Board System.

Bulletin Board System (BBS)

Bulletin Board Systems are particularly useful for larger campaigns or party organizations that need to serve many different users. With the proper software, a Bulletin Board System can be set up to run on any personal computer, and users far and wide will access the system by telephone. Bulletin Board Systems are used to share files, send messages, participate in ongoing conferences, and exchange software. They are much cheaper and easier to set up than Local Area Networks. BBS's also have the advantage of being able to communicate with any type of computer. That's especially useful in a political campaign, where many of the computers either belong to volunteers or have been donated by friends.

Bulletin Board Systems do have drawbacks, however. They can accommodate only one user at a time. There is no real-time communication between users. They cannot handle complex data-sharing tasks, like updating mailing lists. And they're not as fast as a LAN. A Local Area Network, in fact, processes data nearly five thousand times faster.

Despite these limitations, however, the Bulletin Board System has clearly found a home in American politics. Aristotle Industries was the first campaign software company to offer an off-the-shelf program for starting your own political bulletin board. They call it Billboard.

"With 'Billboard' running on your IBM-PC or compatible computer," says the Aristotle Industries catalog, "your constituents can dial up your computer, receive a welcoming message of your choice, and then be invited to sound off on any issue of concern to him or her.

"You can participate in the dialogue. Or, you can let your computer record the names, addresses and comments of those who took part while you take your wife out to dinner. At the end of the session, you can get a complete report and print-out of those who attended."[1]

One of the most successful political BBS systems belongs to the Republican National Congressional Committee, one of the three main arms of the national Republican Party. The Republican Information Network is not a public board; it's intended only for the use of Republican candidates and Republican organizations, so each user must be given a secret password. Once on the system, the user may find offbeat news stories that support the Republican point of view, or Republican position papers on a variety of current issues. The databank contains how-to articles on fundraising, opposition research, and public relations. It also contains boilerplate press releases on the hot news items of the day. If a congressional candidate in Peoria wants to know what to say to the local press about inflation, for example, he can "download" one of these press releases, type in his own name, and put it out as his own.

Information Utilities

One of the most useful things you can do with a modem is use it to get information. Some of the research for this book was done by accessing "information utilities." These are large databanks, usually stored on mainframe computers, that can be accessed by telephone. In 1979 there were only four hundred such databases in the country, most of them highly specialized. Today there are more than three thousand. And they range from medical databanks that can be used only by physicians to general-information networks that can be used and enjoyed by children.

There are three major databanks that specialize in political information: Legi-Slate, Washington Alert Service, and Washington Online. By plugging into one of these, challengers can gain some leverage against the enormous advantage enjoyed by incumbents in securing information.

Legi-Slate, for example, offers the following services:

- An easy-to-search list of all congressional legislation from 1979 to the present, with new bills posted within a day of being presented on the floor.
- Automatic updates on any bill you've told the system to track.
- A complete list of all the current cosponsors of a bill.
- The full text of any printed bill, including every current or past version of the bill.
- The attendance records of every member.
- Biographical profiles of every member of Congress.
- The vote tallies of every vote that has been taken in Congress since 1979.

Legi-Slate, however, does more than just generate lists and tallies. In the hands of a skilled user it also can analyze, process, and manipulate information in a variety of interesting ways. It's possible, for example, to match the voting records of one member with that of another. Thus a Republican challenger may use it to discover that his opponent has voted with Teddy Kennedy 97 percent of the time.

By rapidly searching through the complete texts of bills, it's possible to uncover valuable nuggets of information. An apparently harmless appropriation bill, for example, may contain an amendment calling for the drowning of stray puppies, or something equally unpopular. If your opponent voted for the bill, you can nail him on the "puppy issue" and probably take him by surprise.

Often the incumbent himself won't know he voted in favor

of such a bill, so incumbents can use the system to follow the ancient Greek admonition "Know thyself." Many an incumbent has lost the election because he was insufficiently familiar with his own voting record. By searching and analyzing his attendance and voting history in advance, a smart incumbent will identify his weaknesses ahead of time and prepare a strong defense.

Political candidates also need fast access to *breaking* news, and for this they may want to subscribe to a more general information network, like The Source or Comp-U-Serve.

Suppose a U.S. Navy vessel is attacked by the Libyans in the Gulf of Sidra at two o'clock in the afternoon, and local reporters call campaign headquarters to get a statement from the candidate. "Let me wait until I see it on Dan Rather" is not an acceptable response. Candidates are expected to be on top of such situations. But short of putting a UPI ticker in the office, it's hard to do.

When a candidate subscribes to The Source, however, he not only gets his own UPI ticker, he also gets the AP wire and the latest edition of *The Washington Post . . .* all on the screen of his personal computer. For ten dollars a month (plus access time), members of The Source enjoy many of the telecommunications functions already mentioned in this chapter, including computer conferencing, real-time conferencing, file transfer, bulletin boards, software sharing, and a very good system for electronic mail.

Electronic Mail (E-Mail)

As futuristic as it sounds, electronic mail has been around longer than most people think. Western Union's "Mail-Gram," for example, was one of the first electronic mail delivery systems, and it's still one of the best.

A hard-copy electronic mail system like Mail-Gram works by electronically transmitting the text of a letter to a location near the recipient. From there it is printed on paper, folded into an envelope, and dropped into first-class mail, usually to be delivered on the next business day. "Soft" electronic mail can be used only when both the sender and the receiver are equipped with computers. Soft e-mail can be sent through a Local Area Network, a Bulletin Board System, an information utility like The Source, or directly from modem to modem. Soft-copy electronic mail is delivered instantaneously.

Whether it arrives within an instant or within a day, electronic mail is considerably faster than conventional postal delivery, and therein lies its big advantage. Soft e-mail alleviates "telephone tag"—especially when it's transmitted across time zones. And hard-copy electronic mail is not only more reliable than conventional mail, but also, with the look and feel of a telegram, it has more impact.

Political direct marketers have used Mail-Grams on special projects for years, but they are just now beginning to experiment with the less costly and more flexible forms of electronic mail. The advent of laser printing on hard-copy electronic mail has given it an added dimension that greatly appeals to political direct marketers. It's now possible to reproduce logos, signatures, graphics, and even multiple colors with hard-copy electronic mail. The only thing keeping political direct mailers from using it more often is its price.

Plotted on the same graph, the cost curves of conventional mail and e-mail are on a collision course, with postal rates heading rapidly up and e-mail rates heading just as rapidly down. As the two lines come close to intersecting, expect to see political direct mailers using more and more hard-copy electronic mail for both fundraising and targeted voter contact.

Soft-copy electronic mail costs *less than* conventional postal delivery. But the impact of soft-copy e-mail on political direct marketing will have to await the day when more people own personal computers. For now it's fairly impractical to use soft e-mail for fundraising or voter contact. As an organizational tool, however, it has already proven itself useful in many campaigns.

Electronic Funds Transfer (EFT)

Again, electronic funds transfer is something that sounds very futuristic. But it's more a part of our everyday lives than many of us think. It you've ever used the automatic cash machine at your bank to switch money from your savings account to your checking account, you've used a rudimentary form of electronic funds transfer. If you've used a cash machine that was *not* located at your bank (in other words, one of the "cash networks"), then you've used an even more sophisticated form of EFT. The only thing that distinguishes that kind of transaction from the "futuristic" kind is that it's taking place at the shopping mall rather than at your home. Imagine this same technology being available to you by pushing buttons on your telephone or typing on your personal computer, and you can imagine what the EFT of tomorrow will be like.

Clearly, this will be a boon to political telemarketing, where the problem of collecting pledges is critical. Since telemarketers have their prospects on the phone anyway, it should be a simple matter to have them push their Touch-tone buttons to make a contribution.

I have my doubts, however, about how quickly EFT will catch on in political direct mail. There's something satisfying to the soul about pulling out a checkbook, writing a check, and dropping it in the mailbox. It makes the donor feel as if he is really taking action on the problem, and as such it's an important component of the emotional dynamic of political direct mail. Credit cards, for example, have never caught on in political direct mail, although they've virtually revolutionized the world of commercial direct marketing.

Fiber Optics

The advantages of fiber optic telephone lines have been somewhat misreported to the public. In a television commercial for the long-distance phone company GTE Sprint, a man in New York listens intently to a man in Chicago dropping a pin on a tabletop. Both are dressed in lab coats and surrounded by a lot of high-tech equipment. Yet when the sound travels across the lines clearly, the man in New York is so excited that he drops his scientific veneer for a moment and says, incredulously, "That was a *pin*?" The idea, I guess, is to let America know that fiber optic telephone lines will be much clearer than conventional copper wires. True enough. But that's like saying the big advantage of flying the Concorde is that the food is better.

No, speed is the major consideration in both cases. The speed with which data can be transmitted and the sheer volume of the information that can be transmitted are what give fiber optics its distinct advantage over copper wire. Copper wires, for example, can transmit data at about nineteen thousand bits per second. Fiber optic wires will routinely transmit about 275 *million* bits per second, and in some experiments they've gone higher than two *billion* bits per second.

"At 275 million bits per second," says political computer expert John R. Tkach, "you will be able to transmit data files on 342,750 voters in one second. That should help with your long-distance phone bills."[2]

To put it another way, it's possible to transmit the amount of information contained in a thirty-volume encyclopedia about a hundred miles in one second. Or, if you had a few *minutes* to spare, you could send the entire contents of the Library of Congress over fiber optic lines from Washington to Baltimore. Two billion bits of information is the equivalent of twenty-eight thousand telephone calls or twenty-two different channels of television pictures. Fiber optics has justifiably been called an "inexhaustible" medium for communication.

It will take time, but eventually the day will come when every telephone in America will be hooked into this mighty river of information. When that day arrives the very nature of communications in America may change dramatically. Among other things it may bring about the advent of something that has come to be known as the "HCS," or Home Communications Set.

The HCS, in one form or another, has been speculated about in fiction, nonfiction, and science fiction since George Orwell first got everyone worried about "Big Brother" in his novel *1984*. As its name implies, a Home Communication Set would be a combination of computer, television, cable television, telephone, facsimile machine, and perhaps several other technologies in a hybrid system capable of both sending and receiving information over fiber optic lines. It's the enormous information-carrying capacity of fiber optics that makes such a vision possible. But the Home Communication Set's real power rests primarily in the simple marriage of the two most important technologies of our time: television and the computer.

The Home Communications Set has already achieved a kind of primitive incarnation in the form of two-way, or "bidirectional," cable television. Approximately six-hundred thousand of the homes now served by cable television are wired with a certain type of coaxial cable that allows electronic signals to be sent "upstream" as well as down. The most famous of these systems is owned by a joint venture of Warner Communications and American Express, and the nationwide programming network that serves it is called "QUBE."

Bidirectional Cable: QUBE

"Let's find out how many of you know homosexuals," says the attractive hostess of *Columbus Alive*.[3]

Until now, *Columbus Alive* has looked like a rather typical local television program, in a typical town (Columbus, Ohio), dealing with a fairly typical subject: What it's like to be a homosexual in middle America. But now, as the hostess turns away from her typical panel of experts and casts her eyes directly into the camera, something truly unusual is about to happen. She's going to talk to the television audience, and they're going to talk back. As she speaks, the following words are superimposed on the screen below her: "I have a friend, relative, or acquaintance who I know is homosexual."[4]

At home, viewers sit in front of their television sets holding a small box with five buttons on it. Button 1 stands for "yes," and button 2 stands for "no."

"Touch in now," says the TV hostess. And all over Columbus, people who know homosexuals push button 1 on their little consoles, while people who don't push button 2.

Within seconds, a mainframe computer in the television studios of *Columbus Alive* conducts an electronic sweep of all the homes connected to the QUBE system. And moments later the results appear on the screen: 65 percent of the people watching *Columbus Alive* on QUBE know homosexuals; 35 percent do not.

Launched in 1978, QUBE is the first two-way cable television system in the United States. After its initial test in Columbus, Warner Amex Cable Communications expanded the system to its franchises in Cincinnati, Pittsburgh, Dallas, Houston, and St. Louis. A nationwide programming network serves all six QUBE outlets, and each local cable system also produces its own interactive programming, shows like *Columbus Alive*.

Talk shows, however, are not the only things you can see on QUBE. You can shop at home, order movies for private viewing (including soft-porn movies), second-guess the quarterback during an Ohio State football game, get college credit for a televised course on English Lit., or give someone "the hook" on a local talent show. With a little extra wiring in your home, it's even possible to use QUBE as an automatic alarm system that will notify the police if it hears a loud noise or call the fire department if it smells smoke.

According to the ratings, the most popular programs on QUBE are game shows, especially those in which cash and prizes are given to the home audience. But the *second* most popular type of programming is politics.

Since its debut in 1978, the QUBE system has been used repeatedly for political polling and even direct political participation. In 1979, QUBE attracted nationwide attention when NBC News used the system to get an instantaneous reaction to a Jimmy Carter speech on the gasoline shortage.

QUBE subscribers, in fact, have been polled to death on every subject under the sun. And occasionally their opinions have been solicited in a context where they actually made a difference. For example, there have been several "town meetings" held on QUBE. One such meeting was held outside Columbus, in the suburban community of Upper Arlington, Ohio. Using the QUBE system it was possible to "narrowcast" the meeting only to subscribers who lived in that particular suburb. And although two previous town meetings dealing with the same subject had attracted only about 125 citizens each, the QUBE telecast garnered an audience of more than two thousand active participants.

But QUBE has not been an unqualified success. In March 1984—the year George Orwell predicted Big Brother would find his way into our homes and just six years after QUBE was launched—Warner Amex chairman Drew Lewis announced that QUBE programming on both the national and local levels would be drastically curtailed.

In six years QUBE had lost nearly thirty million dollars. Despite all the fanfare and publicity generated by the system, it came down to the fact that not enough people were willing to part with the ten or eleven bucks a month it cost to subscribe. Cynics pointed out that despite its losses, QUBE served Warner Amex well, since it was instrumental in helping the company win many cable franchises. Bidirectional cable sounds very appealing to City Council members who make the decision on awarding cable licenses. It sounds exciting to viewers, too, until they tune in and find out how dull it is. There are only so many times you can be polled about your opinion of federal excise taxes before you lose interest and turn back to Johnny Carson, who never pesters you with silly questions.

"Out-of-town writers," said one weary resident of Columbus, "talk about this as if it were the second coming of Christ."[5] But the people of Columbus apparently know better.

The demise of QUBE raises an important point to remember when trying to assess the political impact of any new communications technology. To achieve widespread public acceptance, a new technology must have an economic viability apart from politics. No one, in other words, is ever going to pay ten dollars—or even ten cents—for the thrill of participating in a town meeting on rezoning. New communications technologies must prove themselves in the marketplace, usually by offering worthwhile entertainment, before politicians should even bother thinking about them.

Addressable Cable Television

Along those lines, it should be mentioned that there was, and still is, one very profitable aspect of QUBE:

Pay-per-view movies.

The technology that allows one house to receive a TV signal that the house next door cannot receive is called "addressability." A cable system does not have to be bidirectional fully in order to be addressable. In fact, addressable cable systems are less expensive to build and maintain than bidirectional ones, so addressable systems are much more common. Industry statistics project eight million addressable cable homes by 1990, compared to only 3.5 million bidirectional homes. Most significantly, the installation of new addressable systems is being driven by two very strong economic factors.

The first is pay-per-view (PPV) entertainment. Unlike pay-cable programming services such as HBO or Showtime, which charge subscribers a monthly fee no matter how often they use the service, pay-per-view systems charge the viewer only for what he chooses to see. If *The Godfather* is playing on the PPV channel at 9:00 P.M., the cable subscriber will call the cable company at about seven o'clock, tell the operator he wants to watch *The Godfather*, and his set will be electronically prepared to receive it. When he gets his regular monthly invoice for cable service it will contain a note saying that he watched *The Godfather*, and he will be billed an additional four or five dollars. I use *The Godfather* as an example, but the real attraction of pay-per-view is that the films are quite recent. PPV uses the same distribution "window" as home video, so major films can be seen long before they appear on pay cable or broadcast television. In some cases a movie will be shown on pay-per-view while it's still in theatrical release.

The second economic factor driving the installation of addressable systems is that they can be very cost-effective for the cable operator. Running a modern cable system is a highly labor-intensive business, especially when it comes to dealing with what the cable industry calls "churn."

Subscribers stop paying their bills and must be disconnected. People sign up for HBO for a while, decide they don't like it, and call to disconnect. Or they decide they *do* like it, and they call to sign up for *more* services. Each time a subscriber requires a change of this kind, the cable operator must send a technician out to fiddle with the converter box. It's very costly, and most cable operators have a hard time keeping up with it. Yet with an addressable system, all this work is done automatically and electronically. The savings in labor is substantial. And that key economic factor, combined with the increasing popularity of pay-per-view, have poised addressable cable on the verge of tremendous growth.

Political advertisers may eventually find some uses for addressable cable. It's possible, for example, to play a documentary film about the candidate in homes that have been selected on the basis of some geographic or demographic characteristic, or to have the film sitting there waiting to be played for anyone who requests it. Theoretically, as Robert Squier imagined (see page 189), eventually it may be possible to play one set of political commercials in one house and a completely different set in the house next door.

More likely, though, is the possibility that addressable cable systems will re-create some of the political programming formats pioneered by QUBE. Any time you have an addressable cable television set and an ordinary Touch-tone telephone in the same home, you have a fully interactive electronic communications medium capable of doing anything QUBE can do and more. Programming is sent downstream via addressable cable, while responses and instructions are set upstream via Touch-tone phone. The town meetings, interactive political discussions, and opinion polling that showed such promise on QUBE may attain a kind of rebirth with addressable cable.

Videotex

Videotex is another technology that once was thought to depend on bidirectional cable television but that has attained a struggling life by marrying television, telephones, and computers into a hybrid system resembling computer-based information utilities like The Source and Comp-u-Serve.

It's best to define videotex in terms of what it is rather than how it gets to you, since its many different means of distribution can be rather confusing. As its name implies, videotex consists of letters and numbers that appear on your television screen. It also can contain very simple, nonanimated graphics.

News and information are the staples of most videotex systems. In fact, a simple way of defining videotex is to call it an electronic newspaper. But a good videotex system will do a lot more for you than your morning edition of *The Daily Bugle*. You can use it to make a reservation at a local restaurant or to buy an airline ticket for a trip to Hawaii. You may want to check the area real-estate listings to see what your house is worth this morning, or spend the morning shopping at home by leafing through the pages of an electronic catalog. With videotex you can play computer games, bank at home, participate in public-opinion polls, access libraries of information, or send electronic mail. Altogether you can read more than a quarter of a million electronic "pages" of information simply by pressing buttons on a keypad and branching through the system using "tree logic" until you find exactly what you're looking for.

Now, briefly, a word about how videotex is distributed. There are four basic ways to send and receive videotex:

1. Send it over bidirectional cable television and receive it on an ordinary television set with a hand-held keypad.
2. Send it over telephone wires and receive it on a television set using a hand-held keypad/decoder.
3. Send it over telephone wires and receive it on a television set using a personal computer.

4. Send it over telephone wires and receive it on a personal computer, displaying it on the computer's own screen.

Generally this is the order the videotex industry itself has followed in trying to come up with a winning formula. Videotex began on bidirectional cable, just like QUBE. When it became clear that bidirectional cable was not going to take over the world, it switched to telephone lines and hand-held decoders. When the decoders proved too expensive for most consumers, videotex changed its focus to aim at people who already owned PC's.

That's where the industry stands today, although "stands" may be too strong a word. The videotex industry is more or less lying on its stomach and groping at the ropes like a fighter who has been knocked down twice in a single round.

In recent years two major American videotex ventures have hit the deck. Both were backed by giant newspaper chains, Knight-Ridder and Times Mirror, so the problem was not a lack of financing or expertise in the news business. In each case, it appears the biggest problem was the high cost of the hand-held keypad.

In Britain and France, videotex has been a big hit, but that's because the national governments have subsidized it. France's videotex system, Minitel, has been particularly successful. But the government-owned French telephone company installed decoders in thousands of homes *free*, thinking it would save them money in publishing phone books. Don't hold your breath waiting for the U.S. government or AT&T to do the same.

If videotex ever achieves widespread penetration in the United States, political advertisers should find it a very useful medium. It seems particularly well suited to giving voters an opportunity to learn about the candidate's positions in depth. For example, a candidate may want to put a quarter-page advertisement in the news section of the system. Such an ad might say, "To find out where George Bush stands on military spending, turn to page 67." When the viewer types "67" on his keypad, he will be able to read a five-, ten-, fifteen-, or twenty-page document outlining Bush's views on national defense. When he's finished reading, the viewer will be asked to leave his name and address so he can be sent additional material. Once he's on the campaign database, of course, he can be mailed, solicited, visited, and tele-marketed into submission. The viewer gets all this information free, and the candidate pays for the advertising only on a per-use basis.

Videotex is not limited in space, as newspapers are, and it's not limited in time, as broadcasting is. Nor is videotex limited by government regulation, as just about everything is. It's a wide-open communications medium with many conceivable political applications, from commercial advertising to electronic mail. The question is, will it ever find its way into a sufficient number of American homes to be politically useful?

In that regard, videotex is quite different from *teletext*, which is already in seventy-three million American homes.

The problem faced by teletext is that no one knows it's there.

Teletext

Just when you think there's absolutely no use for something—like your belly button, let's say, or the little loop on the back of a shirt—scientists always manage to come up with some clever application for it.

So it was with teletext, which works by utilizing something you probably thought was totally worthless: the annoying vertical black line on your television set.

Although it appears rarely (and usually only during the Super Bowl), everyone knows the vertical line is there. It's there because television works by using a *scanning* process. A TV camera scans a scene from left to right and from top to bottom, dividing everything it sees into tiny dots of light and dark. These dots are transmitted over the air and re-created on the home screen in a manner similar to the way in which they were photographed. An electron beam activates phosphorescent dots on the screen one at a time as it scans from left to right. Dropping down another line, it sweeps from left to right again until it has gone through all 525 lines on a conventional TV set. When it finally reaches the bottom of the screen, it jumps back to the top and starts all over again. During the brief period of time it takes to jump from the bottom of one picture to the top of the next, a television signal transmits the "vertical blanking interval" (VBI), or, as it's more commonly known, the annoying black line.

Until recently, the annoying black line was devoid of information. But communications technology abhors a vacuum. And in 1966, scientists in England discovered a way to pack the vertical blanking interval with digital data. Today nearly two hundred electronic pages of letters, numbers, and simple illustrations can be transmitted on the VBI.

Although anyone can see the vertical blanking interval just by fiddling with the dials on their TV set, one must have a decoder to translate the data carried on it into readable form. The decoder can be used to cast the data over the entire screen, replacing the rest of the television picture. Or it can run a "crawl" of superimposed text beneath the regular picture. It is in the latter mode that teletext has achieved its best-known application, as a means of captioning TV shows for the deaf.

Aside from captioning, though, teletext can be used to provide services very similar to those offered by videotex. The viewer uses menus to choose from a hundred to two hundred pages of news, sports, weather, stock market information, and, of course, advertising. From the perspective of a political advertiser, teletext is similar to videotex in its ability to transmit a large volume of detailed material about the candidate. But teletext does not have videotex's capacity for capturing names and addresses.

"For the political communicator," write electronic media consultants William Paley and Shelly Moffett, "teletext is a marvelous medium for dispersing information on current events. A political position paper, sponsored by a candidate and/or party, can be made readily available to viewers. A constituent may then take the time to absorb information too complicated or lengthy to cover in a short television or radio message, or that, very possibly, could be ignored in a direct-mail effort."[6]

There's no doubt political advertisers would find teletext useful. The big question, once again, is whether teletext has any economic viability outside of politics. CBS and NBC are both transmitting news and information services on their vertical blanking intervals. ABC has been a pioneer of captioning for the hearing-impaired. In one form or another, teletext is in seventy-three million American homes, making it by far the most widespread of the so-called new electronic media. More people have teletext in their homes than cable, personal computers, VCRs, or videodiscs. But only a few hundred people are equipped to use it.

Teletext is suffering from a severe chicken-and-egg dilemma based on the high cost of decoders and the lack of a standardized transmission code. Until U.S. broadcasting companies make up their minds regarding which of several teletext formats to use, the manufacturers of home electronics won't be able to mass-produce the decoders. And until the decoders are mass-produced, their cost will be too high for the average consumer. For the time being, only a deaf person would consider a teletext decoder to be a good investment. And until a politician comes along who can win by directing his message primarily to the hard-of-hearing, teletext will be a political disappointment.

Laser Optical Videodiscs

"Disappointment" also is the first word that comes to mind when one considers the brief and unhappy history of videodiscs.

The laser optical videodisc has been disappointing not only because it was a total bust in the consumer marketplace but also because—and this is not widely appreciated—it probably is the most powerful of all the new video technologies.

In head-to-head competition with VCRs, videodiscs failed miserably among consumers because they could not record television programming off the air. But lost in the shuffle was the fact that videodiscs can do many things VCRs cannot. A modern videodisc player is, in fact, the ultimate marriage of the computer and television.

The key to videodisc technology is the fact that a laser optical disc is not a recording of a television program per se, but a digital rendering of it. Thus it has more in common with a floppy disc than it does with a videocassette. Each videodisc contains about a hundred thousand frames of information. Those frames can be the still pictures of a television program, or they can be electronic "pages" full of text. Most importantly, each single frame can be called up and put on the screen individually. You can say, in effect, give me frame 215, and follow that with frames 6,001 through 7,892.

The result is a computer that behaves like a TV set, or a TV set that acts like a computer. The viewer interacts with the videodisc player by answering various questions, and the machine, in turn, responds by displaying specific frames of text or playing specific sequences of film.

Imagine, for example, a videodisc called "Meet Jack Kemp." When I put it in my videodisc player and turn on the television set, I see a short film biography of the candidate. I see him on the campaign trail, speaking in the well of the House, playing with his dog, tossing a football with his son, and so on.

After five minutes or so, an announcer appears on the screen and says, "Now that you've had a chance to get acquainted with Jack Kemp, what question would *you* like to ask Jack?"

The screen says:

A. How did being a professional football player prepare you for your career in politics?
B. Is supply-side economics really "voodoo"?
C. Do you think your experience as a congressman from Buffalo is sufficient to help you meet the demands of the White House?

I push "A."

Jack comes on the screen.

"Ha, ha, ha. Yes, a lot of people wonder if being a quarterback for the Buffalo Bills really qualifies me to be president. Well, only if Gorbachev can catch! But seriously, leadership is an important quality in both politics and sports. In fact, I remember one time when we were down twenty-one points with less than two minutes to go. In the huddle I called a 'Right Slant, Red Dog Four.' Would you like to see what happened next?"

The screen says:

A. Yes.
B. No.

I press "Yes," and I see a two-minute clip of Jack exercising his leadership on the field. Then we return to Jack.

"I guess that goes to show you that the qualities of leadership forged on the football field can be important on the world stage, too."

You get the idea.

Of course, producing such an electronic extravaganza would be very expensive. But having made that upfront investment, the cost of distribution is relatively low. Since videodiscs are stamped out like record albums, they're much cheaper to duplicate than videocassettes are.

Even so, it's more likely that political parties, rather than individual campaigns, will be the major users of videodisc technology in the future. Both the Republican and Democratic national committees spend a great deal of time and money training candidates and campaign staff. They run seminars in Washington and around the country to bring local candidates and campaign managers up to speed on the techniques of fundraising, advertising, organization, and voter contact. In the future it may be possible to put these training programs on videodisc. By doing so the parties would not only save time and money, but also would get the information into the hands of more candidates.

None of this, however, will happen until videodisc players catch on in the consumer marketplace. And that won't occur until engineers can figure out how to make videodiscs record television programming off the air. Until that time, videodiscs will continue to suffer by comparison with their major competitor:

The VCR.

Videocassette Recorders

"People aren't going to spend a lot of time reading in-depth stories anymore," Stuart Karl told *Mother Jones* magazine in 1986, "because we're all tube-oriented.

"How many housewives in Oshkosh really have the time to sit down and read *A New Democracy*? But they do have time to plug in a videocassette that very graphically shows them: 'Here's a smokestack, and here's Silicon Valley—no smoke. We'll rebuild this.' It's in a format that's more enjoyable to 'read.'"[7]

Stuart Karl knows something about what goes into the making of a popular videocassette. As founder and president of Karl/Lorimar Home Video, he created the best-selling nontheatrical videocassette of all time, Jane Fonda's *Workout*. But Karl isn't talking about another exercise tape. He's talking about a home video version of Gary Hart's campaign manifesto *A New Democracy*.

"Gary Hart would make a better president than he is a candidate," says Karl. "I think it's awkward for him to be a candidate. The tape could become a way for him and other people to maybe not have to be the politician, the campaigner with the smile and the babies."[8]

As it turned out, of course, Gary Hart had a problem with kissing that went beyond babies. As a result, his home video never saw the light of day. But elsewhere on the political landscape, videocassettes have started to make their presence felt:

• Young Joe Kennedy used home video in his successful bid to win the congressional seat once held by JFK.
• A coalition of conservatives in California distributed a videotape attacking the record of Rose Bird, California's controversial Supreme Court judge.
• Political advocacy groups like People for the American Way and The Better World Society are experimenting with videotape as part of their effort to use television as a tool for social change.
• Roger Craver and Frank Greer produced a videotape for the Democratic Senate Campaign Committee that showcased some of the committee's television commercials and asked fat cats for money to help put them on the air.

As a medium of political communication, videotape has many advantages. Unlike film, it requires no developing or laboratory work, no complex lighting, no special studios. The new hand-held cameras are relatively inexpensive and easy to operate. Forty-five minutes in a computerized editing room yields a finished product with graphics and special effects that look much more costly than they really are. All things considered, videotape is almost as cheap and easy to work with as pencil and paper.

But videotape's greatest advantage is that, like a turtle, it comes wrapped in its own delivery system. The cassette itself, in other words, is a medium of distribution. A campaign doesn't have to pay for airtime, or cable time, or satellite time, because the cassette delivers programming directly to its viewers. It can be sent in the mail, handed out at rallies, shipped overnight, distributed on the streets, or passed hand-to-hand from one voter to the next.

The candidate may give a cassette to the local Kiwanis Club, for example, to serve as a springboard for discussion at its next luncheon. He may distribute copies to his biggest contributors as a way of encouraging them to give more money. Or he may hold a series of "watch parties" using the cassette to ask people for modest donations. Videocassettes could be used as part of a highly targeted direct-mail effort, especially in situations where the campaign has identified a few thousand persuadable voters. Several dozen videocassettes could be mailed out like chain letters, with notes saying, "After you've seen this tape, please send it to a friend." In certain key neighborhoods it might even be worthwhile to hand out a few hundred cassettes on the streets. Again, voters would be urged to watch the tape and pass it on.

Unlike many of the video technologies discussed in this chapter, politicians won't have to wait to make use of the VCR. It has achieved a remarkable level of acceptance in the consumer marketplace, and as a result it's ready to have a substantial impact on the 1988 election cycle.

In a way, the advent of videocassettes brings the history of political campaign technology (and brings this book) full circle. It is a high-tech version of the oldest political technology of them all: pamphleteering. If Tom Paine were alive today, *Common Sense* would be on videotape.

"It hasn't happened yet," says Jim Eury, director of the Democratic Congressional Campaign Committee's Media Center. "But I guarantee you we'll be doing VHS and Beta tapes for lots of candidates in 1988—especially for campaigns that don't have a lot of money.

"I guarantee it."

*   *   *

There are very few guarantees when it comes to predicting the impact of new communications technologies on politics. I've tried very hard in this book not to "blue-sky" the outlook by assuming that simply because a certain technology exists it will necessarily find widespread application in the real world. In this chapter, alas, a certain amount of blue-skying has been inevitable. Direct mail, telemarketing, cable television, satellites, and computers are not the "coming things" in politics. They're here. Whether the same can be said for electronic mail, computer conferencing, bidirectional cable, teletext, and videotex remains to be seen.

Predicting the future is a dangerous business. It's always easy to tell what will be possible. It's much harder to tell what will be probable. And it's downright difficult to tell what will eventually be profitable.

Profitability is the key, because without attaining some kind of viability in the consumer marketplace, no communications technology can achieve a sufficient audience to be of value to politicians. Too often we make the mistake of assuming that just because something is technologically possible it also must be economically feasible. That kind of thinking led futurists in the 1940s to speculate that soon we would be commuting to work in personal helicopters.

Politics is a backward business, not given to experimentation and innovation. A new communications technology must be tried and proven in the commercial sector before politicians will consider using it. And who can blame them? Politicians face an inexorable deadline and a chronic shortage of money. There are no "holdover" sales in politics, no extensions, no second chances. Only candidates who are utterly certain they're going to win, utterly certain they're *not* going to win, or so loaded with money that it doesn't matter will dare to try something new. As a result, the pace of technological change in politics is painfully slow.

One wild-card factor in the development of political communications technology is the question of government regulation. After many years of rather heavy-handed control by the FCC, the Reagan administration has pursued an eight-year-long policy of "hands off." Cable television in particular underwent a massive deregulation during the Reagan years, and the FCC completely disavowed the Fairness Doctrine. Meanwhile, as new communications technologies pop up almost every day, they are born into a regulatory environment of almost total laissez-faire.

Personally I think this policy is appropriate. The more ways we have of communicating with each other, the less need we have for the federal government to play traffic cop. The FCC's policies regarding electronic communications, after all, have been based primarily on the scarcity of frequencies on the electromagnetic spectrum. But with cable television, fiber optics, and satellites, we are entering an era of channel abundance. We are becoming a "broad-band society," with potentially millions of channels of communication. Under such conditions the fairness doctrine is meaningless. Why get upset about what your opponent is saying about you on Channel 215 when you can say nasty things about him on Channel 216? Indeed, it seems to me that in this age of burgeoning electronic communications we're approaching the Jeffersonian ideal of a press that is not only free but that is in fact a *free-for-all*, in which thousands of voices are heard and where fairness is guaranteed not by the government but by the very multiplicity of participants.

But not everyone agrees with me on this. In fact, whenever new communications technologies are discussed on TV talk shows, or college classrooms, or in print, the most frequent questions asked are: "How are we going to control it?" "How do we regulate it?" "How do we make sure no one gets hurt by it?" I strongly suspect that if the Democratic Party takes control of the White House in 1988, we'll see a burst of new activity from the FCC as it hurries to make up the ground it lost during the Reagan years. Lightly regulated or unregulated technologies like direct mail, telemarketing, satellites, bulletin board systems, electronic mail, teletext, and videotex may wake up one morning in 1989 to find themselves playing under a whole new set of rules. And that could substantially impede their development as tools of political communication.

Another impediment to the political development of these technologies is that peculiar phenomenon first noticed by *Megatrends* author John Naisbitt called "high-tech/high-touch."

"What happens," writes Naisbitt, "is that whenever new technology is introduced into society, there must be a counterbalancing human response—that is, *high-touch*—or the technology is rejected."[9]

As mentioned earlier in this chapter, credit cards have been very slow to catch on in political direct mail because donors apparently *like* the sensation of writing out checks. It makes them feel like they're really doing something, a feeling they apparently don't get when they simply write their Visa number on a reply card. For this reason I'm skeptical about the impact of electronic funds transfer on political fundraising. And high-tech/high-touch makes me skeptical about a number of other new technologies as well.

For example, electronic mail is being used in Congress right now to convey messages from one office to the next. But the age-old system of congressional pages exists right alongside it, with no member of Congress expressing any interest in giving up the political patronage and, frankly, the charm that the obsolete page system represents.

By turning on my modem, changing the floppy discs in my computer, and pressing a few buttons on my keyboard, I can get today's edition of *The Washington Post* on my computer. But I can also get it by running downstairs to the newsstand in the lobby of my office building. It takes me roughly the same amount of time, and the printed version costs a lot less. Once downstairs, I can also take a horse-and-buggy ride around Central Park. New technologies don't arrive as fast as we imagine, nor do the old ones disappear as quickly as we suppose.

Many writers have taken the electronic polling on bidirectional cable systems like QUBE to be a precursor to in-home voting. But I don't think we'll ever see in-home voting in this country . . . at least not for the next five thousand years or so. Not only would we be giving up the high-touch aspect of traveling to the local high-school cafeteria or church basement, but we would also be opening a Pandora's box of problems, both technological and philosophical.

Do we really want to abandon a two-hundred-year tradition of representative democracy in favor of an entirely new—and completely different—system of "pure democracy"? Although ballot initiatives and referenda are becoming increasingly common in many states, the American people would think twice before they'd institute a system of government by plebiscite. If we did create such a system, who would be in charge of posing the questions? And how exactly is "pure democracy" different from what used to be called "mob rule"?

Even if the American people could be persuaded of the value

of such a system, maintaining the integrity and honesty of it would be a technological challenge. "Voiceprints" have been suggested as a way of verifying the identity of voters. But can we really trust such fancy-pants technology with something so important? Even our current system of computerized vote counting is not as reliable as most people think. Several major computer errors have been discovered in local elections around the country in recent years, and perhaps hundreds more have gone unnoticed. It's hard to tell how much integrity our democratic system would lose if it became totally electronic and, in effect, untraceable. More than one QUBE subscriber has come home to find their preschool toddler happily responding to opinion polls on import trade quotas and oil depletion allowances.

There's a kind of tyranny to widespread public polling that needs to be examined more closely in this country. There are about five people in America who know how to conduct a scientific and reasonably reliable political opinion poll. There are another five thousand people who *think* they know. Unfortunately, the latter group supplies information not only to many state and local political candidates but also to local television and radio stations.

By some accounts, Jane Byrne lost her last Chicago mayoral election to the late Harold Washington because bad opinion polling paid for by local television stations consistently showed her losing the race when (at least according to her own pollsters) she was running quite close.

We also have to deal with the whole question of whether the networks should be permitted to do their exit polls, which serve no purpose other than to discourage people in western time zones from voting.

Clearly, this country would be better off with fewer opinion polls, not more of them. And to institute a system of government by opinion poll—on QUBE, videotex, or even by telephone—would be an electronic nightmare that I don't believe the American people would ever knowingly allow. As far as I'm concerned, in-home voting is a nonissue.

But this is not to say that a substantial portion of tomorrow's political dialogue won't take place inside the living room. In fact, voting may become the only political activity that does *not* happen at home.

Another nonissue, in my opinion, is the question of whether

new communications technologies in politics are creating an "information underclass" of people who can't afford to put the technology in their homes.

Lincoln said, "God must love the common man, because he made so many of them." And from Lincoln's day until now, sheer numerical superiority has always been the source of the common man's political strength. We needn't worry if poor people can't afford to get information into their homes, because if they can't get it on their own, politicians will always figure out a way to get it to them. America's poor will never be disenfranchised as long as we have a (small "d") democratic system in this country and a (large "D") Democratic Party. In fact, if these communications technologies ever become widely used in American politics, I wouldn't be surprised if a Democratic-controlled Congress decides that it's an *unalienable right* to have a personal computer, a satellite dish, and a coaxial cable in your home . . . and proceeds to spend several billion dollars of public money installing them, free.

Don't laugh. It happened in France.

The demise of the national political parties is another non-issue that has been widely circulated by the press, to the point where most people nowadays take it as a matter of faith that the two parties, like Broadway, are practically dead. Yes, the advent of television had a disruptive effect on the national political parties. But direct mail, telemarketing, computers, and most recently satellites have had a highly salutary effect, with the end result being that both parties are stronger today than they've been in the past thirty-five years. The prospects for the immediate future look even brighter, especially as the Democrats begin to catch up with the GOP's early lead in direct mail. Far from being supplanted by new technologies, the parties will become the ultimate masters of it.

I do think, however, that it's quite possible the "two-party system" as we know it today might undergo some significant changes in the future. Although it's usually mentioned right up there next to God and apple pie, the two-party system was never a sacred part of the American political heritage. It's not mentioned in the Constitution, and it's a relatively recent arrival on the political scene. Communications technology will open the door to new political parties. And as those parties gain strength at the polls, Congress may have to alter its outmoded two-party bureaucracy. Within our lifetimes we might just see a U.S. Congress that resembles the parliaments of many foreign countries, in which four or five viable political parties govern by forming majority coalitions.

The question of privacy is *not* a nonissue. It's a very real issue, but not in the way that most people think.

Most people are worried about politicians and government officials using the new communications technologies to *invade* our privacy—the Big Brother syndrome. But I'm worried about new communications technology making our participation in government and politics *too* private.

Don't get me wrong. Concern about personal privacy when it comes to the new electronic media is quite justified. Many of these technologies—particularly bidirectional cable, direct mail, computers, telemarketing, and videotex—possess a frightening capacity to collect, store, and manipulate information about people. Some housewives in Columbus, for example, were distraught when their husbands looked at the monthly QUBE bill and found out their wives had been watching soft-porn movies in the afternoon. The ability of bidirectional cable television to set off burglar alarms at the police station, fire alarms at the firehouse, medical emergency alarms at the hospital, and even to give meter readings at the local utility company has a vaguely Big Brotherish sound to it. But I believe the American people are very alert to this problem. Our public antenna, so to speak, is extended and very much engaged on this issue. It's unlikely we will allow a bidirectional communications system of any kind to be put in place without some government-imposed or self-imposed controls on how the data will be used.

What we are much less alert to, I fear, is the possibility that these new communications technologies are making participation in the American political process much more private than it ought to be. Politics, after all, used to be the most public, the most highly social of all forms of human behavior. Today, politics is more private than masturbation.

I can be very active—*extremely* active—in politics nowadays without ever leaving my desk. I can watch the candidates carry on their endless punch/counterpunch commercials on my nineteen-inch color television. Contribute to the candidate of my choice by responding to a direct-mail letter or a telemarketing call. Respond to a survey on the phone. Peruse the candidates' position papers on teletext. Watch a "town meeting" on cable television, or a filmed biography of one of the candidates on my VCR. I can read my persuasion mail or answer my voter-contact calls. I can participate in a political discussion on The Source, or dial my favorite candidate's BBS and leave a message that I'd like to volunteer. Once I've volunteered, I might be assigned to do data-entry via modem, or write speeches I can send in by electronic mail. Only when it comes time to *vote* do I have to go out in public. And even then I walk into a tiny booth, pull the curtain closed behind me, and mark a secret ballot.

These technologies are creating a kind of political cocoon where the greatest danger is not that our behavior will be watched by Big Brother but that it is going entirely unobserved by anyone other than ourselves. Not by the press. Not by the government. Not by our fellow citizens. Not by anyone. As a result, our political behavior may become quite self-indulgent, whimsical, selfish, emotional, peevish, nasty, greedy, foolish, biased, impulsive, and all those other unpleasant words that refer to how we sometimes behave when we're home alone and nobody's watching.

Politics always has been a crazy business. Funny hats. Noisemakers. Balloons. But at least in the past, we were looking into each other's faces, shaking hands, arguing, compromising, kissing babies, touching, feeling.

Nowadays the level of our political dialogue is roughly equivalent to staring at the bathroom mirror and lip-synching to the radio.

I wonder if one day soon we will look into our home communications set and say, "I have seen Big Brother . . . and he is me."

Notes

Chapter One

1. As quoted in John F. Nugent, "Positively Negative," *Campaigns & Elections* (March–April 1987), p. 47.
2. Ibid.
3. George Will, "So Much Cash, So Few Ideas," *Newsweek* (November 10, 1986), p. 96.
4. Tom Wicker, "The Road Not Taken," *The New York Times* (October 24, 1986), p. 35.
5. As quoted in Neil Hickey, "It's High Noon Now for Political Mudslingers—Let the Targets Beware," *TV Guide* (October 18, 1986), p. 5.
6. Ibid.
7. Ibid.
8. As quoted in Ron Suskind, "The Power of Political Consultants" *New York Times Magazine* (August 12, 1984), p. 56.
9. As quoted in Howard Fineman, "How the Voter Brokers Operate" *Newsweek* (November 10, 1986), p. 22.
10. As quoted in "Tony Schwartz: Radio's Responsive Chord," personal interview, *Campaigns & Elections* (Spring 1981), p. 22.
11. Ibid.
12. Bill Peterson, "Jesse Helms's Lessons for Washington: Big Bucks, Streetfighter's Skills, Racist Appeals and Charisma Still Work," *The Washington Post* (November 18, 1984), p. C-1.
13. J. Brian Smith, "Train Tour Traumas: The Anatomy of a Successful Media Event," *Campaigns & Elections* (July–August 1986), p. 6.
14. As quoted in "Campaign '86 Ads: Strong Medicine for Voter Apathy," *Adweek* (October 13, 1986), p. 36.

Chapter Two

1. Daniel Boorstin, *The Americans: The Democratic Experience* (New York: Vintage Books, 1974), p. 126.
2. Joe Karbo, advertisement headlined "The Lazy Man's Way to Riches."
3. Ibid.
4. Ibid.
5. Joe Karbo, *The Lazy Man's Way to Riches* (Sunset Beach, Calif.: self-published, 1973), front cover.
6. Ibid., p. 6.
7. Ibid., p. 7.
8. Ibid., p. 74.
9. Richard Viguerie, *The New Right: We're Ready to Lead* (Falls Church, Va.: Caroline House, 1981), p. 28.
10. Ibid., p. 29.
11. Ibid., p. 30.
12. Ibid., p. 32.
13. Ibid., p. 33.
14. Ibid.
15. James Aldige, "Political Mail Will Raise Money for Image Makers," *Fund Raising Management* (March 1980) as reproduced in "Campaign Finance Reform Hearings Held Before the Task Force on Elections," p. 426.
16. Larry Sabato, Research Plan and Proposal for "The Party's Just Begun: The Revival of Political Parties in America" (January 1986), p. 36.
17. As quoted in "Liberal Causes Had a Banner DM Year in 1985, Craver Sees Benefit from Conservative Victories," *DM News* (February 15, 1986), p. 49.
18. Richard Viguerie, p. 34.
19. Ibid.
20. As quoted in "McGovern Mailings Emphasize Issues, Motivation, $ Needs," *Direct Marketing* (September 1972), pp. 26–39.
21. Ibid., reproduction of McGovern direct-mail letter.
22. Ibid.
23. Karbo, *The Lazy Man's Way to Riches*, p. 74.
24. Direct-mail letter produced by National Republican Congressional Committee and reproduced as Illustration A in "Campaign Finance Reform Hearings Held Before the Task Force on Elections, Committee on House Administration" (Washington, D.C.: U.S. Government Printing Office, 1984), p. 92.
25. Ibid., p. 95.

Chapter Three

1. As quoted in Jay Mathews, "Absentee Ballots GOP Opposed Swung the Vote for Deukmejian," *The Washington Post* (February 27, 1983), p. A-9.
2. John Myers as quoted in Tony Quinn, "How Governor Deukmejian Won in the Mailbox, Not the Ballot Box," *The California Journal*, Vol. 14, No. 4 (April 1983), pp. 148–150.
3. Roger Craver, "The Direct Mailbox: Launching an Effective Fundraising Effort," *Campaigns & Elections* (Spring 1985), p. 57.

4. Roger Craver, "The Direct Mailbox: Ask and Ye Shall Receive," *Campaigns & Elections* (May–June 1986), p. 42.
5. Ed Nash, *Direct Marketing: Strategy, Planning, and Execution* (New York: McGraw-Hill, 1982), p. 215.
6. Ibid., p. 216.

Chapter Four

1. Stephen H. Winchell, "The Role of Direct Marketing in Republican Election Plans," *Fund Raising Management* (January 1986), p. 34.
2. "Ethical Business Practices," rev. ed., pamphlet published by the Direct Marketing Association (July 1984), p. 6.
3. Bruce Eberle, *Political Direct Mail Fundraising* (self-published), unnumbered pages.
4. Ibid.
5. Ibid.
6. Larry Sabato, *The Rise of Political Consultants*, New York: Basic Books, Inc., 1981, p. 242.
7. Bruce Eberle, *Political Direct Mail Fundraising* (self-published), unnumbered pages.
8. The source for this material is Roger Craver, "Dollars for Democracy," *WHO'S MAILING WHAT!* (January 1985).
9. Bruce Eberle, *Political Direct Mail Fundraising* (self-published), unnumbered pages.
10. Herschell Gordon Lewis, *Direct Mail Copy That Sells!* (Englewood Cliffs, N.J.: Prentice-Hall, 1984), p. 29.
11. Bruce Eberle, *Political Direct Mail Fundraising* (self-published), unnumbered pages.
12. Sabato, p. 245.

Chapter Five

1. As quoted in John Johnson, "Roosevelt Defends His Social Security Lobbying," *The Sacramento Bee* (April 13, 1984), p. AA7.
2. As quoted in Spencer Rich, "Roosevelt Fund-Raising Appeal Letter On Social Security Criticized," *The Washington Post* (April 3, 1984), p. A11.
3. As quoted in John Johnson, p. AA7.
4. Ibid.
5. As quoted in David Goeller, "Big Lobbying Groups Claim Big Successes on Capitol Hill," Associated Press (August 12, 1985).
6. Roger A. Rosenblatt, "Congress Investigates Group Headed by Roosevelt Son," *The Los Angeles Times* (March 10, 1987), p. 13.
7. As quoted above in Roger A. Rosenblatt, "Congress Investigates Group Headed by Roosevelt Son," *The Los Angeles Times* (March 10, 1987), p. 13.
8. James Roosevelt, in a statement before the House Committee on Ways and Means, Subcommittee on Social Security (March 10, 1987), p. 8.
9. James Ridgeway, "The New Right's Campaign to Defund the Left," *The Village Voice* (January 11, 1983), p. 19.
10. As quoted in Elizabeth Drew, *Politics and Money* (New York: Macmillan Publishing Company, 1983), p. 131.

Chapter Six

1. As quoted in Ithiel de Sola Pool, *Forecasting the Telephone: A Retrospective Technology Assessment* (Norwood, N.J.: Ablex Publishing Company), p. 78.
2. As quoted in David S. Boim, "The Telemarketing Center: Nucleus of a Modern Campaign," *Campaigns & Elections* (Spring 1984), p. 76. The voter's responses are hypothetical.
3. Theodore Levitt in the Foreword to Murray Roman, *Telephone Marketing* (New York: McGraw-Hill, 1976), p. ix.
4. Lester Wunderman, as quoted in the Introduction to *Telephone Marketing*, p. xvi.
5. Stephen H. Winchell, "Challenge of the 1980s: Keeping Up with Technology," *Fund Raising Management* (February 1981), p. 30.
6. Murray Roman, *Telephone Marketing*, New York: McGraw-Hill, 1976, p. 46.
7. Winchell, p. 31.
8. As quoted in Murray Roman, *Telemarketing Campaigns That Work* (New York: McGraw-Hill, 1983), p. 187.
9. Bruce McBrearty, "Computerization Improves Fund Raising Production," *Fund Raising Management* (May 1985), p. 102.

Chapter Seven

1. Barney Frank, verbal presentation before the Cabletelevision Advertising Bureau's (CAB) seminar on politics and cable television, Cannon House Office Building (February 14, 1984).
2. Ibid.
3. John Florescu, at CAB seminar.
4. Ibid.
5. Ibid.
6. Barney Frank, at CAB seminar.
7. Tom Belford, "Political Applications of Cable Television," white paper prepared for the Democratic National Committee (January 1982), p. 3.
8. Robert Squier, at CAB seminar.
9. Ibid.
10. As quoted in Steven Marcus, "The First Hurrah," *Home Video* (October 1982), p. 44.
11. David Skylar quoted in "A New Ball Game," *Broadcasting* (November 8, 1982), p. 39.
12. As quoted in "Political Ads Slow Start: Just the Tip of the Iceberg," *CableAge* (October 4, 1982), p. 17.
13. Robert Squier, at CAB seminar.
NOTE: Oral presentations made at the CAB seminar have been lightly edited for the sake of clarity.

Chapter Eight

1. Ed Dooley, personal letter to the author.
2. As quoted in Michael Kramer, "Are You Running with Me, Jesus?," *New*

York (August 18, 1986), p. 27. Kramer says this passage is a "composite of segments from various shows."

3. As quoted in ibid., p. 24.

4. As quoted in "Vanguard Net Mulls Plans," *CableVision* (March 26, 1984), p. 12.

5. As quoted in Victor Livingston, "Cableline to Launch New Service," *CableVision* (February 20, 1984), p. 22.

6. As quoted in "AFL-CIO Outlines TV Promotion Plans," *MultiChannel News* (October 18, 1982), p. 45.

7. Donald Goldberg, "Captain Midnight, HBO, and World War III," *Mother Jones* (October, 1986), p. 29.

8. Charles Wick, "Communicating Democracy-in-Action Overseas," speech before the Public Relations Society of America, Washington, D.C. (November 9, 1986), p. 6.

9. As quoted in Andrew Nagorski et al., "Moscow Faces the New Age," *Newsweek* (August 18, 1986), p. 22.

Chapter Nine

1. *PRIZM: The Marketer's Handbook,* copyright 1984 (The Claritas Corporation), p. 17.

2. Ibid., p. 101.

3. Ibid., p. 39.

4. Jonathan Robbin, "Geodemographics: The New Magic," *Campaigns & Elections* (Spring 1980), p. 30.

5. Joseph Mockus, "Geodemographics II: Targeting Your Turnout," *Campaigns & Elections* (Summer 1980), p. 62. This article was the source for much of the material printed here regarding the 1978 Missouri anti-right-to-work campaign.

6. As quoted in ibid., p. 63.

7. Ibid.

8. As quoted in ibid., p. 55.

9. Matthew Reese, "From Telephone to Telelobby: Two Decades of Targeted Communication," *New Communications Technologies in Politics,* Robert G. Meadow, Ed., p. 102.

10. Larry J. Sabato, *The Rise of Political Consultants* (New York: Basic Books, 1981), p. 199.

11. Frank Tobe, "New Techniques in Computerized Voter Contact," *Campaigns & Elections* (Summer 1984), p. 59.

12. Ibid., p. 57.

13. Ibid., p. 64.

Chapter Ten

1. "Campaign Survival Kit," promotional literature published by Aristotle Industries, p. 5.

2. John R. Tkach, "Ballots and Bytes: Dr. Tkach Predicts the Future," *Campaigns & Elections* (May–June 1986), p. 26.

3. As quoted in John Wicklein, *Electronic Nightmare: The New Communications and Freedom* (New York: Viking Press, 1981), p. 18.

4. Ibid.

5. As quoted in Margaret Yao, "Two-Way Cable TV Disappoints Viewers in Columbus, Ohio, as Programming Lags," *The Wall Street Journal* (September 30, 1981), p. 31.
6. William C. Paley and Shelly Moffett, "The New Electronic Media—Instant Action & Reaction," *Campaigns & Elections* (Winter 1984), p. 11.
7. As quoted in "Hart Woos the Couch Potatoes," *Mother Jones* (February–March 1986), p. 14.
8. Ibid.
9. John Naisbitt, *Megatrends* (New York: Warner Books, 1982), p. 39.

Selected
Bibliography

Anders, Christopher, and Howard Marlowe. "On-line Opposition Research," *Campaigns & Elections* (March/April 1987): 61–64.

Arlen, Gary. "Pols and the New Media," *Emmy Magazine* (May/June): 46–47.

Barone, Michael, and Grant Ujifusa. The Almanac of American Politics 1986, Washington: National Journal, Inc., 1985.

Beiler, David. *The Classics of Political Television Advertising: A Viewer's Guide*, Washington: Campaigns and Elections, Inc., 1987.

Benjamin, Gerald, ed. *The Communications Revolution in Politics*, New York: The Academy of Political Science, 1982.

Blumenthal, Sidney. *The Permanent Campaign*, New York: Simon & Schuster, 1980.

Bonafede, Dom. "Part Science, Part Art, Part Hokum: Direct Mail Now a Key Campaign Tool," *National Journal* (July 31, 1982): 1332–36.

———. "Strides in Technology Are Changing the Face of Political Campaigning," *National Journal* (April 7, 1984): 657–661.

———. *Campaign Finance Reform: Hearings Held Before the Task Force on Elections of the Committee on House Administration*, Washington: U.S. Government Printing Office, 1984.

Clancy, Frank. "Hart Woos the Couch Potatoes," *Mother Jones* (February/March 1986): 14.

Collins, Thomas. "McGovern Mailings Emphasize Issues, Motivation, $ Needs," *Direct Marketing* (November 1972): 26–39.

de Sola Pool, Ithiel, *Forecasting the Telephone: A Retrospective Technology Assessment of the Telephone*, Norwood, New Jersey: Ablex Publishing Corporation, 1983.

Drew, Elizabeth. *Politics and Money*, New York: Macmillan, 1983.

Eberle, Bruce W. *Political Direct Mail Fundraising*, Vienna, Virginia (self-published): 1985.

Elshtain, Jean Bethke. "Democracy and the QUBE Tube," *The Nation* (August 7–14, 1982): 108–110.

Fineman, Howard. "The Technology of Politics," *Newsweek* (October 25, 1982): 29.

Gross, Lynne Schafer. *The New Television Technologies*, 2nd edition, Dubuque, Iowa: William C. Brown Publishers, 1986.

Haskell, Ann. "Live from Capitol Hill," *Washington Journalism Review* (November 1982): 48–50.

Hessek, Scott. "New Venture: Satellites Impact on Fund Raising," *Fund Raising Management* (May 1981): 24–25.

Hiebert, Ray, et al., eds. *The Political Image Merchants*, Washington: Acropolis Books, Ltd., 1971.

Katz, Nick. "King Midas of the New Right," *Atlantic* (November 1978): 52–61.

Kramer, Michael. "Are You Running with Me, Jesus?" *New York* (August 18, 1986): 22–29.

Lautman, Kay, and Henry Goldstein. *Dear Friend: Mastering the Art of Direct Mail Fund Raising*, Washington: Taft Corporation, 1984.

Lewis, Herschell Gordon. *Direct Mail Copy That Sells*, Englewood Cliffs, New Jersey: Prentice-Hall, Inc., 1984.

Light, Larry. "Direct Mail Bids Do Not Ensure Pot of Gold," *Congressional Quarterly* (October 23, 1982): 2714–2715.

Marcus, Steven. "The First Hurrah," *Home Video* (October 1982): 44–46.

Meadow, Robert G., ed. *New Communications Technologies in Politics*, Washington: The Washington Program of the Annenberg School of Communications, 1985.

Mockus, Joseph. "Geodemographics II: Targeting Your Turnout," *Campaigns & Elections* (Summer, 1980): 55–63.

Nash, Ed. *Direct Marketing: Strategy, Planning, Execution*, New York: McGraw-Hill, 1982.

Paley, William C., and Shelley Moffett. "The New Electronic Media—Instant Action and Reaction," *Campaigns & Elections* (Winter, 1984): 4–12.

Perry, Roland. *Hidden Power*, New York: Beaufort Books, Inc., 1984.

Peterson, Bill. "Direct Mail Writes New Chapter in How to Run a Political Campaign," *Washington Post* (November 17, 1982): A1–A2.

Reid, T. R. "Public Trust, Private Money," *The Washington Post Magazine* (November 26, 1978): 12–31.

Roberts, Steven V. "Politicking Goes High-Tech," *The New York Times Magazine* (November 2, 1986): 38–52.

Robbin, Jonathan. "Geodemographics: The New Magic," *Campaigns & Elections* (Spring, 1980): 25–34.

Roman, Murray. "The Telephone as Political Tool," *Campaigns & Elections* (Fall, 1980): 53–56.

——. *Telemarketing Campaigns That Work*, New York: McGraw-Hill, 1983.

Rosenberg, Tina. "Diminishing Returns: The False Promise of Direct Mail," *Washington Monthly* (June 1983): 33–38.

Sabato, Larry J. *The Rise of Political Consultants*, New York: Basic Books, 1981.

Schwartz, Tony. *The Responsive Chord*, Garden City, New York: Anchor/Doubleday, 1973.

Thimmesch, Nick. "The Grass-Roots Dollar Chase—Ready on the Right," *New York* (June 9, 1975): 58–63.

Thompson, Randall. "Computerized Video Wizardry: Winning Elections at the Studio Control Board," *Campaigns & Elections* (July-August 1986): 31–34.

Tobe, Frank. "New Techniques in Computerized Voter Contact," *Campaigns & Elections* (Summer, 1984): 56–64.

Viguerie, Richard A. *The New Right: We're Ready to Lead,* Falls Church, Virginia: Caroline House, 1981.

Weintz, Walter. *The Solid Gold Mailbox,* New York: John Wiley & Sons, 1987.

Wicklein, John. *Electronic Nightmare,* New York: The Viking Press, 1981.

Winchell, Stephen. "Challenge of the 1980's: Keeping Up with Technology," *Fund Raising Management* (February 1981): 30–39.

Readers who wish to receive a complete bibliography are invited to write the author directly at 250 West 57th Street, Suite 1527, New York, NY, 10019. Please enclose a self-addressed stamped envelope and $3.00 for photocopying.

Index